e-Discovery

CURRENT TRENDS

and

CASES

RALPH C. LOSEY

ABA
Defending Liberty
Pursuing Justice

Cover design by ABA Publishing

11 10 09 08 07 5 4 3 2 1

Cataloging-in-Publication data is on file with the Library of Congress

e-discovery: current trends and cases / Losey, Ralph C.

Discounts are available for books ordered in bulk. Special consideration is given to state bars, CLE programs, and other bar-related organizations. Inquire at Book Publishing, ABA Publishing, American Bar Association, 321 North Clark Street, Chicago, Illinois 60610.

www.ababooks.org

Contents

Preface

This book is derived from the Internet blogs I wrote on electronic discovery in 2007, with a few from late 2006, called the "e-Discovery Team Blog." Here I share the latest trends, events, cases, and analysis in this new and exciting area. The book also includes several of the more interesting comments that readers of my blog left, and where applicable, my responses. In that sense this book is unique—it includes prior interactivity and has already been peer-reviewed. The book provides a broad view of this subject because it contains not only my own views and analysis, but those of leading experts, lawyers and judges as I report on their presentations, writings and decisions.

As an underlying theme I explore what most experts consider the most effective solution to the significant problems posed by electronic discovery: an e-discovery team. This is an internal interdisciplinary corporate team that combines the skills of law, IT and management. This has now become a consensus view, and not just my own proposal. I strongly endorse this solution, so much so that e-discovery team formation and leadership has become the primary focus of my legal practice.

This blog-to-book project would not have been possible without the many positive comments, suggestions and support from my fellow bloggers and blog readers. I know from their feedback that this book, like the blog, is very accessible to all types of readers. Litigation attorneys with years of experience in e-discovery will enjoy the analysis and finer legal points made here. So too will sophisticated in-house counsel, and academicians. Still, the material is also very accessible to lawyers just beginning in this area, or those who only want to learn something about e-discovery, including paralegals, law students, and law firm IT support professionals. Since most of these blogs explore recent events and technology issues, as well as the law, they have also been of interest to many technologists and management professionals outside of the legal profession. Many of my regular blog readers are non-lawyer IT experts and management involved in some way with e-discovery or general information management services.

I would like to thank my law firm, clients, and fellow professionals in the e-discovery world for helping make this book possible. Of course, thanks also go to my ever tolerant and loving wife and adult children, and to my readers of the "e-Discovery Team" blog, which can be found at: http://ralphlosey.wordpress.com. You may also want to visit my personal website at: http://www.floridalawfirm.com.

Please let me know your ideas and comments concerning any of the topics in the book. Perhaps I will include them in a future edition? You can send me a personal email at ralph.losey@gmail.com.

Ralph C. Losey

Introduction to e-Discovery

1

OVERVIEW OF THE PROBLEMS POSED BY E-DISCOVERY AND THE TEAM-BASED SOLUTION

Computers and other technologies dominate the world as we know it today. This is not a passing fad; it is a new culture. An information and technology age is rapidly replacing the old ways in every field, including the law. This is particularly true for companies and attorneys involved in litigation. Since most of the evidence today is digital, litigators must not only understand the law, and the facts of a dispute, but also the parties' computer systems and data retention practices. Without this understanding they will be unable to preserve or discover the evidence they need to prosecute or defend a case.

The Problem

The IT systems that contain this digital evidence are extremely complex and technical. Most in-house legal counsel and trial lawyers are trained only in the law and paper chases. They have only a poor understanding of the technicalities required to find the needles in today's vast system of computer haystacks. The business executives in most organizations are also ill-prepared in this field and fail to grasp the importance of information management. This has led to many well-known, spectacular losses over the past decade, from *Zubulake* to *Morgan Stanley*.[1] The largest corporations in the country, and the top law firms that represent them, have all made huge, embarrassing errors, some of them many times.

Litigation is now more expensive and risk-filled than ever before, but not, as many believe, because of runaway juries or expensive trials. Although these possibilities remain as real threats, in fact 98% of all federal court cases are resolved without trial. Litigation today is difficult primarily because of *discovery*. In the areas of commercial, regulatory and employment litigation, discovery can involve forced disclosure of massive amounts of internal, otherwise secret, business records and information. The most burdensome discovery today is for email and other electronic documents located on a litigant's computers, so-called "electronic discovery" or "e-discovery." The costs associated with e-discovery requests can be enormous, sometimes far exceeding the total amount in controversy. These same issues also apply to state and federal government investigations where no suit has been filed.

The problem of e-discovery reached such epidemic proportions that on December 1, 2006, the Supreme Court promulgated new Rules of Civil Procedure for all federal courts to follow to try to address these issues. The new rules govern what is referred to as Electronically Stored Information (ESI), which includes not only all computer files, but all other electronic information, such as voice mail and videos. Although the rules clarify certain issues, they also impose very stringent time requirements. For example, the rules now require companies to preserve and produce within 100 days of the commencement of a lawsuit the relevant ESI within their employees' computers and other storage devices (such as thumb drives and cell phones), no matter where they are located. Most U.S. businesses are ill-prepared to meet these deadlines. The situation is worse for foreign companies doing business in the United States for a variety of reasons, including conflict of laws and the widespread dispersion of technology and ESI in different locations around the world.

The new rules, combined with the new email and Internet-oriented culture in both business and society, create serious information manage-

---

1. Zubulake v. UBS, 229 F.R.D. 422 (S.D.N.Y. 2004); Coleman (Parent) Holdings, Inc. v. Morgan Stanley & Co., Inc., 2005 WL 674885 (Fla. Cir. Ct. 2005).

ment difficulties for everyone. The courts tire of mistakes and delay, and are increasing the pressure upon litigants to get their ESI house in order. Strict compliance is starting to be enforced by judges across the country who no longer tolerate the "pure heart, empty head" defense in the area of e-discovery. All litigants are now subject to severe penalties for the accidental deletion of ESI that might be relevant to a lawsuit or government investigation. Liability may accrue, even if the ESI is lost before notice of the suit or investigation, if a court later determines that the proceeding should reasonably have been anticipated. Penalties will almost certainly accrue if the destruction of ESI occurs *after* suit is filed. Business and the legal profession are now more challenged than ever before to solve these problems.

The $1.5 billion verdict against Morgan Stanley in the *Coleman* case in Florida, even though preliminarily reversed on other grounds, shows how important effective preservation procedures have become. So too does the well-known *Zubulake* case in New York against the Swiss bank UBS Warburg, which resulted in a $28 million jury verdict for sexual discrimination. Most agree that UBS Warburg lost the case in large part because of sanctions for missing emails, and not the actual merits of the case. In a world where 60 billion emails are sent daily, and most large corporations have more information stored on their computers than the biggest libraries in the world, the accidental loss of ESI can easily occur. The *Zubulake* and *Coleman* cases show that these mistakes can be very costly.

The Solution

If a large organization is involved in litigation, and that includes almost every large company and branch of government, then it must now solve this problem, *fast*. The consensus solution to this problem is the formation of an e-Discovery Team, an interdepartmental group comprised of lawyers, IT and management. It rests on the three pillars of knowledge essential to effective e-discovery: Information Science, Law, and Technology.

The multidisciplinary team approach to e-discovery unquestionably works, but it is also true that these teams are notoriously difficult to set up, train and function effectively. The cultures of these three groups, even within an otherwise close-knit company, are very different, and so too are their languages and gestalt. Special efforts have to be made to bridge these gaps. For instance, members of the team should be carefully chosen and rewarded for participation, and typical team-building techniques employed. But the most important components for success are training and group work on a detailed, specific set of tasks. (An overview of these tasks is shown in the standard nine-step chart of e-discovery work that follows.) The group work establishes the common language and understanding that will eventually bring the members together and allow them to function as an effective team.

A few companies, such as Cisco, Pfizer, Halliburton and Merrill Lynch, began working on e-discovery teams years ago. They now have successful teams operating that demonstrate the enormous cost-saving and risk-management benefits of the internal team approach. Some of the leaders of these teams provide advice later quoted in this book.

Although all experts I know in the field now advocate for e-discovery teams, and we already have a few success stories as guidance, the vast majority of large organizations today do not have an e-discovery team. They are either in denial about the scope and severity of the e-discovery problem or they have not yet caught on to the fact that an internal e-discovery team is the best solution to this problem. Other companies are aware that they need an e-discovery response team but are still in the early stages of team formation, or their early efforts are floundering for a variety of reasons. Most companies have not been able to get off the ground on this because they lack the necessary expertise or knowledge of the tasks to be performed. They are unfamiliar with the types of e-discovery protocols and procedures they need and underestimate the challenges mentioned with bridging the different cultures of IT and law. The few that have succeeded received help from outside attorneys with special expertise in this field or from consultants and vendors. The best success stories have used all three. This is one reason this is such a rapidly growing field, ripe with potential for lawyers, consultants and e-discovery vendors alike.

Nine-Step Process

The graphics below provide an overview of the entire e-discovery process from the organization's perspective. The nine-step flow chart is based on the industry standard "Electronic Discovery Reference Model" now under development by a group of e-discovery vendors.[2] This model is already widely accepted and employed by most e-discovery specialists. After the graphics, a short synopsis is provided for each step. If you are not ready yet to get into the technical details of how e-discovery functions, or perhaps you are already very familiar with this, you can always skip over this part and come back to it later. The rest of the book will still make sense.

Under my version of the model, the first four steps are performed by the client's internal corporate team, as coached by a law firm or other outside expert, which below is called the "Expert Team Nodes." The last four steps are performed by local legal counsel, with help and assistance as needed by the internal corporate team. The middle step of Processing is begun by the internal team with initial file filtering, but completed and supplemented by local counsel in connection with their Review and Analysis. The first chart illustrates how the volume of data decreases and the relevance increases as the work progresses. The second chart traces the life cycle of the first step, Records Management, which includes the key step of formation of the internal corporate e-discovery team, and the next eight steps: Identification, Preservation, Collection, Processing, Review, Analysis, and Production.

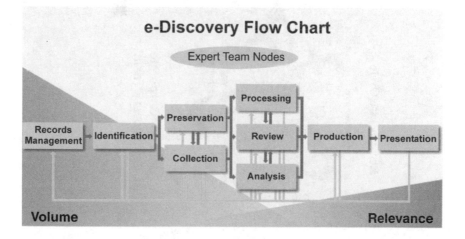

2. http://www.edrm.net/wiki/index.php/Main_Page

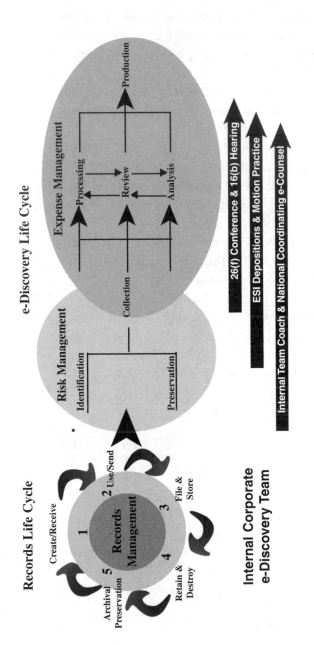

1. Records Management

The first step is for the company to establish or refine an internal e-Discovery Preparedness and Response Team. It typically consists of one or more outside attorneys or other experts in the field of e-discovery, who serve as coach and trainer, and representatives from the client's law department, IT department, key business units, and, where applicable, records management and compliance departments.

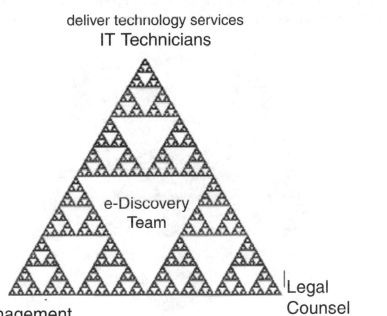

deliver technology services
IT Technicians

e-Discovery
Team

Legal
Counsel
relate to
external forces

Management
establish business policies

Then the outside e-discovery experts assist in articulation of the initial tasks of the team, which typically are as follows: a) identify and retain any outside experts and e-discovery vendors as necessary to meet the specific needs of the client; b) meet with IT and records personnel to perform a complete inventory of client's electronic data and understand the life cycle of the records, and, in the process, obtain a clear and detailed understanding of the client's overall IT architecture and computer systems; c) prepare a computer network and data location map (discussed in the New Technologies chapter) and consider possible technology redesigns to facilitate preservation and production, including E-Mail Filtering and document Archiving systems; d) prepare a form affidavit on computer systems and data, costs and inaccessibility; e) establish or refine standard litigation hold procedures; and f) totally rewrite the existing Records Management Policy Manual, addressing issues of duplicate management, metadata, storage and disposition, and thereafter assist in implementation, ongoing audits and enforcement, and all subsequent technology upgrades. The last one is a particularly big undertaking, but very important to the long-term success of the program.

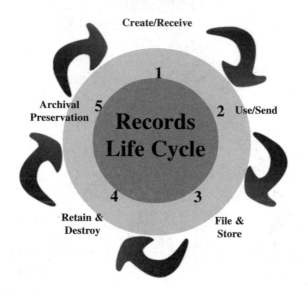

The last step in Records Management, which is tied to the revision of the Policy Manual, is to analyze and, where appropriate, implement a Rule 37(f) Safe Harbor Destruction program in accord with a record life cycle desired by the company and in compliance with all governing laws. Most companies have enormous amounts of unneeded, redundant or legacy data that should be purged. This is a particularly difficult task, but critical to future efficient operations.

2. Identification

The second step is triggered by a lawsuit, subpoena or anticipation of a dispute. You begin a litigation response in the usual fashion by study of the complaint or reasonably anticipated dispute or government investigation. You evaluate the general scope of the electronic and paper data that may fall within the discovery requirements of the dispute, including initial disclosure, and any outstanding discovery requests, retention letters, or orders. Here you analyze possible objections and defenses to unreasonable requests and formulate counter-e-discovery plans.

Next you identify the key witnesses, all sources of discoverable information and the location of all discoverable data, including distributed data or third-party data still owned or under control of the company. As part of this task, you identify and directly communicate with the key witnesses, all relevant centralized IT personnel and data custodians and ascertain what relevant ESI they have. If you have already done a full inventory and map, this function can now proceed quickly and easily.

You then categorize possible relevant data sets by degree of accessibility, such as live, ready-archival, and backup. Again, this is something you should have already done as part of the first-step inventory. At this point you also analyze the metadata and embedded data characteristics of the identified databases and whether this may be relevant to the dispute.

At this early stage in federal litigation, you prepare for and participate in the initial "meet and confer" sessions with opposing counsel and the court. The outside counsel members of the team are also involved in any subsequent hearings related to e-discovery. The purpose here is to reach agreement with opposing counsel or apply for relief from the court early in the case as to identification, preservation, collection, processing and production procedures, including format of production (native or TIFF), confidentiality agreements, and clawback agreements to protect against accidental waiver of privilege.

3. Preservation

After you roughly identify what ESI is at issue, you need to make sure it is preserved and protected against destruction or alteration. Generally in this step you segregate and preserve ESI for later possible collection. You begin the process by preparation and circulation of a Litigation Hold written communication. Ideally this occurs within a few days' notice of the dispute. The hold notice should come from senior management or in-house legal counsel, with a copy to all relevant data custodians, including witnesses. At the same time, you implement litigation holds where feasible by automated processes, and, where a large number of players are involved, by utilization of systemwide keyword searches or more intelligent concept-type searches. Preservation is done on a very broad-brush basis, and it is common to simply copy all PST email files of key players and image (fully copy) their hard drives.

At this point you also consider whether forensic data capture may be necessary. This might be appropriate if you have reason to suspect that relevant files have been deleted, written over or damaged, or if there is reason to believe there is hidden or encrypted data on a system.

As part of the preservation efforts you may also calendar the applicable backup deletion schedules and place on hold where appropriate. You also suspend or modify all "janitor programs" and related procedures that automatically delete ESI that may be relevant.

Generally you preserve on a very broad basis, you are more selective in the next collection step, and even more selective in production. For example, it would not be unusual to preserve 100,000 emails, but only collect 50,000, and produce 10,000.

4. Collection

After the ESI has been preserved, you next collect from the preserved data the information you think is most likely relevant or responsive. This is, in effect, a second round of weeding out data. ESI is narrowed for many reasons, all of which must be carefully documented and considered for reasonability. First, there may be a certain amount of ESI that you have preserved but do not intend to further search or collect, because you have identified it as inaccessible under Rule 26(b)(2) (which primarily means unreasonable or disproportionate cost and effort). Other ESI may have been preserved, but you consider its relevance to be too unlikely to justify any collection efforts.

At this stage, it is important to have further interviews with key players regarding keywords used and networks of people involved so as to prepare appropriate search terms and Boolean logic and concept searches. You also confirm date ranges, identities of witnesses, and file-type inclusions.

In the Rule 26(f) conference with opposing counsel, you should try to reach agreement on applicable search terms and de-duplication parameters. At this point in the process, you prepare a technical plan for the actual data gathering with significant input from outside vendors.

Next you implement the plan and begin data collection from all applicable sources (tapes, drives, portable storage devices, networks, etc.). The team directs supervision of technician activities to confirm valid chain of custody and authenticity protocols, including preservation of metadata, MD5 or SHA-1 Hash authentication, labeling, and identification. Meticulous record keeping and documentation of procedures and sources are required throughout the collection process. Data sampling of backup tapes may also be required at this stage, wherein later processing will determine whether additional restoration is required.

5. Processing

The initial processing of the ESI collected, primarily de-duplication, is performed in tandem with the collection itself to avoid unnecessary vendor search charges. In this step, you reduce the overall set of data collected by filtering out files that are duplicates or known to be irrelevant after further investigation. Files that are probably not relevant because of factors such as date, type, or origin may also be excluded at this step, if they were not previously excluded. Hot files may also be flagged at this stage, including obviously adverse or potentially embarrassing materials, and brought to the attention of trial counsel.

In processing, you need to consider the relationships between the files or documents obtained to better understand what data has been collected and determine whether additional data extraction may be required. All of these steps may in some circumstances have to be employed on an iterative basis, which means to make changes to the prior task and do it again.

Again, in this step, as before, you prepare reports to document the reduced set of computer files to be transferred to local counsel, marking what has been filtered out and why. To the extent necessary, you may also convert electronically stored information from the native form in which it was used to another format required by local counsel or the court.

The e-Discovery Team should maintain a full copy of all data collected and maintain originals of any media as necessary, including backup tapes. After the team's initial processing, a full duplicate set of the culled data is delivered to local counsel and vendors for further de-duplication, processing, review, analysis, production and presentation. Quality control is important throughout the processing and review phases to avoid spoliation or other problems. The backup set in the team's custody will serve as a safeguard should any such problems arise.

6. Review

The ESI collected now has to be studied. You review for relevance, confidentiality and privilege, and related activities such as redaction. Appropriate search techniques and strategies often vary but can include keyword, Boolean, proximity and, again, concept searching. The review team segregates all privileged and confidential documents located and prepares a Privilege Log. Large attorney teams may be involved in this stage to review large quantities of documents. A full chapter of this book is devoted entirely to the critical step of search and review. Suffice it to say that over half of the expenses of e-discovery are incurred in that step.

7. Analysis

Analysis is the process of evaluating the data reviewed to determine relevant summary information, such as key issues, witnesses, specific vocabulary and jargon, and important individual documents. Typically, this step involves integration of the data into trial preparation software. Analysis is performed throughout the remainder of the process as new information is uncovered and issues of the case evolve. This is a traditional legal step that competent trial lawyers are already qualified to perform. Only large quantities of ESI and unusual forms and authentication issues will pose special challenges for analysis, and in the last steps of Production and Presentation.

8. Production

Here, if not before, you perform hash marking (explained in the "New Technologies" chapter) and labeling of all ESI culled for production. Then you deliver the ESI to opposing counsel and various other recipients (co-counsel, corporate legal department, service providers, etc.) on various types of media (CD, DVD, tape, hard drive, portable storage device, other). You may also deliver the ESI to other members of your litigation team for use in other systems (automated litigation support system, Web-based repository, etc.). Before production to opposing counsel, you should verify proper execution of clawback and confidentiality agreements.

9. Presentation

Although this is the last stage, you should always keep in mind possible methods to present the ESI effectively at depositions, hearings and trial. Will you use projections of a computer screen, video, still image enlargenents, etc.?

Blog Reader Comment

E-discovery is upon us! We can ride the wave or get swamped by it! Thanks for setting up this blog!

INTELLECTUAL FOUNDATION OF ELECTRONIC DISCOVERY

Technology

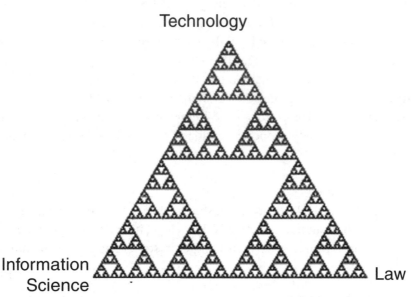

Information
Science

Law

Electronic discovery is a new, multidisciplinary field of knowledge that arises out of the law, but goes beyond it to include information science and technology. This new fractal[3] synthesis is emerging by necessity to meet the many radical challenges imposed upon our system of justice by the rapid acceleration of technology.

Our writings and other forms of communication are being digitized at a dizzying pace. In one generation we have moved from a primarily pa-

---

3.   A fractal is a geometric figure with self similarity over different scales of size. They are key to finding hidden order in what otherwise appears to be random chaotic systems. The Sierpinski Triangle shown in the diagram above is an example of a fractal. Fractals are found everywhere in nature, but can also be created on computers using iterative mathematics with complex imaginary numbers. The best-known computer-generated fractal is the Mandelbrot set. Fractals and the math underlying them are essential to modern chaos theories, which are at the core of advanced physics, information science, and many new forms of technology. Although this subject is beyond the scope of this book, most e-discovery experts today are beginning to explore iterative processes and statistical sampling in the "collection and search" stages to improve the quality of the processes and cut costs.

per-based, tangible information culture to a culture based on intangible binary code. We have moved from a society that stores and retrieves information locally in paper files, filing cabinets, books and libraries to one that stores information globally in electronic devices and the Internet.

This revolution is necessarily having a profound impact upon the law, because information is the foundation of our justice system. We determine what is just and right based on the evidence. As Judge Scheindlin stated in *Zubulake IV*: "Documents create a paper reality we call proof." *Zubulake v. UBS Warburg, LLC*, 220 F.R.D. 212 (S.D.N.Y. 2003). For lawyers to adapt to this new world, we need to rethink what we mean by documents—to understand and revisualize them as electronically stored information. Then we will see the electronic reality we call proof.

As information scientist Jason Baron put it in the law review article he recently wrote with attorney George Paul: "Information is fundamental to the legal system. Accordingly, lawyers must understand that information, as a cultural and technological edifice, has profoundly and irrevocably changed." *Information Inflation: can the legal system adapt?*, 13 RICH. J.L. & TECH. 10 (2007).[4] Baron and Paul argue that litigators must move beyond the gamesmanship model of paper discovery into a more cooperative search for truth in e-discovery. They point out how the sheer volume of electronic documents makes this new collaborative model imperative. They do not suggest that the adversarial system of dispute resolution be abandoned entirely, just that the discovery model be changed. They also argue for the creative adoption of new technologies and records management systems by lawyers. They observe correctly that:

> All this equates to perhaps the biggest new skill set ever thrust upon the profession—a revolution for the practice. What it means to be a lawyer will change rapidly in the years to come.

The new skill set needed to comprehend the electronic reality we call proof does not come easily. Many are unwilling to take the time and effort needed to begin to master the rudimentary elements of computer technology and information science. The younger generations have some advantage in familiarity with technology, but still most have never studied information technology and records management in college. Very

---

4. http://law.richmond.edu/jolt/v13i3/article10.pdf

few move from out of these disciplines into the law. Unfortunately, these subjects are ignored altogether in most law schools. Therefore, until academia catches up with these new trends and radically alters curricula to match the new reality, most lawyers will have no choice but to try to learn these new fields on their own, or in CLEs. Unfortunately, most of the CLEs on information management and technology in e-discovery are sponsored by vendors and have not-so-hidden agendas. They often make competing and confusing claims on what technology to use and how to manage the flow of information. Until you have had a few decades of experience with all this, it can be very difficult to sort out.

I expect (hope) that the quality of continuing education for lawyers in the areas of Information Science and Technology will improve dramatically in the next few years. Most of this will come in the context of litigation and e-discovery, but other areas of the law are also burdened with the flood of information. In the meantime, we will all have to struggle and do the best we can on our own, attending seminars given by vendors and others with a healthy dose of skepticism.

One good place to start is The Sedona Conference;[5] although most of the materials relate to the law, they also contain a heavy dose of IT. Other places to look and learn are *Computer World*,[6] the IEEE Computer Society,[7] the Association of Records Managers and Administrators,[8] and many technology law review periodicals. For Web sites on information science, try the Digital Library of Information Science and Technology,[9] an open-access archive for the information sciences; the *Journal of Information Science*;[10] and the American Society for Information and Technology.[11]

There are other "fun" and entertaining sites and blogs where you can keep up with the latest trends and learn as you go, such as IT Wire,[12] the ever-popular WIRED,[13] the venerable *PC World* Magazine,[14] the hip

---

5. http://www.thesedonaconference.org./
6. http://www.computerworld.com/
7. http://www.ieee.org/portal/site
8. http://www.arma.org/
9. http://dlist.sir.arizona.edu/
10. http://jis.sagepub.com/
11. http://www.asis.org/
12. http://www.itwire.com.au/
13. http://www.wired.com/
14. http://www.pcworld.com/

headliner SlashDotOrg,[15] the GigaOm,[16] the Register,[17] the DIGG,[18] and Tech Crunch,[19] to name just a few. A few minutes with Google will uncover many more.

TOP TRENDS IN E-DISCOVERY NOTED AT ILTA CONFERENCE

I attended the annual convention in 2007 of the International Legal Technology Association (ILTA). This is a big event for law firm IT staff and a few lawyers like me. More than 2,300 "techies" turned out to attend 190 different educational sessions and check out the 150 vendors on display. The ILTA event is also a networking and geek social heaven; the big multivendor-sponsored party is rumored to have cost over a half million dollars. The seminars related to e-discovery were filled to capacity, whereas other areas seemed nearly empty. My favorite CLE-type event was a panel presentation on e-discovery trends by attorneys and IT specialists from several large firms, including DLA Piper and Sullivan & Cromwell. Browning Marean, the chair of Piper's e-discovery team, was particularly effective in delivery. I understand from panelist Art Smith, of Husch & Eppenberger, that Art prepared most of this list, and so kudos to him too. Here is their list of top ten trends.

1. Courts Set Minimum Standards to Supplement the New Rules.
2. Discovery Battles Take Center Stage.
3. Sanctions Become Meaningful Threat.
4. Erosion of the Attorney-Client Privilege.
5. Inaccessible Data Not Really Inaccessible.
6. "Best Practices" Standards Begin to Emerge.
7. Abundance of Electronic Resources.
8. Law Firms Adopt New Approaches.
9. Corporations Finally Starting to Recognize the Risks.
10. Vendors Consolidate and Expand.

---

15. http://slashdot.org/
16. http://gigaom.com/
17. http://www.theregister.co.uk/
18. http://digg.com/
19. http://www.techcrunch.com/

Although for the most part I think the panel got it right, I do have a few points of disagreement. Here is my take on the trends they discuss.

1. Courts Set Minimum Standards to Supplement the New Rules. All Rules of Civil Procedure are typically general in nature and deliberately avoid specifics of application or detail. A certain degree of vagueness and ambiguity are inevitable. The new Federal Rules of Civil Procedure (FRCP) on e-discovery are no exception. They substantially change the conduct of e-discovery, especially its timing. Parties are now required to confer within the first 100 days and reach agreement on e-discovery issues. But the rules do not spell out the details of the conferences and agreements. This leads to vastly different interpretations and implementations between practitioners. It can also lead to unfair "gotcha" situations caused by noncompliance, either through inadvertence or lack of knowledge.

Everyone expects years of litigation before any bright lines of conduct come out of the new e-discovery rules. In the meantime, several district courts have begun to issue guidelines of conduct they expect from counsel to comply with the new rules, especially new Rule 26(f) on "meet and confer" conferences. This trend is very likely to continue and accelerate, and eventually to spill over into the state court systems. See the Appendix for a list of district courts that have already issued some kind of local rules or guidelines for e-discovery. Many of the new guidelines specify exactly what the local court expects the parties to discuss and agree upon. These guidelines thus serve an important function to supplement and clarify several aspects of the new FRCP, and thereby help establish minimum standards of professional conduct.

While I agree this is indeed a current trend in e-discovery, I do not think it is the number one trend, or even close. In truth, there are still only a small number of judges involved in this infant effort.

Chief among this still-small group of minimum standard-setters is Magistrate Judge Paul Grimm. He is a leader in e-discovery whose thoughts and published decisions in this area are discussed frequently in this book. With the help of the local bar in Baltimore, he has written "suggested protocols" of what should happen at 26(f) conferences and the "best thinking" on minimum standards for the kind of information to be exchanged.[20] His suggestions include an extensive list of discussion topics for any case involving discovery of electronic documents, including: the scope of the litigation hold; identification of key custodians; nature and types of ESI involved; metadata concerns; IT network infrastructure; backups; legacy systems with potentially discoverable ESI; records management policies; form of production; de-duplication issues; preservation of data on "dynamic" systems and application of the Rule 37 "safe harbor" for document destruction; quick-peek or clawback strategies for privileged documents; ESI "deemed not reasonably accessible"; document tracking or Bates numbering; cost-sharing issues; possibility of two-tiered discovery; protective orders for confidential information; and Rule 30(b)(6) depositions on IT systems.

2. Discovery Battles Take Center Stage.

This trend is for discovery battles to take on a life of their own and become far more important to a case than the actual merits. This trend in e-discovery started several years ago and is still increasing every year In fact, I would call this the number one trend. The new rules were designed in part to try to counter this trend, because discovery battles often result in cases being tried or settled based on side issues instead of the merits of the underlying dispute. Unfortunately, I predict that this trend will continue for the next five to ten years, if not longer.

Although not discussed by the panel, this trend, in my view, is driven by four forces: (1) businesses and governments have not spent the time and money required to organize and control their electronic records and prepare for e-discovery; (2) the bar, especially litigators, have not learned enough about e-discovery, nor their clients' IT systems, and do not yet understand the importance of e-discovery to dispute resolution today; instead, most law firms still tend to relegate e-discovery to young associates, just like they did paper discovery; (3) the judiciary also needs to improve its understanding in this area and recognize the special problems inherent in the preservation, search and production of ESI; and (4) the plaintiff's bar is starting to recognize that e-discovery is a powerful litigation weapon, especially when suing companies with large IT systems and voluminous ESI storage.

---

20. http://www.mdd.uscourts.gov/news/news/ESIProtocol.pdf

protection requires disclosure of what was previously hidden from opposing counsel under the veil of attorney-client or work-product secrecy.

5.   Inaccessible Data Not Really Inaccessible.

Here the panel was observing the beginning of a trend to extensively litigate Rule 26(b)(2)(B). This rules states that a party does not have to produce ESI that is "not reasonably accessible by reason of undue burden or
costs." But the rule also provides that even if a party proves no reasonable
accessibility, it may still be required to produce that ESI if the requesting
party proves good cause. To make matters more complex and ripe for
litigation, if good cause is shown, the court may still order cost shifting,
where all or part of the production expenses are shifted to the requesting
party. Rule 26(b)(2)(B) is discussed at length in the "New Rules" chapter,
and the rule with commentaries is included in the Appendix.

Although the panel pointed to litigation of 26(b)(2)(B) as a trend, I
would enlarge that trend to include litigation of all of the new rules, but
especially new Rule 34. Rule 34(a) includes for the first time, but does not
define, "electronically stored information." This is already a hot button, as
is shown by the recent decision in Los Angeles interpreting ESI to include
RAM memory, even though the electronic information may only be stored
for less than a second. *Columbia Pictures Industries v. Bunnell*, Case No.
CV 06-1093 (FMC(JCx)) (Doc. No. 176).[23] The *Columbia Pictures* case
and its implications are discussed at length in the "New Technologies"
chapter. Litigation of the requirements of Rule 34(b) as to form of production is another important trend, one that is here to stay for many years. It
allows parties to specify the form of production of the ESI, and states that
if no form is stated in the requests, the default is the form in which it is
"ordinarily maintained," or in a "reasonably usable form."

This in turn raises the whole issue of native files and metadata, addressed at length in the "Metadata" chapter. This is directly related to
Rule 34(b) form litigation because ESI is "ordinarily maintained" in its
native state with full preservation of metadata. In fact, concern and disputes about metadata is an important trend by itself, one which, oddly
enough, the panel completely overlooked. Based upon the case law and
interest among attorneys I have seen on this subject, I would put metadata

---

23.   http://i.i.com/cnwk.1d/pdf/ne/2007/Torrentspy.pdf

in the top five of trends. Attorneys are concerned with whether they should produce ESI in native format with full metadata or convert first to an image file, such as TIFF. They are also paranoid about inadvertently disclosing confidential information by not properly stripping metadata, and even about whether it is ethical to look at the metadata in another party's production.

6. "Best Practices" Standards Begin to Emerge.

In addition to some courts setting minimum standards, at least two private groups are working on the related task of establishing best practices standards. The dominant group by far in e-discovery is The Sedona Conference[24] and its numerous publications in this area, but primarily the Sedona Principles. These principles were updated in 2007 and are described in detail later in this chapter. Another group made up primarily of vendors is starting to have more influence—the previously mentioned Electronic Discovery Reference Model Project.[25] This group developed the now industry-standard nine-step description of e-discovery described previously. Like almost everyone else, I consider this a very effective model to understand and explain how e-discovery should work. In the future, several new groups will probably emerge to help establish best practices for e-discovery. The most likely candidate is the ABA itself, which convened the First Annual National Institute on E-Discovery in 2007 (described in the "Ethical Standards" chapter). Moreover, in 2004 the ABA completed a well-conceived e-discovery addition to the ABA Civil Discovery Standards, a copy of which is included in the Appendix.

Perhaps even more important than these public groups to the actual practice of law are the efforts of private law firms around the country to establish their own internal best practices standards. The panel pointed out that such standards and forms have already been developed by a few of the leading firms in the country and circulated to all litigators in the firm, but they knew of only one firm so far that actually required all litigators to follow the rules. Litigation shareholders in law firms are an independent bunch and resist being told what to do. Browning Marean

---

24. http://www.thesedonaconference.org/. As a member of this group I am admittedly somewhat biased, but at this point everyone seems to agree with this assertion.

25. http://www.edrm.net/

admitted what everyone in the profession already knows—that trying to get the litigators to follow the guidelines he has developed for his firm was like "herding cats." Instead, they are more likely to wait until something goes wrong and then ask for help. Most of the best practices and forms that have been developed by law firms are kept secret and not circulated outside of the firm. I know I have spent many days, if not weeks, working on creating and refining my law firm's best practices standards, which I call checklists and forms, and these will most certainly not be found in this book.

7.   Abundance of Electronic Resources.

This is the trend of increasing quality information on e-discovery. It is now relatively easy to find valuable resources in both electronic and paper form. Google will lead you to dozens of on-line sources, such as my blog (http://ralphlosey.wordpress.com). In addition, several more paper books like this one are being published. Of course, when you have a superabundance of information, a quality control problem arises. Many contradictory statements are being made, especially among competing e-discovery vendors, some of whom make shockingly inaccurate statements or routinely engage in hyperbole and misstatements of the law. The misstatements are especially rife in summarizing what the new rules supposedly require companies to do (typically, buy their software).

8.   Law Firms Adopt New Approaches.

Private law firms are beginning to form interdisciplinary teams to render e-discovery services where litigation attorneys, litigation support paralegals and IT technicians, and other experts in the firm are blending their expertise. This is indeed a trend, but an even more important trend, in my opinion, which the panel only briefly mentioned, is the formation of interdisciplinary teams in business and government to address e-discovery issues. This is the client's e-discovery team concept discussed at the start of this chapter, and which you will see repeated as a theme throughout this book.

Instead of recognizing this all-important client trend, the panel focused on internal law firm teams. They also pointed out that law firms are now outsourcing document review to lower-paid contract-lawyers to try to cut costs. Actually, this contract-lawyer trend started years ago, and some firms have even gone so far as to outsource relevance and privilege review to lawyers in India. This trend is expected to continue—not only for cost-savings, but also to fight the "boredom factor" for young associates and paralegals in some large firms. They would rather quit, no matter what the pay, than spend all of their time for weeks on end reading other people's email, most of it boring. It may require cultural familiarity and speed-reading skills, but no real legal expertise. So let the hungry lawyers in India do it. But do they have the cultural familiarity to do it right? Many doubt that, and so almost all outsourcing today is to laid-back U.S. lawyers who do not want a regular nine-to-five job at a law firm for a variety of reasons. Many question the quality of their work.

The panel also suggested that it was a trend for law firms to keep e-discovery IT-type processing in-house, instead of shipping it to outside vendors, or allowing the clients to do it themselves. Personally I disagree, and do not think this is a new trend, but rather the final gasps of an older e-discovery paradigm. For years, many large law firms have tried to keep all of these services in-house. The firm would take responsibility for all e-discovery IT services and would bill *a lot* for it. This became a significant profit center for many law firms. In my opinion, this old model accounts for some of the high costs in e-discovery, and clients will no longer stand for it. Moreover, it turns law firms into IT business ventures with their own agendas and moves attorneys away from the profession they were trained for. There are also many ethical issues raised by this questionable model of legal services, although I am sure that most firms do a good job balancing the competing interests involved.

Even the panel admitted that management in law firms with large in-house capacity were now struggling with these issues and subjecting their business model to careful risk-and-reward analysis. I believe that the real trend here is, or soon will be, to move away from this captive exclusive model into the new paradigm promoted in this book of discovery teams paired with clients and assisted by vendors. In the new model, a law firm IT department would only infrequently process client data, typically only in smaller and less complex projects. The larger projects would be performed by clients and vendors under the supervision of law firms. This would not be a popular message at an ILTA conference, many of whose members make a living processing the data of the firm's clients and so would be at risk in the new paradigm. For that reason, I am not surprised that it was never mentioned at this event as an emerging trend.

9. Corporations Finally Starting to Recognize the Risks.

The panel thinks that corporate America is finally starting to get it—to recognize that they must get a better handle on their records and be prepared for e-discovery. They correctly noted that for many years most large organizations have taken a kind of "ostrich" approach to the looming problem and tried to ignore the disastrous lawsuits that happen to other companies. Consistent with that policy of denial and avoidance, they have instructed their legal counsel to adopt what the panel called "don't ask, don't tell" agreements with opposing counsel. This has worked in the past when two large companies were suing each other. It is usually referred to as the "MAD" approach ("Mutually Assured Destruction"), and e-discovery is the nuclear weapon that both sides informally agree not to use. If one company did dare to drop a bomb of an e-discovery request, the other would respond in kind. It kept the peace for many years but is now as passé as the Cold War itself. Of course, this approach has never worked in the "David and Goliath"-type lawsuits typical in employment claims, as *Zubulake* shows. It is impractical today even in suits between "big boys," because if you "don't ask, don't tell" with e-discovery, you will never find out what really happened. Because almost all of the evidence is now electronic, if you ignore e-discovery, you ignore discovery. This is especially true for email, which is where most of the "smoking guns" in litigation today are found.

The panel contends that these days are now over, and the trend is for companies to wake up and get with the program. They are getting ready by: (1) appointing an e-discovery liaison within corporate hierarchy, which is a start to the full-blown internal e-discovery team that I advocate in this book; (2) updating records retention policies on electronic records; (3) adopting new software tools for data recovery; (4) adopting new content management strategies; (5) selecting preferred e-discovery vendors; and (6) retaining one or two law firms to act as national e-discovery counsel to coordinate all e-discovery issues in litigation pending in various jurisdictions around the country.

They put this as the second to last trend, and I tend to agree with that, not because it is not important—it is obviously very important—but because this is a new trend, still in its infancy. Many companies have not yet received the message; or they have heard the buzz but do not understand its importance, and so continue to put it off until later. The truth is, most of the companies that are already pursuing e-discovery programs are driven by past e-discovery disasters, or at least big problems. Maybe they lost a case outright because of e-discovery mistakes, or they were slapped with sanctions, or maybe they won a case but in the process had to pay outrageous e-discovery costs and fees. More likely they had to settle a case, or pay too much to settle, just because of the e-discovery exposure. Some companies have had to be burned several times before they reacted. The sanctions and forced settlements continue as the number one trend in e-discovery due in large part to the failure of businesses to respond promptly or take proactive measures.

10. Vendors Consolidate and Expand.
The final trend noted was in the e-discovery vendor industry, which by all accounts now has income of several billion dollars a year. The larger vendors are buying up the smaller ones, and services are moving away from multiple specialty vendors to a few full-service vendors. The trend appears to be toward the one-stop-solution vendor that handles all stages of e-discovery from records creation and retention to collection, review and production.

There are a few more major trends in the vendor area that they did not mention. First is the move to all on-line review, using secure connections to vendor computers instead of storing ESI on law firm servers. Related to this trend is the move to a pricing structure based solely on ESI size alone—that is, a charge per gigabyte for everything, including the software needed for attorney review. Another trend only briefly mentioned by the panel is the move away from simple keyword searching to more efficient "concept searches." This is very significant and will become much more so in the coming years. I explore this further in the "Search and Review" chapter. Finally, there is the strong but controversial trend toward pure "native file review" and away from image file review in TIFF-like formats. Many promote this development as a way

The one-day event that included Justice Breyer on a panel was held at the Georgetown University Law Center and sponsored by e-discovery vendor H5.[28] The panel discussion was moderated by Harvard's famous civil procedure professor, Arthur Miller.[29] Other panelists included Richard Braman of Sedona, Jason Baron from the National Archives, and Judge John Facciola. The discussions and recommendations of this distinguished faculty are well summarized in the Gartner Research Note: *Cost of E-Discovery Threatens to Skew Justice System.*[30] I recommend reading this in full, but here is my summary of the highlights:

1. The expense of e-Discovery has risen dramatically along with the massive profusion of technology in society, especially the Internet and email, and the general explosion in the amount of information.

2. The costs of e-discovery today are too high, and this great expense is having a negative impact on society and the practice of law.

3. There is a danger that only the rich will be able to afford the costs of e-discovery inherent in the lawsuits of today and tomorrow.

4. There is a danger that lawsuits will be decided on the basis of process instead of merit, especially if an organization does not effectively manage its electronic information.

5. The problem of e-discovery should be a high priority for both the legal profession and business.

6. Lawyers and senior management do not understand or comprehend the complexity of the technology or the volumes of information produced by organizations today.

7. The high cost of e-discovery can be attributed to (a) the adversarial nature of litigation, (b) bad or nonexistent document retention polices, and (c) undisciplined deployment of technology.

8. Lawyers need to make better use of technology in e-discovery and to adopt a more collaborative approach to discovery.

---

28. http://www.h5technologies.com/
29. http://www.law.harvard.edu/faculty/directory/facdir.php?id=44
30. http://www.h5technologies.com/pdf/gartner0607.pdf

9. Businesses and other large organizations need to better manage and control their storage of information. Specifically, the panel recommended they: (a) develop reasonable document retention policies that support the needs of the business and destroy information when it is no longer needed; (b) communicate, educate and enforce document retention policies; and (c) use technology to automate document retention policy and compliance.

10. There is a need for neutral third parties in litigation to help determine what needs to be discovered.

The Gartner Research Note concluded that:

> The long-term trend that emerges from this panel is the fact that the legal community is under an obligation to learn about the IT infrastructure, topology and architecture of the organizations they represent.
>
> Information technology has created the problem of massive amounts of data that the court system must deal with. Only technology can solve the problem if it includes well-designed business processes and policies. Throwing technology at the e-discovery problem is in itself ineffective. In a perfect world, the solution to the e-discovery problem would combine the expertise of lawyers, line-of-business owners, IT professionals and a host of other disciplines.

In other words, Gartner here recommends the multidisciplinary team approach. Gartner goes on to specifically recommend that its clients address e-discovery readiness now, beginning with an inventory of all information assets, de-duplication, and destruction of redundant and unneeded data "in a legally sanctioned and policy-driven way." I could not agree more.

| **Blog Reader Comment** |

Gartner raises some excellent points in its call for a multidisciplinary team approach to electronic discovery. In my experience, this approach is the only way to conduct truly effective e-discovery. Attorneys provide the overall legal guidance and management. IT professionals are the keepers of the computer and network systems where the data is to be found. And e-discovery vendors provide the specialist expertise that ensures that the process is conducted in a manner that is both legally and technically sound. On the issue of cost, corporations can help themselves by implementing good compliance procedures that support efficient e-discovery processes. At the same time, third-party software companies can provide advanced technologies that significantly reduce manual processes—a major component of the cost of any large discovery effort—while simultaneously reducing risk.

TOP TEN REASONS E-DISCOVERY IS A MAJOR HEADACHE FOR MOST COMPANIES AND LAWYERS

Most corporate counsel agree that electronic discovery is *the* major problem in litigation today. Here are the top ten reasons:

1. The costs to preserve, find and review electronic evidence, including emails, are astronomical and getting worse every day. See, for example, *Kentucky Speedway v. NASCAR*, 2006 U.S. Dist. LEXIS 92028 (E. D. Ky. Dec. 18, 2006) ($3 million in expenses in five months for e-discovery alone). According to an unconfirmed report by a Microsoft insider, it now spends an average of $20 million per case. It is no surprise that e-discovery is now the hot field for entrepreneurs, and that it has mushroomed into a $2 billion a year industry.
2. The unacceptably high risks of losing a case, or being forced to settle a case, because of e-discovery rather than the merits. The mistakes in e-discovery are pervasive and often disastrous. The biggest of them all is the *Coleman v. Morgan Stanley* case in

Florida, which resulted in a $1.5 billion verdict. *Coleman (Parent) Holdings, Inc. v. Morgan Stanley & Co., Inc.,* 2005 WL 674885 (Fla.Cir. Ct. 2005) (Although the decision has preliminarily been reversed, the Florida courts are not through with this yet.). Also see: *GTFM, Inc. v. Wal-Mart,* 2000 WL 1693615 (S.D.N.Y. Nov. 9, 2000) (sanctions); *Exact Software v. Infocon,* 2006 WL 34999992 (N.D. Ohio) (Dec. 5, 2006) (more sanctions); *Phoenix Four, Inc. v. Strategic Resources Corp.,* 2006 WL 1409413 (S.D.N.Y. 2006) (still more sanctions).

3. Electronic records are easy to destroy or alter, but the bad emails and instant messages never seem to go away! The smoking guns in courtrooms today are found in computers, not filing cabinets. In fact, 98% of all business records are now electronic, and 80% of them are never converted to paper or any other tangible form. So if you don't look for the ESI, you will miss the key evidence.

4. The amount of electronic information stored by most corporations today is staggering. In the *Enron* case, they found twice as much information stored in its computers than in the Library of Congress—over 78 billion pages. As of 2006, the world was sending 60 billion e-mails per day. The volume makes it impossible to retrieve and review everything in most large cases today, and nearly impossible for anyone not an expert to find the needles in the digital haystack.

5. The computer systems and information storage systems have become extremely complex. It is difficult for any one expert to understand it all. The complexity makes mistakes almost inevitable, and explanation to supervising judges and magistrates nearly impossible.

6. Most companies do not have functional ESI management policies. If they do, they are not monitored, much less enforced. With thumb drives and on-line accounts today so commonplace, most companies have no idea where all their business records and communications really are, even if they know where they are supposed to be.

7. There have been so many mistakes with e-discovery in the past several years that many judges and magistrates are now upset.

They will no longer tolerate mistakes. As one judge puts it, "The 'pure heart, empty head' defense will no longer work in my courtroom." Most judges today are reacting by imposing high standards and duties upon the parties and legal counsel. See, for example, *Zubulake v. UBS*, 229 F.R.D. 422 (S.D.N.Y. 2004) (Zubulake V) as discussed further in the "Ethics" chapter.

8. The New Federal Rules of Civil Procedure make the problem worse by accelerating all deadlines and prohibiting the avoidance of e-discovery issues until the end of a case. The only way to comply with the new rules is to be extremely well prepared, even before a lawsuit is filed, and that requires tech-savvy legal counsel and well-prepared litigants.

9. Most lawyers and law firms are unprepared for e-discovery. Attorneys need to know the basics of information management and computer technology to handle e-discovery issues correctly, but in fact, most do not. They do not even like the subject. As everyone in the profession knows, most trial lawyers are big talkers, not geeks. If a law firm does have one or two attorneys with some tech expertise, they are typically the youngest, with little or no litigation experience.

10. Most corporations and in-house legal counsel are unprepared for e-discovery. They may have fine IT departments and great inside legal counsel, but the two departments speak very different languages and do not work well together.

The only viable solution to the problem of e-discovery is for a company to create its own internal e-discovery readiness response team. The alternative of delegating everything to expensive e-discovery vendors, and dozens of outside counsel around the country, has been tried and does not work. Of course, vendors are still key, and so are outside counsel, but the corporate client needs to be in charge of its own destiny. The internal e-discovery team is the best hope to reduce costs, manage risks, and better control quality.

As discussed before, the team is composed of in-house attorneys, IT personnel and management. It rests on the three pillars of law, information science, and technology. The team functions to implement litigation holds, collect data within the time line of new rules, retain e-discovery vendors, supervise local counsel, and improve electronic records systems. A few companies such as Pfizer, Halliburton and Merrill Lynch have done this already, and it works. But experience shows it is hard to get Law and IT to work together and communicate. Most companies want and need outside help to set up their team. That is where e-discovery specialists come in, and the services of law firms with special expertise in this area.

Geek lawyers make the team happen! Ideally, they empower the client by helping the company to start and run its own team. The techno-lawyer serves as team coach and trainer. The client is the owner, which has its own team captain. Just like a coach sometimes has to step up and argue with the referees, the lawyer must sometimes appear in court when necessary to advocate the team's position and assist local counsel on these issues. In that sense, the lawyers on the team also serve as a national e-counsel, coordinating the activities of local counsel. It is a challenging service but a joy to perform once you have a basic understanding of the three pillars underlying this new field: law, technology, and information science.

Blog Reader Comment

I completely agree. The need to be prepared in electronic discovery for litigation purposes has already been established, but as companies start to realize the benefits of taking a pre-emptive approach, they also notice the need for a change in the IT system. That is why many e-discovery software vendors are encouraging companies to move the e-discovery practice in-house and use the outside vendors as a customer support forum for the technology. The "team" approach is exactly what we are looking for in the future of this industry, and we as a company would like to aid in this transition. Electronic discovery and record management are changing the litigation field, but it is also affecting the infrastructure of businesses, and companies need to respond accordingly.

NATIONAL E-DISCOVERY COUNSEL AND THE 98% RULE

I attended a national CLE panel on e-discovery yesterday with a first-class faculty of judges, in-house counsel and attorneys. They all reported observing a new trend in legal practice: national e-discovery counsel. One attorney or law firm serves as a corporation's national counsel to handle or supervise the electronic discovery aspects of all of its cases around the country. The corporation's various local counsel handle all other aspects of the case. The faculty said they are seeing this new model now more and more. All agreed that it makes good sense, especially in view of the tremendous time and effort it takes for an attorney to learn the complexities of today's typical IT environment. It is far too expensive to try to educate all of a corporation's various outside counsel. Besides, most of them are not yet up to the task. The panelists noted that there are not many lawyers around today with an IT background that allows them to learn these complex systems. Most lawyers like that have already formed their own specialty IT firms or have been hired by e-discovery vendors.

The panelists all agreed that there appears to be a sea change under way in the litigation world, where the importance of discovery is coming to be recognized. Merrill Lynch's Jonathan Eisenberg noted that for all practical purposes, discovery today means electronic discovery. This is consistent with his experience, and is also consistent with recent studies of business practices indicating that 98% of all records today are ESI.

The 98% statistic comes up again in the world of federal litigation. The panel of federal judges noted that only 2% of their cases ever go to trial. An astounding 98% of all cases in federal court settle. The settlements occur after sufficient discovery has been conducted to allow the parties to assess their relative positions and evaluate the strengths and weaknesses of their case. Therefore, most of the attorney fees and costs of litigation today are for discovery to evaluate and narrow the issues, and only a small amount to actually try the issues. Litigators are, like it or not, not really trial lawyers at all; they are discovery lawyers, negotiators and mediators. This means that the task of discovery, which used to be assigned to new associates and was considered unimportant, is in reality the key task of litigation. It is also the task that consumes the bulk of the attorney fees and costs.

Clients are starting to realize this and to understand the importance of attorneys who specialize in electronic discovery. Merrill Lynch and Halliburton are two good examples, but there are several others, including Cisco, Verizon, Wal-Mart and Pfizer. Since 98% of the evidence today is in electronic form, and 98% of all cases settle, corporations need national e-counsel to evaluate settlement on a cost-efficient basis. They are in the best position to address the client's need for economic resolution of disputes.

THE ADMISSIBILITY OF ELECTRONIC EVIDENCE

Judge Paul Grimm has written a scholarly treatise on the admissibility of ESI, which is cleverly disguised as a district court opinion denying cross-motions for summary judgment. *Lorraine v. Markel American Ins. Co.*, 2007 WL 1300739 (D. Md. May 4, 2007). Judge Grimm is the chief magistrate judge for the district court in Baltimore. He is a well-known expert in this field, and a pretty nice guy with whom I had a chance to chat at length in Sedona (Arizona) last month. At 101 pages, it is a long read, but I recommend you give it a try, and keep it handy for the next time you need to have ESI admitted into evidence at trial or considered with a summary judgment motion. I predict this will be an often-quoted opinion as lawyers struggle not only with discovering ESI but with getting it admitted.

The facts of *Lorraine* are interesting, involving a yacht named *Chessie* that was struck by lightning and an ambiguous arbitration agreement, but ultimately the case itself is not too important. Suffice it to say the parties filed cross-motions for summary judgment, and both attached emails to their motions without affidavits or any other type of authentication. Judge Grimm denied both motions because they failed to lay a proper predicate for the emails. No doubt the attorneys on both sides were feeling a bit like *Chessie*, as neither saw this ruling coming in a case over $21,900!

Judge Grimm then wrote the long opinion explaining how ESI should be admitted into evidence. Obviously, this advice was intended for a larger audience than the two attorneys in *Lorraine,* and he has been thinking this over for a long time. In Judge Grimm's words:

Because neither party to this dispute complied with the requirements of Rule 56 that they support their motions with admissible evidence, I dismissed both motions without prejudice to allow resubmission with proper evidentiary support. I further observed that the unauthenticated e-mails are a form of computer-generated evidence that pose evidentiary issues that are highlighted by their electronic medium. Given the pervasiveness today of electronically prepared and stored records, as opposed to the manually prepared records of the past, counsel must be prepared to recognize and appropriately deal with the evidentiary issues associated with the admissibility of electronically generated and stored evidence. Although cases abound regarding the discoverability of electronic records, research has failed to locate a comprehensive analysis of the many interrelated evidentiary issues associated with electronic evidence. Because there is a need for guidance to the bar regarding this subject, this opinion undertakes a broader and more detailed analysis of these issues than would be required simply to resolve the specific issues presented in this case. It is my hope that it will provide a helpful starting place for understanding the challenges associated with the admissibility of electronic evidence.

So now we have guidance aplenty from Judge Grimm. He states that five evidence rules must be considered, and he provides a detailed elaboration on each:

Whenever ESI is offered as evidence, either at trial or in summary judgment, the following evidence rules must be considered: (1) is the ESI relevant as determined by Rule 401 (does it have any tendency to make some fact that is of consequence to the litigation more or less probable than it otherwise would be); (2) if relevant under 401, is it authentic as required by Rule 901(a) (can the proponent show that the ESI is what it purports to be); (3) if the ESI is offered for its substantive truth, is it hearsay as defined by Rule 801, and if so, is it covered by an applicable exception (Rules 803, 804 and 807); (4) is the form of the ESI that is being offered as evidence an original or duplicate under the original writing rule, or if not, is there admissible secondary evidence to prove the content of the ESI (Rules 1001-1008); and (5) is the probative value of the ESI substantially outweighed by the danger of unfair prejudice or one of the other factors identified by Rule 403, such that it should be excluded despite its relevance.

Judge Grimm happily noted that the above rules may not apply to every exhibit offered into evidence. Still, attorneys should make sure that they have satisfied the relevant criteria prior to submitting ESI as evidence for a motion or at trial. This case will serve as a good checklist and reference to help us all to do that.

SECOND EDITION OF *THE SEDONA PRINCIPLES* AND THE NEED FOR PROPORTIONALITY

In 2007, the Sedona Conference published the second edition to *The Sedona Principles: Best Practices Recommendations & Principles for Addressing Electronic Document Production (June 2007)*. As a Sedona Conference member, I may be somewhat biased, but it is safe to say that everyone in the e-discovery world considers *The Sedona Principles* a key document for understanding electronic discovery and best practices. This is especially true of the judiciary, who play an active role in *Sedona*. Many district court judges across the country cite to *The Sedona Principles* and consider it to be authoritative. The new *Principles* can be downloaded for free at the Sedona Web site, as long as the copy is for your personal use only.[31]

If you have not read the first edition published in 2004 (with annotations revised in 2005), I strongly recommend you now go ahead and read this new and improved second edition. To those who have studied the original *Sedona Principles*, relax—the 14 Principles remain the same, although they have been reworded somewhat. This is a refined and updated version, not a radical rewrite, which is hardly necessary or appropriate after only three years. But you will still want to download and

---

31. http://www.thesedonaconference.org/dltForm?did=TSC_PRINCP_2nd_ed_607.pdf

begin using this new version ASAP. It is a significant improvement over the first edition in several respects.

First, and most important, the second edition now ties directly into the new *Federal Rules of Civil Procedure*, most of which were significantly influenced by the *Principles*. The interface between the 14 Principles and the new rules is well explained. All of the Principle Commentaries have been updated and refined, but especially the Commentaries for Principle 12 on metadata and Principle 14 on the imposition of sanctions. The resources and authorities provided with each comment have been updated to include several new e-discovery cases and articles. In the process, the total text has grown 30%, from 56 to 73 pages (excluding Appendixes). Finally, the second edition is more user-friendly and better written than before. For instance, it now includes a handy chart in the front that lists topics correlating to the Principles, Federal Rules, and Sedona Commentary.

The new preface makes the point that the Conference tried to keep the "rule of reasonableness" foremost in mind when writing and revising these e-discovery principles and best practices. That rule is embodied in Rule 1 of the Federal Rules of Civil Procedure (courts should secure the just, speedy and inexpensive determination of all matters) and is applied through former Rule 26(b)(2) (now renumbered as Rule 26(b)(2)(C)—proportionality test of burden, cost and need) and in many state counterparts. The rule of reasonableness means that litigants should seek—and the courts should permit—discovery that is reasonable and appropriate to the dispute at hand while not imposing excessive burdens and costs on litigants and the court.

The best practices recommended by *Sedona* must always be tempered by proportionality. In other words, what may be reasonable for a ten-million-dollar case may be impractical for a routine case that barely makes the federal jurisdictional minimum. That point is also embodied in Principle 2, which counsels application of the proportionality standard in making a costs-versus-needs analysis to determine what e-discovery efforts are appropriate. The preface goes on to expand upon this point as follows:

Electronic discovery is a tool to help resolve a dispute and should not be viewed as a strategic weapon to coerce unjust, delayed, or expensive results. The need to act in good faith also extends to the efforts taken to reasonably preserve relevant electronic information, to the form of the production, and to the allocation of the costs of the preservation and production. All discovery issues should be considered in light of the nature of the litigation and the amount in controversy, as well as the cost, burden, and disruption to the parties' operations.

If only all counsel would remember and follow these wise dictates, and judges would enforce them, we would all be better off. The reality is that many litigants are misusing e-discovery as a strategic weapon, including the so-called "weapons of mass discovery," as discussed in my blog on discovery of computer RAM memory found in the "New Technologies" chapter of this book.

This is a key point for me, and so I am pleased that the newly revised Comment 2.b, now emphasizes how the *total* costs of e-discovery must be considered, not just the costs of retrieval and production:

> Costs cannot be calculated solely in terms of the expense of computer technicians to retrieve the data but must factor in other litigation costs, including the interruption and disruption of routine business processes and the costs of reviewing the information. Moreover, burdens on information technology personnel and the resources required to review documents for relevance, privilege, confidentiality, and privacy should be considered in any calculus of whether to allow discovery, and, if so, under what terms. In addition, the non-monetary costs (such as the invasion of privacy rights, risks to business and legal confidences, and risks to privileges) should be considered. Evaluating the need to produce electronically stored information often requires that a balance be struck between the burdens and need for electronically stored information, taking into account the technological feasibility and realistic costs involved.

Sedona Principles, page 17, Comment 2.b.

This point about hidden costs needed to be emphasized. It has been overlooked multiple times in the last several years, especially by overreaching plaintiffs and less-discerning judges. The disruption and privacy factors are hard to quantify but are very real and burdensome. Further, the cost of review is skyrocketing out of control, despite some attempts to export the work to low-paid hourly lawyers in India. The attorney fees incurred to review ESI for relevance, privilege, confidentiality, and the like now constitute the bulk of all e-discovery expenses. The estimates I have seen range from a low of 40% to a high of 60% of total e-discovery costs.

All of these costs, especially review expenses, should, in my opinion, be considered by the courts in any proportionality analysis of whether to allow discovery or to shift the costs of discovery. These costs should be considered regardless of whether the ESI at issue is "reasonably accessible." Unfortunately, Rule 26(b)(2)(B) does not expressly say that. It provides for cost-shifting only if the ESI is inaccessible. For that reason, a request for accessible ESI that would impose unreasonable expenses on the producing party must be opposed on the proportionality test under Rules 1 and 26(b)(2)(C), Federal Rules of Civil Procedure, and Sedona Principle 2. Only in this way can the integrity of the judicial system be protected from the intentional misuse of e-discovery to force settlements based on expense avoidance instead of merit.

Blog Reader Comment

With respect to the point you make in the last paragraph, you may be interested to read "'Peskoff,'Cost-Shifting and Accessible Data." an article by H. Christopher Boehning and Daniel J. Toal that was published in the 6/26/07 edition of the *New York Law Journal.*

Ralph's Reply

Thanks for that heads-up. It is a good article that echoes my own views. It can be found at: http://www.law.com/jsp/legaltechnology/pubArticleLT.jsp?id= 1182935154681. I recommend you read the whole article, but here are a few excerpts from Boehning and Toal:

> Although the new Rule 26(b)(2)(B) now explicitly acknowledges that "conditions" can be imposed on the discovery of inaccessible data, neither it nor any other rule states, explicitly or implicitly, that cost-shifting or other conditions cannot be considered when accessible data is at issue. Indeed, since courts clearly retain the discretion to deny discovery outright under Rule 26(b)(2)(C), it stands to reason that they necessarily have the lesser power to condition production on the requesting party's payment of the costs of production.

> Perhaps most persuasively, Judge Lee H. Rosenthal, chair of the Advisory Committee on the Federal Rules of Civil Procedure that crafted the amendments, also recently addressed this specific issue and reached the same conclusion. In discussing the amended Rule 26, he stated that "[t]he amended rule does not say that judges may only consider cost allocation if . . . the electronically stored information is not reasonably accessible. . . . Nor does the amended rule preclude producing parties from seeking to shift costs of producing electronically stored information that is reasonably accessible." Lee H. Rosenthal, *A Few Thoughts on Electronic Discovery After December 1, 2006*, 116 YALE L.J. 167, 180-81 (2006).

> In these circumstances, a district court should have the discretion to entertain either an outright limitation on the scope of the search under Rule 26(b)(2)(C) or a cost-shifting protective order under Rule 26(c). In the words of a leading treatise on federal practice, "it is not self-evident that every discovery request of electronically stored information on accessible active databases will not entail undue costs and burdens, solely because they are on an active database," and therefore "cost-shifting may be appropriate" even when accessible data is sought. *Moore's Federal Practice* § 37A.36 (2007).

THE SEDONA CONFERENCE RELEASES TWO NEW MUST-READ COMMENTARIES ON "EMAIL MANAGEMENT" AND "LEGAL HOLDS"

The Sedona Conference has done it again and group-written two more excellent guides, one on Legal Holds and the other on Email Management. Both were just released for public comment and may be downloaded from the Sedona Web site[32] for personal use.

Legal Holds Guideline

The Sedona Conference Commentary on Legal Holds: The Trigger & the Process[33] (August 2007 Public Comment Version) provides much-needed guidance on an issue very troublesome to most large organizations: when and how to preserve ESI for purposes of litigation. In their words:

> The basic principle that an organization has a duty to preserve relevant information in anticipation of litigation is easy to articulate. However, the precise application of that duty can be elusive. Everyday, organizations apply the basic principle to real-world circumstances, confronting the issue of when the obligation is triggered and, once triggered, what is the scope of the obligation. This Article, intended to provide guidance on those issues, is divided into two parts: The "trigger" and the "legal hold."

Once again, this is a group effort by a special committee of The Sedona Conference called the Working Group on Electronic Document Retention and Production. The Working Group includes many well-known experts on this tricky topic. Under the guidance of the group's editors, Conor Crowley, Eric Schwarz and Gregory Wood, they agreed upon a set of 11 guidelines with detailed commentary on each.

These are common-sense-type principles that will, I predict, be acceptable to most companies, although still challenging for many to implement. It is also likely that these guidelines will often be referred to by courts when reviewing the reasonableness of a party's legal hold activities

---

32. http://www.thesedonaconference.org/
33. http://www.thesedonaconference.org/dltForm?did=Legal_holds.pdf

in litigation. If you can show that your organization made a good-faith effort to follow these guidelines, then you will be in a strong position to argue that any loss of data that incurred anyway is not sanctionable.

The 11 guidelines include advice and language such as:

- **Guideline 1**—notice of a *"credible threat"* of litigation as the trigger of the duty to preserve;
- **Guideline 2**—the *"adoption and consistent implementation"* of a written policy as a key factor to show reasonableness and good faith;
- **Guideline 3**—the need for established procedures to report potential litigation threats;
- **Guideline 6**—the need to issue a written legal hold notice in most circumstances; and
- **Guideline 10**—the need for legal holds, once issued, to thereafter be *"regularly monitored."*

Guideline 7 provides important input on the scope of a hold, including the key "proportionality" criteria that I have written about before—namely, the consideration of the amount in controversy and related factors.

- **Guideline 7**—In determining the scope of information that should be preserved, the nature of the issues raised in the matter, experience in similar circumstances and the amount in controversy are factors that may be considered.

The proportionality factor in determining the proper scope of a hold is often overlooked, especially by some plaintiffs' counsel who still routinely make outrageously overbroad preservation demands.

The comments to Guideline 7 also point out that accessibility is another important factor to consider in determining the proper scope of preservation. In fact, the wording of Guideline 7 in the commentary is slightly different from the wording quoted above that appears at the beginning of the document. They both begin the same, but the version in the Comments section ends with "accessibility of the information" as a factor that may be considered, instead of the first stated "amount in controversy" factor. I think this is just a mistake that will be cleaned up in the final draft.

The comments do, however, make clear that the issue of the costs and burden to try to preserve certain types of data, including, as the comments mention, "voicemail and instant messaging," should be considered. In my view, this means that in many circumstances, "not reasonably accessible" ESI does not need to be preserved. The Sedona Comments to Guideline 7 do not, however, go quite that far. They instead make the point that just because a type of ESI is not reasonably accessible does not mean that it is outside of the scope of a duty to preserve.

We all agree that it depends on the circumstances. In some circumstances, the inaccessibility of ESI will take it outside of the scope of preservation, but in other circumstances it will not. In my view, the general bias should be to exclude "not reasonably accessible" ESI from preservation. As I frequently mention, I think Judge Scheindlin got it right in *Zubulake IV* when she held:

> The scope of a party's preservation obligation can be described as follows: Once a party reasonably anticipates litigation, it must suspend its routine document retention/destruction policy and put in place a litigation hold to ensure the preservation of relevant documents. **As a general rule, that litigation hold does not apply to inaccessible backup tapes, for example, typically maintained solely for the purpose of disaster recovery, which may continue to be recycled on the schedule set forth in the company's policy.** (Emphasis added.)
> *Zubulake v. UBS Warburg LLC*, 220 F.R.D. 212, 218 (S.D. N.Y. 2003).

Backup tapes are, of course, a prime example of not reasonably accessible ESI.

Guideline 8 is the most detailed guideline:

- **Guideline 8**—A legal hold is most effective when it:
- (a) Identifies the persons who are likely to have relevant information and communicates a preservation notice to those persons;

(b) Communicates the preservation notice in a manner that ensures the recipients will receive actual, comprehensible, and effective notice of the requirement to preserve information;

(c) Is in written form;

(d) Clearly defines what information is to be preserved and how the preservation is to be undertaken; and

(e) Is periodically reviewed and, when necessary, reissued in either its original or an amended form.

Guideline 8 comes with a sample Certification of Completion document (Appendix B) designed to serve as a checklist for the recipient to confirm that he or she has complied with a hold notice. It requires the recipient to certify to the general counsel's office that he or she has searched a long list of locations where responsive ESI might be located, including the office LAN server, laptop and office computer, email, home computers, Blackberries, email trash bin and desktop re cycle bin, "removable storage media, such as disks, CDs, DVDs, memory sticks, and thumb drives," and "files of any administrative personnel working for me."

Many companies will dislike how extensive and complete this list is, especially the inclusion of home computers, removable storage media, and secretarial ESI. The commentary softens the blow somewhat by clarifying that this is not a form; it is only a sample and may not be appropriate for every case. Still, this long list could put a huge search burden on many employees that is not appropriate for many cases, so this aspect of the commentary is likely to be controversial.

Another controversial aspect of Guideline 8 is its placement of the burden for search and preservation upon the individual employees themselves, instead of on the company, its IT department or automated procedures. This let-the-employees-do-everything procedure has been the norm in the past but is beginning to be challenged by many courts, especially where there is inadequate follow-up. See *Cache La Poudre Feeds, LLC v. Land O' Lakes Farmland Feed, LLC,* 2007 WL 684001 (D. Colo., March 2, 2007) and my blog, in Chapter Two of this book, *Litigation Hold Is Not Enough: Sanctions Imposed Under Rule 26(g) for Negligent Collection and Preservation.*

- **Guideline 4**: Any technical solutions should meet the functional requirements identified as part of policy development and should be carefully integrated into existing systems.

Most e-discovery teams studying these issues find that some kind of software and hardware purchases are needed to implement their recommended email practices. Guideline 4 addresses this reality and counsels the importance of carefully integrating the new purchases into existing systems. The commentary notes that there are many different software and hardware solutions offered by competing vendors to solve these problems, and no one approach is superior. The commentary then provides a list of practical issues to consider when evaluating competing vendor proposals.

My congratulations and thanks to the hard work of The Sedona Conference Working Group on Electronic Document Retention and Production, eMail Management and Archiving Special Project Team. They have a long name, but their short, concise guidelines and commentary are a very practical and useful work. Every e-discovery team in America struggles with email issues, and all will benefit from these pioneering guidelines.

INFORMATION EXPLOSION AND THE FUTURE OF LITIGATION

A new law review article raises thought-provoking questions about the impact of the information explosion on the practice of law, especially litigation: *Information Inflation: Can the Legal System Adapt?*, 13 RICH. J.L. & TECH. 10 (2007).[35] In a very highbrow, and some would say "far out," article, they predict that the legal system will adapt by changing in four basic areas. I personally agree with their predictions but suspect that more adaptations will be required than the four they set forth.

The article begins by laying out the recent very rapid acceleration of information and placing this dramatic increase in historical context.

---

35.   The article is available on-line at http://law.richmond.edu/jolt/index.asp. The authors are George Paul, a partner in Lewis and Roca and a graduate of Yale Law School (1982), and Jason Baron, a director of litigation at the National Archives and Records Administration, College Park, Md., and graduate of Boston University School of Law (1980).

Writing has co-evolved with civilization over the past 50 centuries or longer, during which time there has been a slow but steady increase in information as our writing technologies slowly improved. Charted out on a graph, it would look like a gradual curve as our writing moved from chiseled stone to parchment to the printing press. Then with the printing press there was a significant upturn, but still a curve, much like a sine wave. All of these forms of information are, in the author's words, "recorded communications . . . confined to the physical realm—frozen in time as 'information artifacts.'" *Id.* at pg. 4. Then all of a sudden, about 20 years ago, the sine wave spiked straight upwards, far up. The amount of information exploded as mankind invented new and much more powerful writing technologies, including "digitization; real-time computing; the microprocessor; the personal computer; e-mail; local and wide-area networks leading to the Internet; the evolution of software, which has "locked in" seamless editing as an almost universal function; (and) the World Wide Web." *Id.* at pgs. 5-6.

These new technologies allowed for an altogether different form of writing, free from all physical confines. Now the quantity of information humankind can create is virtually unlimited. They point out how anyone today "can distribute thousands or even millions of identical records in an instant." *Id.* at pg. 8. The authors refer to this as an "Information Ecosystem," which as a "whole exhibits an emergent behavior more than the sum of its parts." *Id.* at pg. 7. They contend that:

> Critically for law, such systems cannot be understood or explained by any one person. As a result, writing has now grown into something akin to a new "form of life." Because of its long-standing stasis and the importance of writing as a global technology, such a development may legitimately be said to herald a new phase of civilization. (footnotes omitted)

The authors compare the sudden spike in information to the rapid early growth of the Universe right after the "Big Bang." They use the term "inflation" in the same sense that many cosmologists use the term. *Id.* at 1. Unlike the economic meaning of inflation, in information theory and many cosmologies, there is no countervailing deflation or recession. Our ESI, like the Universe itself, just keeps expanding, and there is no turning back, no downward adjustment. No one knows whether the amount of information we store will continue to increase forever at this rate, or whether the inflation may eventually slow down or maybe even reverse. But we do know that, barring a major world disaster, an exponential increase of information is the most likely scenario for the rest of our lives, and so we had better learn to cope with this rapid change, and learn fast.

The authors then turn to the legal profession and consider how it is "confronting an inflationary epoch." Basically, the problem for dispute resolution attorneys is that the vast quantities of data involved in most cases make it impossible to find *all* of the evidence relevant to the case. We are forced to settle for limited information. To use the old parable, we are all blind men looking at an elephant, except that now the elephant keeps getting bigger and bigger. In the paper world of just a few years ago, this was anathema to the legal profession. Discovery was intended to ferret out all of the key facts. We pretty much knew what we were looking for and where to find it. We would all strive for as much certainty as possible and would routinely review all of the written records involved in a dispute.

Today, the word "all" itself becomes obsolete. In most large lawsuits today, the amount of ESI involved makes it impossible to gather all relevant information. Litigators have to be satisfied with retrieving some of the relevant evidence. To use a common analogy, you know you have a haystack to search through, but you have no real idea of the number of needles in it, if any. You could find one or two, and you may have them all, or there could be hundreds more. You will never know, because the haystack is impossibly large.

For instance, in future suits involving actions by the current administration, the National Archives and Records Administration (NARA) estimates that by January 20, 2009, it will have custody of over 100 million emails from the George W. Bush White House alone. *Id.* at pg. 12. The total number of emails in NARA custody will soon reach the one billion mark. To search through all of those emails would take a team of 100 full-time lawyers *more than 54 years. Id.* at pg. 13. Assuming a very low billing rate of $100 per hour, the cost of review would be

$2 billion. As the authors point out, email is just the beginning; new forms of writing and communication are developing that will continue the flood, such as instant messages, voice mail, Web traffic, "wikis," and the like. *Id.* at pgs.14-15.

The authors predict the legal profession will necessarily have to change and adapt new strategies of practice to cope with this information inflation. Here in a nutshell are their four predictions:

1. "There must be a change in culture among litigation lawyers." What they call the current "game theory" behind litigation must end and be replaced by strategic cooperation and transparency in ESI discovery and production. Lawyers will be forced to collaborate because that will be the only way to discover enough ESI related to a dispute to adequately evaluate the client's position. The traditional adversarial mode of discovery will not achieve that end. As a specific example, they predict what they call "virtuous cycle iterative feedback loops." *Id.* at pgs. 32-36. As I understand it, that means the parties will agree to a preliminary search method, which today is likely to be an agreed set of search terms. The parties will then try out the agreed search on a limited data set, evaluate and share the results, and then meet again to try to refine the terms for the next search. The next iteration of the search will incorporate the lessons learned from the last search, and so on, until the parties (or, barring agreement, the court) are satisfied they have enough information to resolve the dispute (or the funds budgeted for the discovery process have been exhausted).

2. New search technologies and software will have to be employed to get a better handle on the overall size of the haystack and find more of the needles that lie within. The current reliance on mere keyword searches will be replaced by much more sophisticated searches employing various types of concept and contextual searches, artificial intelligence, and statistical sampling techniques. The reliance on expensive human review will significantly diminish, and instead litigators will develop new skills and computer competence.

3. The law will innovate and change to face the reality that all evidence cannot be searched before production, and that no one will ever know if *all* relevant ESI has been located, much less preserved and produced. The law governing inadvertent disclosure of privileged information will have to change, and new, more appropriate rules of waiver developed.

4. There will be a revolution in legal practice as attorneys fully incorporate the continuing advances of technology. This "equates to perhaps the biggest skill set ever thrust upon the profession. . . . Lawyers must embrace creative, technological approaches to grappling with knowledge management as information inflation continues apace. Failure to do so will severely hamper the legal profession's ability to meaningfully retrieve and process evidence." *Id.* at pg. 3. I only wish that the article spent more time exploring this necessary adaptation; instead it is largely left to your imagination. But then, perhaps that is part of the message.

New Ethical Standards for e-Discovery

ZUBULAKE DUTY

The landmark series of opinions by District Court Judge Scheindlin in New York City culminatng in *Zubulake v. UBS*, 229 F.R.D. 422 (S.D.N.Y. 2004) (*Zubulake V*), impose a new discovery responsibility upon attorneys. The essential core of the new duty is to supervise e-discovery by speaking directly with your client's IT personnel and understand what they say. Because this duty was first widely publicized in the *Zubulake* (pronounced "zoo-boo-lake") opinions, it is sometimes referred to as the "*Zubulake* duty." Due to the fact that most lawyers are not trained in IT, and today's technologies are horrendously complex, this new duty can be an enormous challenge. Still, more and more courts are following Judge Scheindlin and require that the IT-legal burdens be met by the counsel appearing before them. Lawyers today must rise to the occasion and learn enough about IT to carry this load, or at least associate with others who can. Failure to do so may constitute a breach of their professional and ethical duty of competent representation and may also lead to sanctions by the court.

Zubulake V requires outside counsel to make certain that all potentially relevant electronic data are identified and placed "on hold." In the words of Judge Scheindlin:

> Once a "litigation hold" is in place, a party and her counsel must make certain that all sources of potentially relevant information are identified and placed "on hold," to the extent required in *Zubulake IV*. To do this, counsel must become fully familiar with her client's document retention policies, as well as the client's data retention architecture. This will invariably involve speaking with information technology personnel, who can explain system-wide backup procedures and the actual (as opposed to theoretical) implementation of the firm's recycling policy. It will also involve communicating with the "key players" in the litigation, in order to understand how they stored information.

This places a high duty on outside counsel to speak directly with their client's IT personnel, and to understand the intricies of their computer systems.

At the end of the opinion in *Zubulake V,* Judge Scheindlin summarizes her requirements for counsel in connection with e-discovery:

> In sum, counsel has a duty to effectively communicate to her client its discovery obligations so that all relevant information is discovered, retained, and produced. In particular, once the duty to preserve attaches, counsel must identify sources of discoverable information. This will usually entail speaking directly with the key players in the litigation, as well as the client's information technology personnel. In addition, when the duty to preserve attaches, counsel must put in place a litigation hold and make that known to all relevant employees by communicating with them directly. The litigation hold instructions must be reiterated regularly and compliance must be monitored. Counsel must also call for employees to produce copies of rel-

evant electronic evidence, and must arrange for the segregation and safeguarding of any archival media (e.g., backup tapes) that the party has a duty to preserve.

Litigants and their attorneys can be sanctioned for their failure to discharge these duties and properly supervise e-discovery. This is based upon the practical reality that "discovery is run largely by attorneys, and the court and the judicial process depend upon honesty and fair dealing among attorneys." *In re September 11th Liability Insurance Coverage Cases,* 2007 WL 1739666 (S.D. N.Y. June 18, 2007).

Still, if attorneys are diligent, and they properly investigate and communicate, they should not be held responsible for their client's failures. As Judge Scheindlin put it in *Zubulake V:*

A lawyer cannot be obliged to monitor her client like a parent watching a child. At some point, the client must bear responsibility for a failure to preserve.

But where the lawyer has not fulfilled her duty, personal sanctions can be imposed. The authority of the court to sanction outside counsel, as opposed to parties, for the failure to properly supervise the client's document production was discussed at length in *Metropolitan Opera Association Inc. v. Local 100, Hotel Employees and Restaurant Employees International Union,* 212 F.R.D. 178, 218-19 (S.D. N.Y. 2003). The *Metropolitan Opera* case discusses the authority of the court to sanction outside counsel, as opposed to parties, for the failure to properly supervise the client's document production. The court found three legal bases to sanction the attorneys:

1. The Rule 26(g)(2) requirement that an attorney sign and so certify discovery responses;
2. Federal statute 28 U.S.C. 1927, which allows an award of attorney fees if an attorney vexatiously multiplies litigation; and
3. The "inherent" or "implied" power of a court to manage its own affairs.

Many courts after *Zubulake* have imposed sanctions on clients and lawyers alike for negligence in the search and production of electronically stored information. In the process, some courts have set very high standards, and imposed a strict duty on attorneys to investigate and comprehend even complex and arcane computer technicalities. This is best exemplified in *Phoenix Four, Inc. v. Strategic Resources Corp.*, No. 05-CIV-4837, 2006 WL 1409413; 2006 U.S. Dist. LEXIS 32211 (S.D. N.Y. May 22, 2006).

In *Phoenix,* a law firm and its clients were both sanctioned for the attorneys' failure to personally investigate and understand that two of the clients' computer servers had hidden partitions containing discoverable ESI. In the words of the court:

> The computer system in Schack's office was configured in such a way that the desktop workstations did not have a "drive mapping" to that partitioned section of the hard drive.

In truth, how many trial attorneys understand what the judge just said, much less what a "partitioned server" is, or that such a thing could be hidden and contain key evidence? This case shows you had better find out, and find out fast, at the beginning of the case, or at least associate with counsel or other experts who already know.

The defendants' law firm in *Phoenix* ended up with a $22,581 sanction order against it for overlooking the hidden server partitions (one-half of the total sanction of $45,162). *Phoenix Four, Inc. v. Strategic Resources Corp.,* 2006 WL 2135798 (S.D. N.Y. Aug. 1, 2006). The court also applied then-future Rule 26(b)(2)(B) and required disclosure of the sources of inaccessible data. In this case, however, the data was not inaccessible at all, it was just hidden in a partitioned section of the hard drive. The attorneys did not understand this and personally paid for that mistake.

The facts in *Phoenix* illustrate just how dangerous e-discovery has become. After suit was filed, defense counsel in *Phoenix* requested that their clients produce electronic and hard-copy documents. The clients produced paper but claimed that they did not have any relevant ESI. Defense counsel repeated that assertion to plaintiff's counsel. Then, a year later, on the eve of trial, during routine maintenance of their computers, the defendants discovered that two of them had hidden partitions, and that these sections of the servers' hard drives held 25 gigabytes (equivalent to 2,500 boxes) of potentially relevant ESI. The clients immediately notified their counsel, who in turn immediately notified plaintiff's counsel. The defendants began to roll out the production of these documents as soon as they could, but at this point it was six weeks after the close of discovery. There was no allegation of bad faith on behalf of the defendants or their counsel, but the court found that the defense counsel was grossly negligent in failing to timely discover the information on the server. In the words of the court:

> [Counsel] failed in its obligation to locate and timely produce the evidence stored in the server that the . . . [d]efendants took with them . . . . [Counsel] affirms that it engaged in dialogue with the defendants on the need to locate and gather paper and electronic documents. . . . But counsel's obligation is not confined to a request for documents; the duty is to search for sources of information.
>
> It appears that [counsel] never undertook the more methodical survey of the . . . [d]efendants' sources of information . . . outlined in *Zubulake V*. [Counsel] simply accepted the defendants' representation that, because [it] was no longer in operation, there were no computers or electronic collections to search. Had [Counsel] been diligent, it might have asked—as it should have—what had happened to the computers. . . . Further, [Counsel's] obligation under *Zubulake V* extends to an inquiry as to whether information was stored on that server and, had the defendants been unable to answer that question, directing that a technician examine the server. In the case of a defunct organization such as SRC, this forensic effort would be no more than the equivalent of questioning the information technology personnel of a live enterprise about how information is stored on the organization's computer system.

. . . The proposed amendments [to the FRCP] essentially codify the teaching of *Zubulake IV & V*, of which [Counsel] should have been well aware. I find [Counsel's] deficiencies here to constitute gross negligence.

Despite the words of Judge Baer, who is in the same New York City court as Judge Scheindlin, that "[T]he proposed amendments [to the FRCP] essentially codify the teaching of *Zubulake IV*," the new rules do not explicitly require counsel to become fluent in "computer network architecture." But revised Rule 26(f)(3) does require parties to discuss during initial disclosure "any issues relating to disclosure of electronically stored information including the form or forms in which it would be produced." Further, Rule 26(b)(2)(B) requires the parties to identify sources of data that support the case or defenses, including sources of data that are "not reasonably accessible." Can you discuss the issues of ESI and fulfill your duty as counsel without speaking "computerese," or affiliating with counsel or other experts who do?

The judge in *Hopson v. Mayor of Baltimore*, 232 F.R.D. 228, 245 (D. Md. 2006) described the obligations under new Rule 26(f) with much greater particularity, making the answer to that largely rhetorical question even more obvious:

[C]ounsel have a duty to take the initiative in meeting and conferring to plan for appropriate discovery of electronically stored information at the commencement of any case in which electronic records will be sought. . . . At a minimum, they should discuss: the type of information technology systems in use and the persons most knowledgeable in their operation; preservation of electronically stored information that may be relevant to the litigation; the scope of the electronic records sought (i.e., e-mail, voice mail, archived data, backup or disaster recovery data, laptops, personal computers, PDAs, deleted data); the format in which production will occur (will records be produced in "native" or searchable format, or image only; is metadata sought); whether the requesting party seeks to conduct any testing or sampling of the producing party's IT system; the burdens and expenses that the producing party will face based on the Rule 26(b)(2) factors, and how they may be reduced (i.e., limiting the time period for which discovery is sought, limiting the amount of hours the producing party must spend searching, compiling and reviewing electronic records, using sampling to search rather than searching all records, shifting to the producing party some of the production costs); the amount of pre-production privilege review that is reasonable for the producing party to undertake, and measures to preserve post-production assertion of privilege within a reasonable time; and any protective orders or confidentiality orders that should be in place regarding who may have access to information that is produced.

If you do not speak directly with the client's IT personnel and come into court unprepared to discuss all of these issues, you are gambling that *Phoenix, Zubulake, Hopson,* and the like are aberrations. You can only hope that the presiding judges in your cases will not impose such high standards. This hope may be misplaced, especially in federal court, where e-discovery training for federal magistrates has been ongoing for several years now, and this training favors the adoption of *Zubulake* duties. See, for example, David Isom, *Electronic Discovery Primer for Judges*, 2005 FED. CTS. L. REV. 1[1] (Section II.M., Defining Lawyer's Responsibilities for Electronic Discovery).

Moreover, the imposition of *Zubulake*-type duties on outside counsel is not new. There are several decisions before *Zubulake* that found fault with counsel for not speaking directly with their client's IT executives. See, for example, *GTFM, Inc. v. Wal-Mart*, 2000 WL 1693615 (S.D. N.Y. Nov. 9, 2000), and WL 335558 (S.D. N.Y. Mar. 30, 2000). In *GTFM,* the plaintiff requested certain local store sales information regarding the purchase and sale of alleged counterfeit goods. Senior Wal-Mart executives told their attorneys that the information had been destroyed pursuant to normal records retention policy procedures wherein the data was only preserved for five weeks. Wal-Mart's attor-

---

1. http://www.fclr.org/articles/2005fedctslrev1(noframes).htm

neys responded to the request accordingly. More than a year later, a Wal-Mart IT vice president was deposed and testified that the information was kept for a year, not five weeks; it was available when the request was made but had recently been deleted. The court sanctioned Wal-Mart ($109,754 and an on-site computer inspection) and criticized its attorneys for an inadequate investigation, holding that the attorneys should not have relied upon representations of the client's business executive; instead they should have also spoken directly with the IT personnel involved.

Ignorance of IT is simply no longer an acceptable cover for mistakes in most federal courts. If you mess up on e-discovery, you may have to pay for it. For instance, in Tampa last year, a trial lawyer and his counsel were sanctioned for producing only paper records and claiming "computer illiteracy" as the reason they did not produce additional electronic records that were eventually found on the plaintiff's computers. *Martin v. Northwestern Mutual Life Insurance Co.*, 2006 WL 148991 (M.D. Fla. Jan. 19, 2006). The magistrate rejected the attorney's excuse of "computer illiteracy" as "frankly ludicrous."

In Orlando, the magistrates have gone on record as saying they will require counsel to talk directly with their client's IT personnel. See my blog entry on this in the "New Rules" chapter. In New Jersey, they have even promulgated a local rule requiring it, L.Civ. R. 26.1(d) of the Local Rules of the U.S. District Court, District of New Jersey. This rule has been in effect since 2003 and thus precedes *Zubulake V*. (Perhaps *"Zubulake* duty" is better named "New Jersey duty"?) The New Jersey local rules state:

> Prior to a Fed. R. Civ. P. 26(f) conference, counsel shall review with the client the client's information management systems, including computer-based and other digital systems, in order to understand how information is stored and how it can be retrieved . . . including currently maintained computer files as well as historical, archival, backup and legacy computer files.

The New Jersey rule also requires counsel to locate an "IT witness":

Counsel shall also identify a person or persons with knowledge about the client's information management systems, including computer-based and other digital systems, with the ability to facilitate, through counsel, reasonably anticipated discovery.

Other jurisdictions are getting on the New Jersey and *Zubulake* bandwagon and explicitly or implicitly requiring interaction between counsel and an IT "liaison." They are, in effect, requiring counsel to assume the *Zubulake* duty and understand their clients' ESI architecture. See, for example, D. Ark. L. R. 26.1 (2002); M. Dist. Pa. L.R. 26.1(a) (2005); D. Wyo. L. Civ. R. 26.1 (2005). Rule revisions are pending in many other jurisdictions, including many state courts. Many other courts, such as the district court in Orlando, do not have an express local rule, but the judges require it nonetheless. If your court is silent so far, you run the risk of being a test case.

Even though no judicial opinion that I know of expressly rejects *Zubulake,* it is not without its critics. The first and only publication of this nature was published by a well-known insurance defense attorney. David Levitt, *Counsel's Obligations for E-Discovery*, FOR THE DEFENSE, Aug. 2007, Vol. 49, No. 10. Mr. Levitt begins his argument with a question: "Where did Judge Scheindlin get all these obligations for counsel, as distinct from obligations of the party that counsel represents?" That is really his main point, that Judge Scheindlin unfairly shifts the discovery burdens from clients to attorneys. He argues that Judge Scheindlin incorrectly premises her burden shifting upon a misinterpretation of Rule 26(e). This rule places a duty to supplement prior discovery responses when the party or attorney learns of an incomplete or incorrect response. He contends that *Zubulake V* unfairly transforms this duty to supplement into a duty to preserve and search, and impose what he refers to as "draconian (not to mention expensive) steps that counsel *must* take."

Mr. Levitt then argues that "the implications of *Zubulake V* are immense, especially when coupled with the new Federal Rules on e-discovery and the approaching application of these principles in state courts." Most people would agree with him on that. He then asserts that the *Zubulake* duties imposed on attorneys create a "blueprint for spawning satellite litigation on discovery." Many would argue that such satellite litigation spawned long before *Zubulake*, and that indeed the whole purpose of the *Zubulake* duties, and the new rules, is to serve as a wake-up call to attorneys to avoid the discovery sideshows. But Mr. Levitt disagrees; he contends that "the combination of *Zubulake V* and the new Federal Rules will create a legion of new areas to probe, to complain about, and on which to file discovery motions." Still, even he admits:

> It may be that it is a wise idea for counsel to become familiar very early on in a case, especially one that has any significant potential value, with the electronic storage systems of the client, so that counsel can explain effectively to the opponent and to the court what it has, and what steps it has taken to preserve and properly produce relevant discovery evidence.

Then, in his next sentence, he voices a concluding protest, one that I have heard several attorneys say but never before put in print:

> But the court goes way over the top when it begins to mandate obligations that ought to belong to the client be met by the lawyer. There is simply no authority for imposing these obligations on the attorneys. It is bad public policy to so mandate.

Still, even this dissenting view concedes at the end of the article that *Zubulake V* and the imposition of these discovery duties on counsel are the "wave of the future" and counsel "would be well advised to learn and follow them."

Your local court may follow the arguments advanced in the Levitt article and may decide to reject *Zubulake, Metropolitan Opera,* and *Phoenix.* Not all courts may impose such strenuous duties on counsel who appear before them as officers of the court. They may let you off the hook when ESI is discovered at the last minute by your client or, worse, by opposing counsel. But until they expressly reject these cases, do you really want to take that chance? Do you want to simply accept at face value a client's representation that the contents of a box or boxes of paper comprise "the file," or some other category of documents, and not discuss all of the ins and outs of their ESI?

In the old days (the early and mid-1990s), before the Information Age exploded (we are now up to 60 billion emails a day), you probably would accept such representations and let it go at that. Legal counsel would rarely, if ever, find it necessary to meet with file clerks and records custodians to verify the contents of paper records. In fact, depositions of paper records custodians have become mere formalities in most "paper" cases, and are usually replaced by a simple production of copies and later authenticity stipulations. But in today's world, it can be unethical negligence, or, as Judge Baer held in *Phoenix*, "gross negligence," to fail to meet with IT personnel and discuss the origins and completeness of discovery. If you do not, you could face sanctions against both your client and your law firm or, even worse, lose otherwise defensible cases with adverse inference sanctions, such as in *Zubulake* ($29 million) and *Coleman (Parent) Holdings, Inc. v. Morgan Stanley & Co., Inc.,* 2005 WL 674885 (Fla. Cir. Ct. 2005) ($1.45 billion). So even the grumblers today agree that these duties are here to stay and counsel "would be well advised to learn and follow them."

LITIGATION HOLD IS NOT ENOUGH: SANCTIONS IMPOSED UNDER RULE 26(g) FOR NEGLIGENT COLLECTION AND PRESERVATION

Sanctions were recently imposed in a district court case in Colorado based on Rule 26(g), *Federal Rules of Civil Procedure,* for errors in the collection and preservation of computer files. *Cache La Poudre Feeds, LLC v. Land O' Lakes Farmland Feed,* LLC, 2007 WL 684001 (D. Colo. March 2, 2007). Rule 26(g) requires an attorney to sign all discovery requests, responses, and objections. The rule further states that:

The signature of the attorney or party constitutes a certification that to the best of the signer's knowledge, information, and belief, formed after a reasonable inquiry, the disclosure is complete and correct as of the time it is made.

Moreover, Rule 26(g)(2) provides that by signing, an attorney is certifying that, to the best of the signer's knowledge, information, and belief, formed after a reasonable inquiry, the request, response, or objection is: . . . (B) not interposed for any improper purpose, such as to harass or to cause unnecessary delay or needless increase in the cost of litigation. . . . (C) not unreasonable or unduly burdensome or expensive, given the needs of the case, the discovery already had in the case, the amount in controversy, and the importance of the issues at stake in the litigation.

Unfortunately, in my experience, these quasi-ethical obligations imposed upon counsel of record by Rule 26(g) are not always followed. The *Land O' Lakes* case provides a rare example of the imposition of sanctions for its violation. Even here, the court held that the conduct in question was also sanctionable as spoliation. Further, the sanctions imposed against the defendant whose attorneys violated the rule were minor, only a $5,000 fee award plus court reporter costs. The mild nature of the sanction is perhaps explained by the court's obvious irritation at the conduct of both parties, including the plaintiff, who had previously been sanctioned for a Rule 11 violation. If the moving party had been wearing a "white hat," I expect that a far harsher sanction would have been imposed.

Even though the sanctions imposed were relatively minor, the case is still important, not only because Rule 26(g) was applied, but also because of the facts found to be sanctionable. These facts make clear that it is not enough to simply issue a litigation hold to key employees and then assume they will properly locate, preserve and produce the relevant computer files and other ESI. Counsel have an ethical duty to the court, clients, and bar to follow up on the hold notice and make reasonable efforts to independently verify that the hold directive has been followed and the relevant ESI has been preserved and produced.

This is part of the so-called *"Zubulake* duties" discussed previously. See *Zubulake v. UBS Warburg LLC*, 229 F.R.D. 422 (S.D. N.Y. 2004).

The defendant in this case, Land O' Lakes, sent out a litigation hold notice to key employees within days after the trademark violation suit was filed. The court found that the timing was acceptable but faulted Land O' Lakes' in-house and outside counsel for the procedure chosen to preserve and collect the ESI and for the poor follow-up to the hold notice.

After the written hold notice was sent, there were interviews with key witnesses, but the Land O' Lakes employees were essentially on their own to locate and preserve the emails and other files that they considered to be related to the trademark dispute. The employees looked through their files, and although they located 50,000 pages of documents related to the mark "Profile," they found only 415 emails. Counsel simply accepted all of this as correct. No attempt was made by either in-house or outside counsel, who signed the discovery responses under Rule 26, to independently verify their efforts. Counsel simply took the files they produced and assumed that they were complete and the search was thorough. Further, no systemwide keyword search was ever run on the defendant's or the key employees' systems, as the plaintiff argued strenuously should have been done.

The court was clearly troubled by this borderline negligent approach under the circumstances. But the court found even more troubling the failure of counsel to prevent the "wiping" of hard drives from computers of employees who left the company after the suit was filed, at least one of whom was undeniably a "key player." The court considered this a failure to preserve evidence that constituted spoliation.

The plaintiff argued that this conduct constituted a clear violation of defendant's *Zubulake* duties. Specifically, as summarized by the court, the plaintiff argued that:

Defendants failed to comply with the following "duties" set forth in *Zubulake V*:

- once litigation is commenced or a party reasonably anticipates litigation, it must suspend its routine document retention/destruction policy and put in place a "litigation hold" to ensure the preservation of relevant documents;

- in furtherance of the "litigation hold," counsel must become fully aware of the client's document retention policies and data retention architecture;
- counsel must communicate with "the key players" in the litigation in order to understand how they stored information;
- counsel must take reasonable steps to monitor compliance with the "litigation hold" so that all sources of discoverable information are identified and searched; and,
- having identified all sources of potentially relevant information, a party and its counsel are under a duty to retain that information and produce information responsive to the opposing party's requests.

Under these circumstances the court held:

While instituting a "litigation hold" may be an important first step in the discovery process, the obligation to conduct a reasonable search for responsive documents continues throughout the litigation. See Fed. R. Civ. P. 26(e)(2) (a party is under a duty seasonally to amend discovery responses "if the party learns that the response is in some material respect incomplete or incorrect and if the additional or corrective information has not otherwise been made known to the other parties during the discovery process or in writing").

A "litigation hold," without more, will not suffice to satisfy the "reasonable inquiry" requirement in Rule 26(g)(2). Counsel retains an ongoing responsibility to take appropriate measures to ensure that the client has provided all available information and documents which are responsive to discovery requests. *Sexton v. United States*, 2001 WL 649445 (M.D. Fla. 2001). As the Advisory Committee Notes make clear, "Rule 26(g) imposed an affirmative duty to engage in pretrial discovery in a responsible manner that is consistent with the spirit and purposes of Rules 26 through 37." In this case, I find that Defendants failed to meet this standard.

SANCTIONS FOR E-DISCOVERY ABUSES—IS THE ATTORNEY TO BLAME?

A district court in Ohio decided that sanctions were appropriate due to the plaintiff's "persistent and egregious noncompliance with a series of discovery orders," but could not decide whether to impose the sanctions against the plaintiff or its attorneys. *Exact Software v. Infocon*, 2006 WL 34999992 (N.D. Ohio) (Dec. 5, 2006).

In an unusual order, the plaintiff software company was granted leave to show cause why sanctions should be imposed against its attorneys, and not the company. The question of blame arose when new counsel appeared for the plaintiff and filed an affidavit by the plaintiff's CEO swearing that the prior attorney failed to inform the company of the court orders and pending motion for default. *Id.* at fn. 25.

The court is ready to sanction the plaintiff by dismissing its case, entering default judgment for the defendant on its counterclaims, and taxing all fees and costs. But as the court noted, it should not sanction a party "where the fault lies with inattentive, inept, or incompetent counsel" so that the "party does not suffer for the ineptness or incompetence of its counsel." As the court only knew that its orders were not followed and did not know why, it provided the plaintiff with an evidentiary hearing to prove that its prior attorneys were to blame.

The opinion at footnote 2 notes that the plaintiff had been represented in this dispute by at least four different attorneys. This is usually a red flag that the client is the problem. Still, the opinion suggests that the third attorney, whose motion to withdraw was still pending, could be partially at fault because most of the discovery failures happened on her watch.

One of the most interesting failings noted in the order had to do with the use of keyword searches of the plaintiff's records. The plaintiff blamed its failure to produce certain relevant documents upon the opposing party's poor choice of search terms. The plaintiff argued that the search terms that defendant used did not produce a hit on these known documents, and so they did not produce them. The court soundly rejected this, saying:

> Their attitude and approach were not appropriate. Just as a party asking for production of a paper document does not have to specify the room, cabinet, drawer, and file in which the document is to be found, a party calling for production of electronically created and kept information is not required to plot the search with exactitude. If the party from whom discovery is sought can comprehend with reasonable certainty what is being asked for, it is up to it to access its storage system to retrieve the document. If problems are encountered due to uncertainty about what is being sought, the party conducting the search of its own system and records is to ask for further clarification.

ABA FIRST ANNUAL NATIONAL INSTITUTE ON E-DISCOVERY

There was a big turnout for this e-discovery event sponsored by the American Bar Association's Section on Litigation in early 2007. It was an experienced crowd of lawyers to be sure, but there were not that many young lawyers, and I had the feeling the room was not exactly filled with bloggers, techies and Web 2.0 aficionados. Three of the faculty that the ABA Section of Litigation assembled for this event stood out as particularly good: Andrea Zopp, the keynote luncheon speaker; Kevin Esposito, a panelist on the "Cost Reduction Strategies" segment; and Judge Paul Grimm, a panelist on the last session on ethics.

Ms. Zopp was the general counsel for Sears for many years and is now serving as the head of human resources for Exelon Corp., Chicago's power company. Her presentation was titled "We Have to Do What? The In-House Perspective." It provided a rare, frank glimpse into the mind of in-house counsel on a number of subjects, not just e-discovery. She was very blunt in saying that it is absolutely imperative that outside counsel personally meet with their in-house counsel clients and closely question and educate them on e-discovery issues. She explained that most in-house lawyers do not really understand e-discovery, nor do they want to. They like "shiny things" and want all of them, but couldn't care less how or why they work. She also jokingly said not to trust what in-house counsel tell you—not because they are ill-intentioned, but because they are so future-oriented, always focusing on the next task at hand, that they do not remember things in the past that well. Also, she pointed out that corporate departments are tribal, and even the larger IT tribe has various subtribes within it. You should never assume that the various tribes and subtribes in a company ever speak to one another or know what the others are doing. So when you meet with IT people, you have to meet with all departments and levels of IT.

This message was emphasized by Kevin Esposito, in-house counsel for Pfizer, who heads up its e-discovery team. He had some good suggestions on how to communicate with the IT techies that we must all depend on in the world of e-discovery. He advised working with them closely before the 26(f) conferences, but never actually bring them to the conference. They are likely to speak out of turn and volunteer information that could get you into a lot of trouble. Mr. Esposito made clear that you have to meet in person with a company's IT staff—and not just the CIO but all levels, especially the "lowest" level of the help desk and backup technicians. Only the "rubber meets the road" techs actually know what is going on in IT and what the ESI storage practices really are. Otherwise you risk falling victim to the old "telephone" game, where the one who receives the final message (the trial lawyer) gets it all wrong.

All of the panelists on the Cost Reduction Strategies panel agreed that the key to costs savings was to spend more up front to create an effective ESI response team, to map the data, and to set up sound processes and procedures for preservation, identification and collection. Conversely, they stated the "worst enemy of cost control is the poorly organized and poorly prepared" internal e-discovery response team. This is all the stuff I regularly preach, so it was affirming to hear all of the panelists agree. In fact, this was one of the underlying themes of the whole conference.

The last presentation was "E-Ethics: Practical Consideration and Ethical Issues in Electronic Discovery." Here Magistrate Judge Paul Grimm of Baltimore, Maryland, made a strong impression with his practical approach. Judge Grimm has gone far deeper than most judges in the area of e-discovery and, as mentioned, has even helped developed a set of e-discovery protocols[2] for the proper conduct of counsel in Maryland. I suggest you take a look at these well-considered local rules. As Judge Grimm said, they make a good checklist to be sure you cover everything. The ethics panel all agreed that the *Zubulake* duty is inherent in the new rules and sets a new standard of care for all attorneys to follow. They called this a "sea change" in discovery duty and responsibility. The distinguished panel, including the current head of the ABA's Litigation Section, agreed that outside counsel has a duty to sit down and meet with the general counsel and IT personnel, that it is not sufficient to just call and write. As Judge Grimm put it, the "empty head, pure heart" defense just won't cut it any more.

NEW YORK JUDGE'S TOP TEN TIPS

One of the better handouts at the ABA's First Annual National Institute on e-Discovery was Judge John J. Hughes's "Top Ten Tips for E-Discovery." Judge Hughes is a district court judge in Trenton, New Jersey. What follows is my paraphrasing and elaboration of his ideas.

1. **Talk to your client.** This is the key to fulfilling the *Zubulake* duty. It means to talk to all the involved people in a client corporation: in-house counsel, IT on all levels, and the business players involved in the dispute. It also means to talk to your client about a records retention program and the formation of an e-discovery team. It is good to see that Judge Hughes makes this his number one tip to improve e-discovery.

2. **Talk to opposing counsel.** The only way for e-discovery to work is through full and open communication between counsel as to what you are doing, what you want to do, and why. This is what Judge Hughes calls "establishing the rules of the

---

2.   http://www.mdd.uscourts.gov/news/news/ESIProtocol.pdf.

game before you start to play it." The new rules of procedure are very bare-bones; they are designed to start dialogues between counsel rather than end them. E-discovery requires a high degree of cooperation and transparency between attorneys, something that has been all too rare in the past. The days of strong adversarial conduct in discovery are over. "Hide the ball" tactics will inevitably lead you to trouble, not victory.

3. **Identify and talk to your client's techies.** You need to get to know your client's IT people, as the judge puts it, to get on the "same wavelength." This requires identifying the IT techs who will locate, preserve, and harvest the ESI at issue in your case. It also requires identifying the techie among them you should prepare and produce for deposition on ESI-related subjects. Not all IT people make good deponents, to put it mildly. This tip emphasizes the importance of establishing lines of communication with your client's techies. If your client does not already have an e-discovery team formed, this step is especially critical, and often extremely challenging. It is far better to have these lines of communication established well before a lawsuit hits.

4. **Educate the judge.** Again, the emphasis is on full and open communication, this time with the presiding judge. Let the judge know what is going on with e-discovery in the case. If there are any issues, bring them to the judge's attention as soon as possible. Do not assume that your particular judge is familiar with e-discovery. Some are, some are not. Some judges may require full briefing on the subject, and almost all will require some education about your client's particular ESI situation. The complexity of most IT systems is beyond the experience of most judges, even technologically savvy ones, and this requires a detailed education process, including, in some instances, testimony by your designated "talking techie."

5. **Continuing disclosure.** Follow up with your clients on IT and be sure that all responsive ESI is being preserved, harvested and produced. You need to be vigilant in preserving and not just rely on a one-time effort. It is way too complicated, and

the amount of ESI at issue in a typical case is too vast, for a single effort to succeed. As a speaker at the ABA conference put it, never use the word "all" in e-discovery. You will never be able to identify and produce *all* responsive ESI; you will never be able to do a perfect job in this area and avoid *all* mistakes. The best you can do is establish reasonable systems and be diligent. This diligence requires follow-up and reminders. As Judge Hughes put it, "Assume somebody will forget to disclose their PDA."

6. **Make specific discovery requests.** Be specific and focused in your e-discovery requests. Judge Hughes says the days of saying "any and all" and "in any form" are over. Overbroad discovery is inappropriate, and objections on that basis should be sustained.

7. **Show "good cause" for production.** Be prepared to establish a factual predicate for the production you request. If an objection is made, be prepared to prove why it should be produced. Never assume that the judge knows your case and knows why the ESI requested is important for you to prepare for trial.

8. **Explain "undue hardship" in opposition.** Again, prove your ESI discovery positions and offer evidence as to why the data requested is inaccessible. Do not assume the judge understands the burdens that a request may place upon your client. As Judge Hughes puts it: "Offer certifications as to precise cost in time/money/loss of productivity."

9. **Connect e-discovery with e-trial.** The judge here makes a valid point that practitioners sometimes lose sight of: The only legitimate purpose of e-discovery is to prepare for trial or negotiated settlement. From the start, you should be thinking about how you will use and present the electronic evidence you uncover at mediation or trial. Further, e-discovery should never be an end in itself, and judges should not allow one party to use the threat of expensive e-discovery as a tool to force settlement.

10. **Be professional.** Judge Hughes reminds us that our reputation is our most valuable asset and, as he puts it, "your most effective litigation skill." He also reminds us that although it takes time and consistent effort to build a good reputation, it is easily and quickly lost.

The New Rules for e-Discovery 3

INTRODUCTION TO THE NEW RULES

The full text and official commentaries of the new Federal Rules of Civil Procedure, Rules 16, 26, 34 and 37, are included in the Appendix. Rule 33 on interrogatories and Rule 45 on subpoenas were also amended but are largely technical to track the other amendments. Several cases that interpret and apply the new rules are discussed in this chapter, along with blogs containing my analysis, and others, of the new rules and how they are impacting legal and corporate practice.

In 2007 the Uniform Law Commission promulgated Proposed Uniform State e-Discovery Rules for adoption by the states. The Appendix includes the full text of these proposed rules. They closely track the federal rules but have a few significant differences, and are discussed at the end of this chapter. The Appendix also includes the American Bar Association's (ABA's) Civil Discovery Standards section on technology that was created in August 2004. These standards largely anticipate the new Federal Rules and are briefly mentioned at the end of this chapter.

Finally, the Appendix contains local rules on e-discovery that have been adopted by several district courts around the country to implement the new Federal Rules. More are expected in the next several years, by both district courts and state courts.

DECEMBER 1, 2006: NEW RULES WENT INTO EFFECT

The new rules went into effect December 1, 2006. It was just another day for most lawyers, with no immediate, profound changes on legal practice. There are two schools of thought on this. One says it is just like the big Y2K scare, much ado about nothing. The practice of law will go on pretty much as it always has before. All the pre-amendment talk about the profound changes the new rules would have on the law was just hype. The other, I think more realistic, view is that the new rules are the start of something big, a kind of point of no return, soon to become a "tipping point." Of course, nothing special happened the day the new rules went into effect. This was never a Y2K doomsday scenario. It is more like a landmark, a time when the process of change begins to accelerate as the legal profession struggles to keep up with the massive changes in society.

The law must inevitably follow the digitization of society. There is no turning back. In today's world, the smoking gun every litigant searches for in discovery lies in a computer, not a filing cabinet. We must follow the evidence, just like the truth, wherever it takes us. That is why e-discovery is here to stay, and why December 1, 2006, was an important day.

In a few years I think that we will look back on the rule change and see that it did indeed have a significant impact on civil litigation in America. It helped our dispute resolution process keep up with the explosion of information and helped our profession adapt to the age of technology. Specifically, it is likely to lead to much greater cooperation between counsel in the discovery process, a more active judiciary in discovery, and to many more technologically competent attorneys.

WHEN DO THE NEW RULES APPLY?

First, to state the obvious, the new rules only apply to cases in federal court, although no doubt the new Federal Rules of Civil Procedure (FRCP) and their commentaries will also be frequently argued in state court e-discovery disputes.

Second, the new FRCP rules certainly apply to all cases filed in district courts on or after December 1, 2006, the date the new rules went into effect. As to federal cases filed before December 1, 2006, the Supreme Court said they should apply "insofar as just and practicable."[1]

Thus, under the Supreme Court guidelines, if a case was filed before December 1, 2006, it will be up to the district court to determine on a case-by-case basis whether application of the new rules will be too burdensome or will result in undue delay. If a court determines it is impractical or unjust to use the new rules, then the old rules will apply. This will almost certainly be the case where discovery has already closed or is in the final stages.

SURVEY: COMPANIES NOT READY FOR NEW RULES

A November 2006 survey by *Computerworld*[2] indicated that most companies were not prepared for the December 1 rule change. The popular magazine reported that a survey of 170 IT managers and staffers showed that 32% were not prepared at all; 6% somewhat unprepared; 4% halfway prepared; 11% somewhat unprepared; 5% completely prepared; and a whopping 42 percent said they did not know the status of any preparation efforts. My guess is that most who said they did not know are, in fact, unprepared. This means the vast majority of IT departments, perhaps as high as 80%, are not ready for e-discovery. The follow-up questions the survey posed seems to confirm that.

When IT personnel were asked if they knew who was in charge of preparing for e-discovery, 35% did not know; 27% said no one; 20% said IT; only 8% said in-house legal counsel; 5% said the compliance department; and the last 5% said other. That 8% percent figure is surprising. You would think that legal departments would have a bigger presence. The survey report does not indicate the size of the companies polled. I would suspect many were small to mid-range, with limited in-house legal staffs. Regardless, this survey confirms the suspicions of many commentators that corporate America is still not prepared to respond to electronic discovery, and that disastrous *Coleman v. Morgan Stanley*-type e-discovery cases are likely to continue for many years to come.

---

1. *See* http://www.supremecourtus.gov/orders/courtorders/frcv06p.pdf
2. http://www.computerworld.com/

the litigation hold process: Atlas LCC, by PSS Systems.[3] It is tied into the company's key databases, and notifies and implements direct transfers of data by custodians as part of a litigation hold. It also keeps a record of the whole process and so facilitates documentation of efforts and up-to-the-minute status reports.

REVOLUTIONARY EFFECT OF REVISED RULES 16(b) AND 26(f)?

The December 1, 2006, amendments to the rules include additions to Rule 26(f) governing "meet and greet" attorney conferences and Rule 16(b) governing scheduling conference hearings. These revisions were short and not particularly controversial, and yet e-discovery experts Adam Cohen and David Lender call them "revolutionary in effect." Rule 16(b) was simply revised to add a new subsection five stating that the scheduling order may include: "(5) provisions for disclosure or discovery of electronically stored information." Rule 26(f) was just revised to add a new subject for the attorneys to discuss: "(3) any issues relating to disclosure or discovery of electronically stored information, including the form or forms in which it should be produced."

Cohen and Lender are the authors of *Electronic Discovery: Law and Practice.* They add a prediction in the just released 2007 Supplement[4] that these additions to Rule 26(f) and 16(b):

> ... are likely to be revolutionary in their effect—elevating electronic discovery to front and center status in many federal court litigations, and potentially "front loading" and defusing many disputes about electronic discovery.

Cohen and Lender go on to explain that the early discussion requirements mandated in the revisions to these rules will necessarily require lawyers to "acquire a firm grasp in understanding the facts about their clients' electronic information systems at the outset of litigation." To support this prediction they point to the Rules Committee Notes to Rule

---

3.   http://www.pss-systems.com/solutions/litigation.html
4.   *Electronic Discovery,* Section 2.03[D], 2007 Supp., Aspen Publishers.

16(b) that state that it "may" be important for counsel to become familiar with their clients' computer systems before the conference.

Most experts speaking or writing on this subject agree with the prediction of Cohen and Lender; indeed, it seems to be the consensus view. This view is also consistent with the duty set out in *Zubulake V* and other cases discussed at length in the "Ethics" chapter. *Zubulake v. UBS*, 229 F.R.D. 422 (S.D. N.Y. 2004). Judge Scheindlin in *Zubulake V* requires outside counsel to make certain that all potentially relevant electronic data are identified and placed "on hold":

> To do this, counsel must become fully familiar with her client's document retention policies, as well as the client's data retention architecture. This will invariably involve speaking with information technology personnel, who can explain system-wide backup procedures and the actual (as opposed to theoretical) implementation of the firm's recycling policy. It will also involve communicating with the "key players" in the litigation, in order to understand how they stored information.

This duty to become fully familiar with your clients' "data retention architecture" is the so-called "*Zubulake* duty" that has so many lawyers concerned. Rightly so, because if your client is a mid-size to large corporation, its data retention architecture is probably horrendously complex. Very few of your client's own IT people are likely to understand the whole thing, much less be able to explain it to you in laymen's language. Still, if you fail to fulfill the *Zubulake* duty, you could face personal sanctions, as the attorney did in *Phoenix Four, Inc. v. Strategic Resources Corp.*, No. 05-CIV-4837, 2006 WL 1409413; 2006 U.S. Dist. LEXIS 32211 (S.D. N.Y. May 22, 2006). The case is fully discussed in the "Ethics" chapter, but suffice it to say the court held the attorney responsible for not thinking to ask about hidden partitions in his client's servers, where, as it turns out, most of the evidence in this case was hiding.

The originator of the *Zubulake* duty, Judge Shira Scheindlin, was quoted in a February 2007 *ABA Journal* article by Jason Krause, "E-Discovery Gets Real," as saying the new amendments to the rules "should make life much easier for attorneys." This seems like an ironic statement from the originator of the *Zubulake* duty. She then points out that attorneys must come to the Rule 16(b) and 26(f) conferences prepared to discuss all aspects of e-discovery, and if they do not, "that's just not accepted by the rules." According to the *ABA Journal,* she goes on to try to reassure attorneys by stating:

> I'd like to put their [attorneys] mind at ease, you don't have to know everything at the first conference. But you at least have to start to assess the situation.

Based on her past decisions, the stress points here were likely on the words "everything" and "first."

DO THE NEW RULES DISCOURAGE IT IMPROVEMENTS?

Do the new *Federal Rules of Civil Procedure* (FRCP) reward the continued use of outdated computer systems where information is hard to find and retrieve? Overall, no. But surprisingly, one of the new rules *does* reward inefficient IT, and it is an important rule at that: Rule 26(b)(2)(B). Although it is not the intended purpose of the rule, there is no getting around the fact that 26(b)(2)(B) is a disincentive to IT upgrades designed to improve accessibility to stored information. It does so by providing special protection from discovery to hard-to-access computer data, protection not afforded to any other type of digital evidence.

Fortunately for hardware and software vendors, the impact of this one "pro-Luddite" rule is outweighed by the terms of the other new rules, primarily Rules 16(b) and 26(f). They require a party in federal litigation to *very quickly* identify, preserve, search, and produce relevant computer data. The new FRCP timelines established by these rules cannot be met by businesses unable to quickly access the high volumes of electronic records stored on their computer systems. For that reason, the overall impact of FRCP, despite Rule 26(b)(2)(B), supports the upgrade and migration of IT systems to improve information accessibility.

A company in litigation today must be able to quickly and efficiently locate and retrieve information relevant to the dispute. It is foolish to continue to use outdated technology that makes it difficult, if not impossible, to do so. In fact, that can often make the difference between win-ning and losing a lawsuit. That is why many companies are now moving away from unsearchable backup tapes to new searchable tape systems, archiving, live mirroring, or other solutions. That is also why they are investing in software to more efficiently search and preserve information, especially emails.

Rule 26(b)(2)(B) FRCP goes against this trend and provides some small comfort to procrastinators who put off these needed upgrades. This rule actually encourages inefficient IT because it places hard-to-find computer data off-limits from discovery, absent a special showing of good cause not required for all other computer evidence. In other words, if you store computer data so that it is hard to access, then, as a general rule, when you are sued, this information is, to a large extent, exempt from discovery. Unlike other relevant computer information that is stored efficiently so that it can be reasonably accessed, if information is very difficult to access, then you do not have to access it at all. You do not even have to search it to see if it contains relevant evidence, and so, of course, you also do not have to produce it. You just have to disclose that it exists, and explain why it is hard to get to. Then it is up to the requesting party to try to persuade the court that special circumstances exist to justify the burden and expense of discovery. This is a so-called "two-tiered" system of discovery, with "not reasonably accessible" data requiring a second tier of good-cause proof to be discoverable.

Here is the full text of Rule 26(b)(2)(B):

(B) A party need not provide discovery of electronically stored information from sources that the party identifies as not reasonably accessible because of undue burden or cost. On motion to compel discovery or for a protective order, the party from whom discovery is sought must show that the information is not reasonably accessible because of undue burden or cost. If that showing is made, the court may nonetheless order discovery from such sources if the requesting party shows good cause, considering the limitations of Rule 26(b)(2)(C). The court may specify conditions for the discovery. (Emphasis added.)

Information considered by the law to be "not reasonably accessible" and thus protected from ordinary discovery by this rule includes backup tapes, "legacy data," and "double-deleted" files. By "legacy data," I mean information stored on hardware or requiring software that is no longer used or easily available. By "double-deleted" files, I mean files no longer listed in the operating system, but still located on a hard drive or other storage device, at least in part, because they have not been written over yet by new information. (For more on what I mean by "double-deleted" as opposed to single-deleted, see the blog *When Should You Search for Deleted Files* in the "Search and Review" chapter.)

The "pro-Luddite" aspect of FRCP inherent in 26(b)(2)(B) seems to have escaped the notice of most IT commentators and vendors, especially those in the information storage and retrieval field. They promote the idea that compliance with FRCP requires companies to upgrade their IT systems. They affirm that FRCP now mandates businesses to make all of their computer data reasonably accessible, especially their email, which is the primary focus of discovery in most lawsuits. To read all of the hype in this area, you would think that the new FRCP contains provisions requiring specific technology improvements, such as archiving of e-mail.

They do not, and in fact, as you can see by the terms of Rule 26(b)(2)(B), this rule protects old, inefficient systems. It serves to put information that is not reasonably accessible—that is, information stored in a manner that is burdensome or expensive to retrieve—outside the scope of normal discovery. Therefore, in that way, Rule 26(b)(2)(B) rewards a company that maintains its data inefficiently by excluding that data from discovery. The company is saved from the expense of preserving or searching for that kind of data. **To put it simplistically, you do not have to produce what you can't easily find. So, why make anything easy to find? If you do, you just make it discoverable.** Following this argument, the best strategy to avoid the high expense of e-discovery is to keep storing your company's business information in sources that are not reasonably accessible. This is what I call a Luddite strategy of "deliberate inaccessibility."

Although I do not agree with this strategy, I recognize that the argument does have *some* merit. I think this aspect of FRCP should be openly discussed and not just swept under the rug. In fact, this language in

26(b)(2)(B) is, in my view and others', one of the most significant weaknesses in the new rules and will cause problems for years to come. See Garrie, Armstrong & Burdett, *Hiding the Inaccessible Truth: Amending the Federal Rules to Accommodate Electronic Discovery,* 25 REV. LITIG. 115 (2006).[5] As Garrie, Armstrong & Burdett point out in another law review article on Sarbanes-Oxley and e-discovery, the *Zubulake* decisions have the same technology-chilling effect insofar as they place a special burden of cost-sharing on a party seeking discovery of inaccessible data, including legacy data and backup tapes:

> *Zubulake* thus creates a perverse disincentive that prevents companies from investing in more efficient data storage technologies, because parties with efficient storage systems are generally forced to produce more digital documents than parties using legacy storage systems. Although companies eventually may determine that the need for a newer storage system exceeds the risks posed by broad electronic discovery, litigants should not be forced to weigh potential adverse legal consequences against the benefits that could be realized by investing in appropriate systems for their business needs. (Footnotes omitted.)

Garrie & Armstrong, *Electronic Discovery and the Challenge Posed by the Sarbanes-Oxley Act,* 2005 UCLA J.L. & TECH. 2, para. 13.[6]

Other commentators acknowledge the problem but then dismiss it too easily by stating that courts will see through any fraudulent schemes to hide evidence in inaccessible systems. This argument assumes fraudulent intent. For authority, these commentators usually cite the *Rambus* saga of cases: *Rambus, Inc. v. Infineon Techs. AG,* 220 F.R.D. 264, 284 (E.D. Va. 2004); *Rambus, Inc. v. Infineon Techs. AG,* 155 F. Supp. 2d 668, 680-83 (E.D. Va. 2001); *Rambus, Inc. v. Infineon Techs. AG,* 222 F.R.D. 280, 286 (E.D. Va. 2004); *Samsung Electronics Co., Ltd. v. Rambus, Inc.,* 439 F. Supp. 2d 524 (E.D. Va., July 18, 2006). These cases expose the deliberate actions by Rambus to change its record retention

---

5.   http://www.utexas.edu/law/journals/trol/abstract.php?volume=25&page=115

6.   http://www.lawtechjournal.com/articles/2005/02_050530_garrie_armstrong.php

policies and physically destroy evidence in anticipation of bringing patent litigation. (See my blog *Rule 37(f) Safe Harbor Requires Routines That Most Companies Lack* in this chapter for further discussion of this interesting case and the employee "shred days.")

This kind of facile response—"don't worry about 26(b)(2)(B) because the courts will pick up on any fraud"—begs the question. Obviously, if a company moves all of the data it does not want found into a legacy system before filing suit instead of just destroying it as in *Rambus*, this is a fraudulent scheme and will likely be exposed. But this does not address the more realistic scenario of a company that simply continues the status quo of maintaining old systems with unreasonably accessible data. It does not address the non-fraudulent scheme. The strategy of "deliberate inaccessibility" is not necessarily fraudulent. In most cases, it will more likely be driven by procrastination, penny-pinching, and short-sighted thinking.

Again, to reiterate, I do not think a company should follow this kind of strategy of inertia. A company should not put off upgrades to its IT systems to make more information accessible just because this might take the information out of the protection of Rule 26(b)(2)(B). The strategy of inaction is too risky. Businesses *should* improve their IT systems, especially email, and move away from old technologies that are hard to search. Everyone, especially businesses involved in frequent litigation, should move toward making their information retrieval more efficient and reliable both for business purposes and for litigation readiness purposes. But it is not a simple black-and-white matter of compliance with FRCP, as some contend. The reality is, FRCP is a mixed bag, and companies should act now to improve information accessibility primarily for business and records management efficiency reasons, and only secondarily because of litigation.

Even from the litigation perspective alone, a full risk analysis counsels in favor of technology improvement, not status quo. Attempts to rely on 26(b)(2)(B) to protect data from discovery by using obsolete storage, such as tapes and legacy systems, are too risky. The risk is unacceptable because the exemption of inaccessible data from discovery is subject to a second-tier "good cause" exception. The vague good-cause exception allowing discovery is not defined by the rules. Under this second-tier analysis, a court can require the production of even inaccessible records, regardless of how much burden and expense this may cause, and the expenses in a situation like that can be enormous. Costs of $3 million in just five months are not that unusual. See *Kentucky Speedway, LLC v. NASCAR*, 2006 U.S. Dist. LEXIS 92028 (E. D. Ky. Dec. 18, 2006). It is true that a court has discretion to shift some of these costs onto the requesting party, but you cannot count on that.

Good cause for discovery of inaccessible data can be shown in any number of ways, depending in large part on how the governing judge views the case and the discovery sought. The Rules Committee Commentary specifies some of the factors they think a court should consider in finding "good cause." These are suggestions only, and are not binding on any court. These Rule 26 Commentaries are quoted in full in the Appendix. Here is my summary of the factors the committee suggested be considered to decide whether there is good cause to allow discovery of "not reasonably accessible" information:

1. The specificity of the discovery request.
2. The quantity of information available from other, more easily accessed sources.
3. The failure to produce relevant information that seems likely to have existed but is no longer available from more easily accessed sources.
4. The likelihood of finding relevant, responsive information that cannot be obtained from other, more easily accessed sources.
5. Predictions as to the importance and usefulness of the requested information.
6. The importance of the issues at stake in the litigation.
7. The parties' resources.

It is a long list, and not exclusive, and everyone knows that it will be one of the most heavily litigated parts of the new FRCP for many years to come.

Since the good cause exception is so general and vague, not to mention hard to predict, it is foolish to keep information in the dark based on the hope that it will, for that reason, never be subject to discovery. You never know when a court may require you to search in the dark at great expense.

Also, and even more important in my opinion, that is no way to run a business or manage records. Why keep information if you don't want it and can't use it? It might all come back to haunt you someday (just ask Morgan Stanley), and in the meantime it costs money to store. The best solution to an archaic computer system is to throw it out and upgrade. The best solution to archaic information is to throw it out, period. If there is no valid business purpose or legal requirement to save records, then destroy them. Do not just save information because you have the ability to do so. That is a natural pack-rat tendency of most IT departments, and the one that annoys lawyers the most. Of course, do not act rashly, either. Think long and hard, and be sure that you do not need the records. Then take the time to purge and destroy, and do it the right way. Follow the guidelines of Rule 37, document everything, and so protect against any later spurious charges of spoliation.

BLOG READER COMMENT

I don't think any company could support archaic/legacy systems for very long, especially if their only motivation was data inaccessibility. They would face too much pressure from other stakeholders (e.g., internal business units wanting tools to improve productivity; executives wanting newer technology to enhance the company's image, etc.).

RALPH'S REPLY

I agree, it is a stupid strategy. But due to mergers, many companies have legacy systems, and especially legacy data, by default, not strategy. Rather than destroy the data and systems, they tend to just hang around, unused. Like I said, some in IT do not like to get rid of anything. The reasoning is that perhaps someday they may be needed or useful. The downside of e-discovery exposure is not even considered by IT. So it is out of sight, out of mind, until an e-discovery request comes along, and they become a problem, perhaps a big problem. You have to disclose them, and run the risk of having to search and produce if the requesting party succeeds on the second tier.

EMPLOYER ALLOWED TO MIRROR EMPLOYEES' HOME COMPUTERS AND OBTAIN INACCESSIBLE ESI

26(b)(2)(B)
26(b)(2)(B)

A district court in Missouri became one of the first in the country to employ the new inaccessibility analysis under Rule 26(b)(2)(B). *Ameriwood v. Liberman*, 2006 WL 3825291, 2006 U.S. Dist. LEXIS 93380 (E.D. Mo., Dec. 27, 2006); clarified 2007 WL 685623 (E.D. Mo., Feb. 23, 2007). This is a trade secret theft case where the plaintiff moved to compel the defendants (former employees of the plaintiff) to allow a complete mirror-image inspection of the hard drives on all of their computers. The request included their home computers and other portable storage devices (like thumb drives). The defendants objected on the basis that the mirror imaging requested sought data that was not reasonably accessible and thus protected under 26(b)(2)(B). They further objected on the grounds the imaging requested was unnecessary and overly intrusive.

A mirror image of a hard drive is an exact duplicate of the entire drive, including deleted files, slack and free space. *Id*. at fn. 3. A trained computer forensic expert can examine a mirror image of a drive and reconstruct files that have been deleted, thus transforming them from inaccessible to accessible. This process can, however, be quite expensive. As a general rule, mirroring or inspection of an entire hard drive is not permitted without good cause. It is analogous to allowing a requesting party to inspect an entire paper filing cabinet instead of just the particular files in the cabinet that are relevant, and search the garbage cans too.

Still, in this case the court granted the employer's motion because of: (1) the close relationship between the plaintiff's claims and the defendants' computer equipment; (2) facts placing in doubt that all responsive documents have been produced; and (3) the plaintiff's willingness to pay for the expert forensic examination costs involved in the mirroring.

The court followed the new burden-shifting analysis of new Rule 26(b)(2)(B) to reach this result. The rule provides:

> On motion to compel discovery . . . , the party from whom discovery is sought must show that the information is not reasonably accessible because of undue burden or cost. If that showing is made, the court may nonetheless order discovery from such sources if the requesting party shows good cause, considering the limitations of Rule 26(b)(2)(C). The court may specify conditions for the discovery.

The defendants first argued that they had already searched their ESI and produced all discoverable information, and thus there was no need for a complete mirror-image production too. In essence, they argued that this was "just a fishing expedition" not permitted under the rules. Plaintiff effectively countered by producing an email to defendants that they had obtained by subpoena of a third party. This email should have been in the defendants' custody and produced by them, but it was not. This cast doubt on the completeness of the defendants' production, and thus supported the plaintiff's argument that the mirroring was needed.

Defendants next argued that the mirror was a request for ESI not reasonably accessible to them because of undue burden and cost. They supported this objection with affidavits of the significant costs involved in mirroring all of their computers and drives, recovering deleted information, and then translating it into reviewable formats. The court agreed that the defendants had established that the ESI requested was inaccessible to them under Rule 26 (b)(2)(B). But that is not the end of the analysis. The rule goes on to still allow discovery of inaccessible data if the requesting party, here the plaintiff, shows good cause.

The plaintiff sustained this burden under the seven-point good-cause inquiry suggested by the Advisory Committee Notes to the rule. The third criterion was particularly persuasive in this case: "(3) the failure to produce relevant information that seems likely to have existed but is no longer available on more easily accessed sources." This factor was met by the email produced by the third party, but not by defendants.

Good cause for the mirroring requested was also found in the allegations of the complaint itself, in that the trade secret theft here was allegedly accomplished by the computers in question. As the court explained:

> Furthermore, in cases where a defendant allegedly used the computer itself to commit the wrong that is the subject of the lawsuit, certain items on the hard drive may be discoverable. Particularly, allegations that a defendant downloaded trade secrets onto a computer provide a sufficient nexus between plaintiff's claims and the need to obtain a mirror image of the computer's hard drive. . . . In the instant action, defendants are alleged to have used the computers, which are the subject of the discovery request, to secrete and distribute plaintiff's confidential information. How and whether defendants handled those documents and what defendants did with the documents is certainly at issue. The Court recognizes defendants' privacy concerns over the information contained on their computers, but finds that the procedure below in addition to the Court's protective order sufficiently addresses these interests.

> In performing the good-cause inquiry, the court is also permitted to set conditions for discovery, including but not limited to payment by the requesting party of part or all of the reasonable costs of obtaining information from the sources that are not reasonably accessible. See Fed. R. Civ. P. 26(b)(2) Advisory Committee's Note. As plaintiff does not object to incurring the costs for the requested procedures and defendants do not perform these procedures in the regular course of their business, plaintiff will incur the costs involved in creating the mirror images, recovering the information, and translating the information into searchable formats, as described below. For the above reasons, this Court finds that plaintiff has shown good cause to allow it to obtain mirror images of defendants' hard drives under the following conditions.

The court then set forth conditions designed to protect the privacy rights of defendants to the ESI on their computers, including their home computers. The court followed the procedures set forth by the seminal case in this area, *Playboy Enterprises v. Welles*, 60 F. Supp. 2d 1050, 1054 (S.D. Cal. 1999). Essentially, under the *Playboy* protocols, a third-party expert does the exam and restoration, and then turns over to defendants' counsel a copy of all ESI found and recovered, including deleted files. Defendants then review the restored ESI and produce all data responsive to discovery requests, and log any responsive but privileged ESI. Thereafter plaintiff may file motions to compel if warranted.

RULE 37 AND THE SUPREME COURT ON DOCUMENT DESTRUCTION

The Supreme Court articulated its policy on corporate document destruction in *Arthur Andersen v. United States*, 544 U.S. 696 (2005). This case considered the appeal of the criminal conviction of Enron's auditor, Arthur Andersen, once the biggest accounting firm in the world. Arthur Andersen was convicted of obstruction of justice because it destroyed records pertaining to Enron, and did so knowing that a government investigation was imminent. The "substantial destruction of paper and electronic documents" by Arthur Andersen was supposedly done in compliance with its records retention policy. *Id.* at 710. It argued that had its policies been followed, these documents would already have been destroyed. But, as the Supreme Court points out, in so doing, Arthur Andersen ignored other sections of its records retention policy prohibiting the destruction of relevant records when litigation is threatened. *Id.* at 700, fn. 4.

There is little doubt that the accounting giant suddenly began to enforce its previously ignored record retention policies in order to prevent the government from getting information on its "creative" accounting services for Enron. The Supreme Court even notes one incident where a document was destroyed by the firm's senior accountant for Enron, David Duncan. This document had already been labeled, believe it or not, "smoking gun," and Duncan destroyed it with the comment, "We don't need this." *Id.* at 702, fn. 6.

Arthur Andersen was convicted of obstruction of justice, and the conviction was affirmed by the Fifth Circuit Court of Appeals. How did the Supreme Court react? It reversed in a unanimous opinion, holding that the jury instruction was too stringent. The Court had this to say on document destruction:

> "Document retention policies," which are created in part to keep certain information from getting into the hands of others, including the Government, are common in business. (citations omitted) It is, of course, not wrongful for a manager to instruct his employees to comply with a valid document retention policy under ordinary circumstances. . . . .
>
> A "knowingly . . . corrupt persuader" cannot be someone who persuades others to shred documents under a document retention policy when he does not have in contemplation any particular official proceeding in which those documents might be material.

Id. at 704, 708.

This same Court the next year (2006) approved all of the recent revisions to the Federal Rules of Civil Procedure, including Rule 37(f), which states:

> Rule 37. Failure to Make Disclosures or Cooperate in Discovery; Sanctions
>
> * * * * *
>
> (f) Electronically Stored Information. Absent exceptional circumstances, a court may not impose sanctions under these rules on a party for failing to provide electronically stored information lost as a result of the routine, good-faith operation of an electronic information system.

Considering the new rule on ESI destruction and the *Arthur Andersen* opinion, you might wonder why some companies are so skittish about following their usual document retention policies. I have heard some well-known e-discovery experts go so far as to state that the entire pharmaceutical industry now never recycles backup tapes; instead they save them all forever, for fear of a later spoliation charge. When I asked Kevin

These inaccessible backup tapes need not be subject to a litigation hold on authority of Judge Scheindlin in *Zubulake IV,* the Supreme Court in *Arthur Andersen,* and new Rule 37(f). Nevertheless, until we get a little more guidance on this issue, in some cases you may still want to take them out of the normal recycle routine, at least until your opposing counsel agrees, or, failing that, you obtain relief from the court on this issue.

BLOG READER COMMENT

As the dispositive element in this seems to be "knowledge" of impeding litigation, isn't this an incentive for corporate officers to bury their heads in the sand to avoid liability? So what's to keep a company from adopting this "ostrich" approach in tandem with a draconian document retention policy (destroy everything every six weeks) in order to protect themselves?

RALPH'S REPLY

Courts usually adopt a known or "should reasonably have known" policy to preempt just such a tactic. The "three monkeys" strategy probably would not work. Besides, the knowledge of a company's employees is usually imputed to the company itself. The *Zubulake* case provides a good example of this. The emails of Laura Zubulake's supervisor showed that he knew Laura Zubulake was sure to sue the company, and also later showed he knew about the EEOC charge before he decided to fire her.

RULE 37(f) SAFE HARBOR REQUIRES ROUTINES THAT MOST COMPANIES LACK

New Rule 37(f) creates a "safe harbor" for a company to destroy ESI as part of its routine electronic records management practices. Unfortunately, this harbor is beyond the reach of most companies because they lack established routines for ESI retention and destruction. The rule states:

> (f) Electronically stored information. Absent exceptional circumstances, a court may not impose sanctions under these rules on a

party for failing to provide electronically stored information lost as a result of the routine, good faith operation of an electronic information system.

The routine good-faith operation of an electronic records storage system can be proven by reference to a company's written records retention policy. That is the document, usually very long and complicated, that tells you when to save records, and for how long, and when to delete them. If the deletion of ESI was in accordance with the company's written manual on the subject, then you may be able to prove that the loss of evidence was the result of routine and good-faith operations. This assumes, however, that (a) the company has such a manual, and (b) the manual is routinely followed. In reality, a company's records retention policies are often ignored and seldom enforced. That makes the routine needed for Rule 37(f) safe harbor protection a difficult element for most companies to prove.

There are many reasons for this, including that the records manual is usually too long and incomprehensible, and everyone finds this whole subject too boring and unimportant to deal with. So people just do what they want with the records they control. This seems to be especially true of IT employees, who, it seems, frequently follow their own rules based on the "we know better" principle. For instance, the manual may say to recycle backup tapes every three years, but in reality you may have tapes going back for decades. The tapes are probably unlabeled, and no one has any real idea what is on them, much less how to restore them. Still, the company may have to produce these tapes someday and pay experts a small fortune to restore them to try to find missing evidence.

In the event a written records retention policy is not uniformly followed, a court will look to actual practices of a company to determine its "routine, good faith operation." Although a written manual will have consistent operation procedures specified, when you turn to actual practices by employees in a large company, consistency is rare. What is routine for one part of the IT department may be different in another part. It is worse when comparing individual employees. Some may be organized pack-rats and keep everything, and others may delete everything as soon as they read it. See, for example, *Playboy Enterprises, Inc. v. Welles,* 60 F. Supp. 2d 1050 (S.D. Cal. 1999) (Defendant explained that she had no emails to produce because she always deleted an email immediately after she read it.).

The result is that it is difficult for most companies today to take advantage of the safe harbor provided by Rule 37(f). They cannot do so because they do not have routines. About the only thing that is likely to fall within the purview of the rule for most companies is the automatic "janitor programs"[7] that delete things without need for any human intervention at all. For instance, if a file is not used within a set time period, it will be automatically deleted. In fact, this is a common practice for ESI but impossible for paper records. (XEROX has, however, recently invented a new kind of printer and paper wherein the document automatically erases itself after a few days.[8])

Even in the case of automatic ESI destruction, the defense will work only if the electronic janitor did its job before the human in IT was, or should have been, told by legal that there was a lawsuit brewing, and the auto-destruction routines should be placed on hold. If a litigation hold was not implemented when it should have been, then the practice probably lacks the good faith needed for the safe harbor, even if it has the routine element.

This is made clear by the rule's commentary, which states:

> The good faith requirement of Rule 37(f) means that a party is not permitted to exploit the routine operation of an information system to thwart discovery obligations by allowing that operation to continue in order to destroy specific stored information that it is required to preserve. When a party is under a duty to preserve information because of pending or reasonably anticipated litigation, intervention in the routine operation of an information system is one aspect of what is often called a "litigation hold."

---

7. http://lifehacker.com/software/geek-to-live/geek-to-live-hard-drive-janitor-133190.php

8. http://www.xerox.com/go/xrx/template/inv_rel_newsroom.jsp?app=Newsroom&ed_name=NR_2006Nov27_TemporaryDocuments&format=article&view=newsrelease&Xcntry=USA&Xlang=en_US

As mentioned, unlike paper records, ESI can automatically throw itself away. This distinction between paper and electronic records is the genesis behind Rule 37(f). The commentary to the new rule, which is quoted in full in the Appendix, explains the difference between paper records and ESI this way:

> The "routine operation" of computer systems includes the alteration and overwriting of information, often without the operator's specific direction or awareness, a feature with no direct counterpart in hard-copy documents. Such features are essential to the operation of electronic information systems.

On the other hand, if paper evidence is destroyed, it is frequently evidence of culpable conduct. For instance, one tech company apparently began preparing for patent litigation by getting rid of evidence that might make its cases more difficult. *Rambus, Inc. v. Infineon Tech. AG*, 220 F.R.D. 264, 284 (E.D. Va. 2004); *Rambus, Inc. v. Infineon Techs. AG*, 155 F. Supp. 2d 668, 680-83 (E.D. Va. 2001); *Rambus, Inc. v. Infineon Techs. AG*, 222 F.R.D. 280, 286 (E.D. Va. 2004); *Samsung Electronics Co., Ltd. v. Rambus, Inc.*, 439 F. Supp. 2d 524 (E.D. Va., July 18, 2006). The company began its records destruction campaign by establishing a new records "retention" policy. It began to implement the new policy with what it called "shred days," where, I kid you not, they gave every employee a burlap bag to fill up with papers to be shredded, followed by pizza parties. They managed to destroy 2.7 million pages of documents this way, but the strategy failed in the end and resulted in spoliation sanctions instead.

JUDGE SHIRA A. SCHEINDLIN VIDEO ON THE NEW RULES IS NOW ONLINE

A video has recently been posted online[9] of a speech by Judge Scheindlin of *Zubulake* fame. She gave the keynote address on October 23, 2006, at the annual meeting of ARMA (formerly known as the

---

9. http://www.arma.org/podcast/rss/Scheindlinkeynote.cfm

Association of Records Managers and Administrators). Although it is unlikely to be a hit on YouTube,[10] it is certainly worth watching.

Judge Scheindlin's speech is on the new rules. She begins with the standard explanation from the commentary on why the new rules were needed:

1. The volume of e-records is much more than paper records;
2. E-storage systems are dynamic, created and destroyed automatically;
3. ESI is difficult but not impossible to delete (you transfer information from an accessible location to inaccessible location); and
4. ESI has to be retrieved, restored and translated before it can even be reviewed.

Judge Scheindlin then talks about the "meet and confer" Rules 26 and 16, pointing out that the revision to Rule 26(f) requiring the parties to discuss "any issues relating to preserving discoverable information" is the first time the Federal Rules have ever mentioned the word "preservation."

She then turned to Rule 26(b)(5)(B) on return of privileged materials, pointing out that the Advisory Committee on the Rules of Evidence has proposed a new Evidence Rule 502. It would provide the procedural rule with much-needed teeth by prohibiting a finding of waiver if reasonable precautions to review were taken.

Then Judge Scheindlin goes into Rule 26(b)(2)(B) on inaccessibility and Rule 37(f) on "safe harbor" destruction. She provides no new comments on either rule; instead she just outlines the text of the rules and commentaries.

Magistrate Judges Share Their Views on e-Discovery and the New Rules

At the Federal Bar Association's e-Discovery CLE session in late 2006 in Orlando, Florida, the final portion of the seminar featured a panel discussion by Orlando Magistrate Judges Spalding, Glazebrook, and Baker. They had many comments on e-discovery, including these 10 points:

---

10.   http://www.youtube.com/

1. All agree that David Baker is the main "techie" on the bench in the Middle District and defer to his expertise in this area. All three judges do, of course, hear these issues. They are beginning to hear more and more of these disputes.

2. Judge Baker is of the opinion, and Glazebrook and Spalding agree, that you [attorneys] "need to grill your client" before the meet and confer session. Further, you need to "talk to their techies" before the conference. They thus follow Judge Scheindlin in *Zubulake*. Judge Glazebrook said that it was not sufficient simply to have the parties' respective techies speak with each other. The lawyers have to participate in the dialogue. Judge Baker indicated that lawyers have to learn "tech-speak." The inability to do so is not an acceptable excuse.

3. Judge Glazebrook also mentioned that you may need to have a computer tech expert at the meet and confer meeting and emphasized that lawyers definitely should meet with the client's IT personnel beforehand.

4. All three judges agreed that it is better to bring up all electronic issues as soon as reasonably possible. They would prefer that the parties not wait until there is a particular discovery request or dispute. If it is possible to frame an issue, then it is better to come to the magistrates early for review and consideration. This is the kind of thing that can be brought up in the initial pretrial conference; no pending motion is required.

5. Judge Baker indicated that he thought that the recent revisions to Rule 34(b) probably did mean that "native file format" production is the default mode. He did, however, qualify that opinion by stating that it is based upon proof of "usual course of business" for a particular business and upon the particular time frames involved. In other words, what is the usual course of business, and what do they do with data on a day-to-day basis, as compared to after a month or a year.

6. All the judges expect that the most difficult areas in e-discovery in the future will involve the so-called "David and Goliath" type of cases and the "M.A.D." (Mutual Assured Destruction) cases between two large companies.

UNIFORM LAW COMMISSION APPROVES MODEL E-DISCOVERY RULES

The Uniform Law Commissioners have now adopted model rules of e-discovery for use by state courts. The full-text of the *Uniform Rules Relating to Discovery of Electronically Stored Information* is included in the Appendix. The Uniform Law Commission[11] issued a press release[12] on August 2, 2007, to announce the proposed e-discovery rules. Rex Blackburn, the Boise, Idaho, attorney who chairs the committee that drafted the new rules, explained why the commissioners thought these new rules were necessary:

> With the emergence of electronic technology, the extent to which information is stored electronically has vastly increased, and will continue to do so. These new uniform rules should provide states with the necessary guidance governing discovery of electronically stored information.

The proposed state rules for e-discovery closely follow the Federal Rules. Just like the Federal Rules, the proposed state rules have provisions requiring early discussion of e-discovery, protection from production of not-reasonably-accessible information with cost shifting, privilege protection procedures, a default "ordinarily maintained" or "reasonably usable" production mode, and a safe harbor from sanctions for routine, good-faith destruction. It is interesting to see how the early discussion requirements contained in model State Rule 3 are required within 21 days of a party's appearance and are not tied into a court hearing or order as in Federal Rule 26. That was designed to appeal to those states that have declined to adopt a counterpart to the federal "meet and confer" obligations of Rules 16 and 26. There are several other more significant differences, some good and some bad. I will review these at the end.

The influential National Conference of Commissioners on Uniform State Laws hopes all states will now adopt these rules so that there will

---

11. http://www.nccusl.org/Update/
12. http://www.nccusl.org/nccusl/DesktopModules/NewsDisplay.aspx?ItemID=188

be uniformity of practice outside of the federal system. The commissioners for this reason will now lobby the state courts and legislatures to adopt these rules. The conference was formed in the early 1890s and claims to be the oldest state governmental association in the country. President Woodrow Wilson, former Supreme Court Justice Louis Brandeis, former Supreme Court Chief Justice William H. Rehnquist, and current Supreme Court Justice David Souter all served as uniform law commissioners. It is the source of more than 250 uniform acts, including the Uniform Commercial Code, Uniform Fraudulent Transfer Act, Uniform Interstate Family Support Act, Uniform Enforcement of Foreign Judgments Act, and Uniform Transfers to Minors Act. The conference seeks "to secure uniformity of state laws where diversity obstructs the interests of all the citizens of the United States." The model Discovery of Electronic Records Act (copy in Appendix) has been over two years in the making. Final approval came at the 116th Annual Meeting in Pasadena, California, on August 2, 2007.

The Draft Text of the Rules[13] included Prefatory and Reporters Notes, which, as always, were excluded from the final version approved as a model to be adopted by the states. The Notes are not intended to be authoritative, but still are interesting to understand the thinking behind the committee that prepared the rules. You might want to review the Draft Text for that reason. Here are a few highlights of the Notes that I found interesting:

> With very few exceptions, when the state rules and statutes concerning discovery in civil cases were promulgated and adopted, information was contained in documents in paper form. Those documents were kept in file folders, filing cabinets, and in boxes placed in warehouses. When a person or business or governmental entity decided a document was no longer needed and could be destroyed, the document was burned or shredded and that was the end of the matter. There was rarely an argument about sifting through the ashes or shredded material to reconstruct a memo which had been sent.

---

13. http://www.law.upenn.edu/bll/archives/ulc/udoera/2007annual meeting_ draft.htm

In today's business and governmental world, paper is a thing long past. By some estimates, 93 percent or more of corporate information was being stored in some sort of digital or electronic format. This difference in storage medium for information creates enormous problems for a discovery process created when there was only paper. Principal among differences is the sheer volume of information in electronic form, the virtually unlimited places where that information may appear, and the dynamic nature of electronic information.

The Notes explain that the Commission Drafting Committee intentionally copied the new revisions to the Federal Rules, cloning their "spirit and direction" and sometimes even using the exact same language.

There are, however, a few substantive differences between the federal and proposed state rules. One in particular caught my eye. Unlike the Federal Rules, the proposed uniform state rules define the term "Electronically Stored Information." The federal drafting committee did not define ESI on purpose, so that tomorrow's not-yet-invented information technologies would more easily come within the scope of ESI. The state commissioners were apparently not as concerned about this possibility, and so they went ahead and defined ESI in Rule 1(3):

"Electronically stored information" means information that is stored in an electronic medium and is retrievable in perceivable form.

They also define "electronic" in Rule 1(2) to mean "relating to technology having electrical, digital, magnetic, wireless, optical, electromagnetic, or similar capabilities."

These definitions seem awkward and ambiguous to me. One wonders why they talk about "retrievable in perceivable form." Why this focus on perception? If it is not perceivable, then how would you know it had been restored? What information could be retrieved, but in an "imperceivable form"? Imperceivable by whom or what? If a human being could not perceive it but a machine could, would it still be imperceivable? What if it were sounds that only my dog could hear? Or infrared light? As to the definition of "electronic," what does "similar capabilities" mean? What if the capabilities of a new technology were completely new? Would all the states have to revise their definitions to clarify that the information the new technology stored or created was covered by these rules? There is ambiguity inherent in these definitions as to what information is, or is not, covered by the rules and what might be in the future. The attempt to gain certainty by defining these terms has, ironically, only added uncertainty. I think the Federal Rules got it right on this point and predict that these proposed state rule definitions will only lead to trouble in the long run.

Another significant difference is found in the approach to protection of not-reasonably-accessible ESI. Federal Rule 26(b)(2)(B) protects such information from production unless the requesting party makes a good-cause showing. The Federal Rule itself does not spell out the considerations for such good cause, but only refers to the limitations of Rule 26(b)(2)(C). You have to look to the Rule Commentaries to find a non-exhaustive list of seven considerations:

1. The specificity of the discovery request;
2. The quantity of information available from other and more easily accessed sources;
3. The failure to produce relevant information that seems likely to have existed but is no longer available on more easily accessed sources;
4. The likelihood of finding relevant, responsive information that cannot be obtained from other, more easily accessed sources;
5. Predictions as to the importance and usefulness of the further information;
6. The importance of the issues at stake in the litigation; and
7. The parties' resources.

Model State Rule 8(c) takes a different approach and specifies the good-cause considerations in the rule itself. Moreover, there are only four considerations listed, instead of seven, and this list of four is exhaustive.

The court may order discovery of electronically stored information that is from a source that is not reasonably accessible because of undue burden or expense if the party requesting discovery shows that the likely benefit of the proposed discovery outweighs the likely burden or expense, taking into account (1) the amount in controversy, (2) the resources of the parties, (3) the importance of the issues, and (4) the importance of the requested discovery in resolving the issues. (Numbers added)

The four considerations listed in the state rule are taken directly from old Federal Rule 26(b)(2)(C), which states in part:

(C) The frequency or extent of use of the discovery methods otherwise permitted under these rules and by any local rule shall be limited by the court if it determines that: . . . (iii) the burden or expense of the proposed discovery outweighs its likely benefit, **taking into account the needs of the case, the amount in controversy, the parties' resources, the importance of the issues at stake in the litigation, and the importance of the proposed discovery in resolving the issues.** . . . (Emphasis added.)

The proposed state rule thus follows the federal big brother by incorporating part of 26(b)(2)(C), but deviates significantly by limiting the court to only these four factors. The wording does not include the rest of 26(b)(2)(C), and does not include the first four federal commentary criteria: (1) specificity of request, (2) quantity available from other sources, (3) failure to produce other more reasonably accessible relevant information, and (4) likelihood of finding other relevant information from more easily accessible sources. Under the proposed rules, a state court would arguably be prohibited from considering anything other than the four rather simplistic 26(b)(2)(C)-type factors specified. This does not appear to be as well thought out and balanced as the federal approach and will, I predict, draw strong opposition from the plaintiff's bar.

Another significant difference can be found in proposed State Rule 8(e), which articulates a "proportionality" limitation on the production of all ESI, even readily accessible live data:

(e) The court shall limit the frequency or extent of discovery of electronically stored information, even from a source that is reasonably accessible, if the court determines that:

1. it is possible to obtain the information from some other source that is more convenient, less burdensome, or less expensive;
2. the discovery sought is unreasonably cumulative or duplicative;
3. the party seeking discovery has had ample opportunity by discovery in the proceeding to obtain the information sought; or
4. the likely burden or expense of the proposed discovery outweighs the likely benefit, taking into account the amount in controversy, the resources of the parties, the importance of the issues, and the importance of the requested discovery in resolving the issues.

Rule 8(e) is an improvement over the wording of the Federal Rules, where you have to consult old Rules 1 and 26(b)(2)(C) to find these proportionality limitations, and even then, they are not as clear as many would like. (See my blog in the first chapter on the *Second Edition of the Sedona Principles and the Need for Proportionality*.) This provision will also be opposed by the plaintiff's bar, but more as a knee-jerk reaction than anything else. The protection from needlessly expensive discovery goes both ways. The costs of e-discovery must be contained somehow. Otherwise, as Justice Breyer pointed out in the H5 Conference on e-Discovery at Georgetown University, in the future only the very rich will be able to afford to litigate. (See my blog, *U.S. Supreme Court Justice Speaks Out on e-Discovery*, in the first chapter.)

ABA CIVIL DISCOVERY STANDARDS ON E-DISCOVERY AND TECHNOLOGY

The ABA added an e-discovery and technology section to the Civil Discovery Standards back in 2004. Although not new at this point, they are still relevant and could be helpful, especially in a state court setting. For that reason, I have included them in the Appendix, along with the committee comments.[14]

The ABA explains the purpose of these civil discovery standards as follows:

---

14. The full text of all of the ABA Civil Discovery Standards can be found at http://www.abanet.org/litigation/discoverystandards/.

The order, by Magistrate Judge Barbara Lynn Major, came on the heels of the 54-page Order on Remedy for Finding of Waiver, entered August 6, 2007, by District Court Judge Rudi M. Brewster. *Qualcomm Inc. v. Broadcom Corp.*, No. 05-CV-1958-B(BLM) Doc. 593 (S.D. Cal. Aug. 6, 2007).[3] There, the district judge found:

> . . . by clear and convincing evidence that Qualcomm['s] counsel participated in an organized program of litigation misconduct and concealment throughout discovery, trial, and post-trial before new counsel took over lead role in the case on April 27, 2007.

Among other things, this first-shoe-to-drop opinion highlighted Qualcomm's production of more than 200,000 pages of relevant emails and other electronic documents four months *after the jury trial* (which Qualcomm lost). Judge Brewster impugned Qualcomm's counsel and their claims that they carried out their discovery obligations in good faith, explaining:

> Qualcomm counsel's discovery responses demonstrate that they were able to locate with alacrity company records from December 2003 forward and find four or more Qualcomm employees participating in proceedings of the [Joint Video Team (JVT)]. Yet inexplicably, they were unable to find over 200,000 pages of relevant emails, memoranda, and other company documents, hundreds of pages of which explicitly document massive participation in JVT proceedings since at least January 2002. These examples of Qualcomm counsel's indefensible discovery conduct belie counsel's later implied protestation of having been "kept in the dark" by their client.

Judge Brewster's 54-page opinion detailed the actions of Qualcomm and its counsel, concluding that these facts demonstrate "aggravated litigation abuse." The court found "constant stonewalling, concealment,

---

3. http://ralphlosey.files.wordpress.com/2007/08/case-qualcomm_8_6_ 07_order_on_remedy.pdf

and repeated misrepresentations concerning existing corporate documentary evidence." In spite of such discovery tactics, Qualcomm lost the jury trial, and the full extent of its abuses were revealed. Qualcomm then fired its lead counsel, and its substitute counsel tried unsuccessfully to explain it all away. In the words of the court, the substitute lead counsel "adamantly denied the obvious and then, when the truth was discovered and exposed by the document production, sequentially contended denial of relevance, justification, mistake, and finally non-awareness."

The end result of the 54-page opinion was to hold and order that Qualcomm had completely waived its rights to enforce the two video compression patents (5,452,104[4] and 5,576,767[5]) at issue in the case. The waiver applies not only against Broadcom, but against anyone. The waiver was caused by Qualcomm's prior inequitable conduct before the Patent Office —conduct that Qualcomm tried to cover up in this litigation.

On August 6, 2007, Judge Brewster also entered an Order Granting Broadcom Corporation's Motion for Exceptional Case Finding and for an Award of Attorneys' Fees (35 U.S.C. § 285). *Qualcomm Inc. v. Broadcom Corp.*, No. 05-CV-1958-B(BLM) Doc. 594 (S.D. Cal. Aug. 6, 2007).[6] Judge Brewster there held that "the enumerated misconduct of Qualcomm establishes the entitlement of Broadcom to all attorneys' fees, expenses, and costs incurred in the defense of this case." If the parties are unable to agree on a reasonable number, an evidentiary hearing is to be held before the magistrate. I would anticipate a very large fee and costs award in this case. It was filed in 2005 and tried before a jury in early 2007.

Back to the Show Cause Order of August 13, 2007, against Qualcomm's many outside counsel. The magistrate advised these attor-

4. http://patft1.uspto.gov/netacgi/nph-Parser?Sect1=PTO1&Sect2=HITOFF&d=PALL&p=1&u=/netahtml/PTO/srchnum.htm&r=1&f=G&l=50&s1=5,452,104.PN.&OS=PN/5,452,104&RS=PN/5,452,104.

5. http://patft1.uspto.gov/netacgi/nph-Parser?Sect1=PTO1&Sect2=HITOFF&d=PALL&p=1&u=/netahtml/PTO/srchnum.htm&r=1&f=G&l=50&s1=5,576,767.PN.&OS=PN/5,576,767&RS=PN/5,576,767.

6. http://ralphlosey.files.wordpress.com/2007/08/case-qualcomm_8_6_07_atty_fee_order.pdf.

writing the file with a new file that contains no bytes of data and is named in a manner inconsistent with Windows operating system naming conventions. Rather than simply eliminating the pointer to the data, the actual recording of the data on the hard disk is erased (like taping over an existing tape recording).

Deleted email leaves a different set of tracks. When a user "deletes" an email in Outlook Express, the "fields" are deleted and sent to the trash or recycle bin. What remains on the hard drive are the HTML internet codes that define the fields, font, graphics, etc., of each message. What also remains is the actual email message. When the trash bin is emptied, the matter itself is deleted. Because typical email files are internet files, each time they are accessed, a temporary internet file ("temp file") is created. Thus, even though the email itself is deleted, the temp file remains on the hard drive, unless it is wiped. . . .

Taylor testified that GhostSurf wipes files by searching the hard drive for files that Windows "no longer knows about" because they have been previously deleted, and writing data over those locations with random data to obscure it from undeleting. Once the files are overwritten in this fashion, an undelete utility cannot recover them. . . . According to the GhostSurf User's Manual, the application may be set to erase files using different strength algorithms. If the weaker algorithms are used, the manual suggests "nearly all" of the targeted files will be erased. In short, GhostSurf is a very powerful tool that Krause could easily have used to purge files and data from his computers before turning them over to the Trustee.
Id. at *5, *7.

The popular file-wiping program did its job effectively. Following Department of Defense computer file erasure protocols,[14] it erased the files multiple times, rewrote the affected hard drive space with zeros, and set up fake file names. There was no way to recover these files. They were super-erased, and the forensic experts could not restore them.

---

14. http://www.qsgi.com/usdod_standard_dod_522022m.htm.

But the lawyer slipped up in at least two ways, and his scheme to destroy evidence was exposed. First, he did not hide his use of the GhostSurf software very well. It was easy for the forensic experts to see how many files were deleted and when (right after the order). Second, a few of the files were not visible to GhostSurf, probably because they were "orphan files,"[15] and so they were not super-deleted. *Id.* at *9. Consequently, a few temporary Internet email and Web Browser files were not wiped from the hard drives. These files showed that the "bankrupt" debtor had recently traveled to Zurich, Switzerland, to pursue investment opportunities and suggested that he had substantial, secret offshore assets.

It is interesting to note that even though the metadata-showing dates had been deleted along with the files, the forensic experts were still able to prove that they were very recent, and thus very relevant. They used an ingenious method to date these files. The debtor's computers used Norton Antivirus software. It keeps its own log of all files checked for viruses when downloaded from the Internet. The Norton logs they located did not have download time information, but the forensic experts were still able to prove that the erased files had been recently downloaded. They could do that because the logs showed that a recent version of the software had been used to inspect these files. *Id.*

When a motion for sanctions for spoliation brought all of this to the attention of the bankruptcy court, the judge gave the lawyer-debtor a choice. He could either turn in backups of his computers that contained the deleted files or go to jail. The judge also ordered him to turn in his passport, entered a partial default judgment, ordered the repayment of $59,710 to the estate, and entered other sanctions.

To reach this result, the court had to consider and reject a series of excuses offered by the debtor to try to explain the wipeout of so much evidence from his computers. He offered the classic hard drive crash excuse and also claimed that he only used GhostSurf for legitimate purposes, a type of routine, good-faith destruction argument under Rule

---

15.   An orphan file is a file that once belonged to a program that was later uninstalled from the computer. The uninstall procedure sometimes fails to delete all of files related to the removed software. The remaining files are called "orphan files."

37(f). Here is the actual language of Chief Bankruptcy Judge Robert Nugent in Kansas City disposing of these arguments:

> Based upon the evidence presented here, it is clear that Krause (a licensed Kansas lawyer) violated his duty to preserve electronic evidence. He candidly admitted that he never reviewed his hard drives to determine if he had electronic evidence that was responsive to the Government's RFP. In fact he took the belated and frivolous position that the RFP did not encompass electronic evidence. He continued his routine practice of deleting e-mails. Finally, he made no claim that he deactivated or uninstalled the GhostSurf wiping software program upon service of the Government's adversary complaint or RFP. Nor is Krause saved by his alleged computer crashes. One, those crashes occurred several months after the adversary was commenced and the Government's document requests were served. If he had backed-up his computers, he has not been forthcoming with the back-up data or files. Two, once Krause restored the computers, he again installed GhostSurf and ran the wiping program on both computers.
> *Id.* at *20.

When a litigant responds to an e-discovery request by installing and using a superdeletion type of software program such as GhostSurf for the first time, he will probably be *hoisted on his own petard.*[16] Once uncovered, such actions provide compelling proof of intentional destruction of evidence. In the words of the court:

> The deliberate and intentional use of a wiping software program such as GhostSurf and the timing of its use further leads the Court to the inescapable conclusion here that Krause willfully and intentionally destroyed electronically stored evidence. Although Krause professed earnest concern for the protection and

---

16.   A petard was the first bomb used in warfare for the assaults of castles. A chain was used to try and hoist the bomb up over the walls. Sometimes that would fail, and the bomb, the petard, would fall back upon the person trying to hoist it. http://en.wikipedia.org/wiki/Petard.

security of his computer files and personal and financial information, he testified to no incidents where his computer or internet security had been previously compromised while using other standard security software or protective measures (e.g., Norton Antivirus) that were also loaded on his computers. No evidence was presented that these standard non-wiping security protections were inadequate for Krause's use of his computers. Apparently, no previous experience or incident prompted him to go out and buy a software wiping program such as GhostSurf 2006. Nor was any credible evidence presented that Krause had run GhostSurf or any other wiping software program on his computers at any period of time prior to the commencement of the adversary complaint in November 2005. The Court concludes that Krause purchased the GhostSurf 2006 wiping program after the adversary complaint was filed and after the duty to preserve attached. He installed and ran it. This constitutes a willful or intentional spoliation of evidence.
Id. at *21.

The producing party here argued that new Rule 37(f) provided him protection from sanctions because he claimed that his use of GhostSurf was routine and made in good faith to try to protect his privacy. The lawyer-debtor argued that he always superdeleted his files in this way. The evidence on this was weak at best. The defense was obviously a ruse, as the software was never even installed until after the order compelling discovery. In any event, even assuming he had routinely used GhostSurf before the order, the Rule 37(f) safe harbor would still not apply. In these circumstances, after the order to produce is entered—and probably well before then, when suit is filed, or even contemplated—the producing party is obliged to suspend such file deletion. In Judge Nugent's words:

> Nor can Krause claim that his use of GhostSurf 2006 was a good faith "routine operation" of his computers. With the 2006 amendments to the Federal Rules of Civil Procedure, a party enjoys a safe harbor from sanctions where electronic evidence is "lost as a result of the routine, good-faith operation of an electronic information system." Fed. R. Civ. P. 37(f) . . . .

The undisputed evidence established that Krause's hard drives were far from being at full capacity, thus making it improbable that electronic information was being overwritten or deleted by routine operation of his computers. Just as a litigant may have an obligation to suspend certain features of a "routine operation," the Court concludes that a litigant has an obligation to suspend features of a computer's operation that are not routine if those features will result in destroying evidence. Here, that obligation required Krause to disable the running of the wiping feature of GhostSurf as soon as the preservation duty attached. And it certainly obligated Krause to refrain from reinstalling GhostSurf when his computers crashed and he restored them.

Id.

In this case there was strong evidence of bad faith, intentional destruction of evidence, and that the files deleted were crucial to the case. In these circumstances, a court will usually impose severe sanctions on the spoliating party. The reasoning is well explained in this case:

Because no one will ever know what was on those computers before they were wiped and purged with GhostSurf, the Trustee and the Government have been severely prejudiced in the prosecution of their claims against Krause. It may have irretrievably lost relevant and probative evidence that supports their case against Krause. A sampling of some of the orphan files and temporary internet files that the Trustee was able to salvage from Krause's hard drives suggest that Krause has been engaged in significant internet activity during the pendency of this case related to investments, more involvement with additional entities, use of off-shore contacts and conduits to conduct business and financial activities and trafficking in frozen assets. Because the computers appear to be the "nerve center" of Krause's business interests, including all of the alleged "sham" entities of which he denies ownership, their alteration significantly harms the Trustee's and the Government's ability to go forward and show Krause's connection. The Trustee has shown enough from the salvaged e-mails and temporary internet files, however, to persuade this Court that the electronic evidence purged by Krause would have been relevant to these proceedings. The Court infers that the lost electronic evidence is relevant, as it is entitled to do, because of Krause's willful and intentional destruction of it. *Id.* at *22.

Spoliation misconduct should not be tolerated in any court, but it is especially harmful in bankruptcy proceedings. In my opinion Judge Nugent was correct to react in a strong and forceful manner to protect the integrity of the system. As he explained:

> Krause's willful misconduct with respect to the spoliation of electronic evidence and turnover of his computers cuts to the heart of a chapter 7 bankruptcy debtor's duties, far more oner- ous than those of a litigant involuntarily snarled in civil litiga- tion. The Bankruptcy Code and Rules are designed to prevent, not foster, a game of "hide the pea" with the Trustee. The Court has repeatedly warned Krause about the repercussions of not making full, complete, and accurate disclosure and not cooper- ating with the Trustee. [FN88] The Court has progressively con- ditioned Krause's conduct, without success. There is nothing left for the Court to do now but administer sanctions that mirror the egregiousness of his conduct. . . . . The willful destruction of electronic evidence has supported the most severe of sanctions, including entry of judgment against a defendant and dismissal of a plaintiff's case. [FN89]
>
> Krause's running of the GhostSurf wiping program after being ordered to produce electronic evidence and before turn- over of his computers is simply inexcusable.
> *Id.* at *23.

The bankruptcy court then entered a whole series of sanctions against the debtor-attorney, including an order to turn over information and com- puters, and gave him 10 days to comply. To make it clear that he meant business, Judge Nugent included the promise of jail should the lawyer- debtor fail to full comply:

3. If after a period of ten (10) days Krause has not satisfied the foregoing sanctions:

(a) default judgment will be entered against Krause declaring that the Krause Children's Trusts I, II, III, IV and V are his nominees and property of the estate subject to turnover; and

(b) a bench warrant will issue for Krause's apprehension and he will be incarcerated until he complies with these orders.

Id. at *25.

After imposing sanctions for spoliation, the court went on to find that the debtor was also in contempt for violation of the court's original discovery order and other violations. For this reason, the court also entered essentially the same sanctions based on contempt. *Id.* at *26-28.

I checked the docket sheet after the entry of this order. It appears that the lawyer-client has since given himself better advice. The docket indicates that he turned in his passport, produced computers and backups apparently as ordered, and filed an appeal. We will wait to see how this is handled on appeal, and whether the spoliating lawyer is able to remain out of jail.

IT TECH'S FAST-TALK HAD ZERO PERSUASIVE VALUE WITH JUDGE

A district court judge in Connecticut recently rejected a defendant's explanation as to why the hard drives of key employees contained only zeros, and imposed sanctions for spoliation. *Jane Doe v. Norwalk Community College*, 2007 WL 2066496, 2007 LEXIS 51084 (D. Conn. July 16, 2007).

First, some background of this "Jane Doe" case. The main defendant here is a state community college. The plaintiff is a student alleging that her college was negligent in its retention and supervision of a professor who sexually assaulted her. The now "former professor" is also a defendant, but with no legal representation. The student was permitted to file suit as "Jane Doe" to protect her privacy.

After two years of litigation, Jane Doe persuaded the court that the college was withholding electronic evidence. The school was ordered to produce the computers of key witnesses for inspection by Doe's computer forensic expert, Dorran Delay of DataTrack Resources. The expert inspected the college computers over a two-day period. Here is where the case gets interesting. Delay's inspection showed that several of the computers had no data: they were literally all zeros.

Jane Doe's next move was to file a motion for sanctions based on spoliation of evidence. She alleged that "the hard drives of key witnesses in this case were scrubbed" or "completely 'wiped' of data." This led to a flurry of affidavits by Doe's expert, Delay and the counterexpert used by the college, its own in-house information technology technician, Wyatt Bissell. Of course, the experts did not agree. Bissell came up with a laundry list of excuses for why two computers were "full of nothing." He tried saying it was the wrong computer, then that it was not wiped at all, just imaged. As a last resort, he settled on the best excuse of many an IT tech, that the "all zeros" problem was simply the result of "computer failure."

The judge responded by scheduling two evidentiary hearings. At these hearings, Delay, Bissell, and other witnesses testified and were cross-examined about the many suspicious circumstances surrounding the missing ESI. Further, at one of the hearings, the college offered the expert testimony of another of its employees, Mr. Olsen, the information technology systems manager, which did not help much. Among other things, both Bissell and Olsen testified that they did not think the state's two-year document retention policy applied to them or "normal computer usage," directly contradicting the hearing testimony of their boss, the dean. The testimony of the defense experts was rejected by the court as not credible, and overall, they only served to make a bad situation worse.

District Court Judge Janet Hall not only rejected the defense expert testimony, she rejected the legal arguments of defense counsel as well. One of the more clever arguments they made, to no avail, was that they could not put an effective hold in place without revealing the true name of Jane Doe. Judge Hall said they should have contacted plaintiff's counsel and tried to work that out. Defense counsel's arguments as to when the duty to preserve commenced were also given zero value. It seems as if the attorneys' credibility was completely nullified by the specious testimony of their experts.

In the end, Judge Hall granted Jane Doe's motion and awarded an adverse jury instruction based on the grossly negligent failure of the college to preserve ESI. She also awarded Doe her expert witness's costs, which, I suspect, will be quite large.

In a case like this, an adverse inference instruction is almost always fatal to the defense. For all practical purposes, even though the case has not yet been tried, it has already been lost because of e-discovery. The only real question remaining has to do, once again, with zeros: How many will be added to the judgment or settlement?

To me, the most interesting aspects of this case are its computer forensic, geek-type technicalities. First of all, the forensic expert, Delay, and the college IT technician, Bissell, could not agree on whether the computers had been "wiped." Delay opined that the "all zeros" condition of the hard drives showed that they had been intentionally wiped or scrubbed of all data. Footnote 3 of the opinion explains:

> According to Delay, wiping is a "process that overwrites exist-ing data on the hard drive, making this information unrecover-able."

Bissell's counter-explanation is set forth in footnote 6:

> At the Hearing, Wyatt Bissell indicated that he disagreed with the term "scrubbed," which overwrites a hard drive, completely elimi-nating all data from it. Instead, Bissell testified the correct word to use is "imaged"– that is, NCC's [the college] technology modi-fies the structure of the hard drive, without scrubbing it.

Bissell also testified:

> . . . that Delay's results, i.e., that it appeared that this particular hard drive had been "scrubbed," were because Schmidt's hard drive was in the process of failing, which can produce inconsis-tent or corrupt results.

The court did not believe Bissell and found that the computers had been "scrubbed" or "wiped." Judge Hall explained what she meant by these terms in footnote 11:

By "scrubbed" or "wiped" the court means more than overwriting or "reimaging;" it means eliminating all data from the hard drive, such that none of the old data can be read or still remains on it.

It is hard to see how you can reach any other conclusion when presented with a computer hard drive filled with zeros. That is what most (but not all) data-scrubbing programs are designed to do. Most data erasure software physically writes zeros (or ones, or random combinations) to all sectors of a hard drive and thereby completely writes over and erases everything, even residual data existing outside of any organized file structures. This process is also known as "shredding," and among Mac users is called "zeroing all data." Supposedly, expensive equipment exists that allows for the recovery of segments of a hard drive even after it has been zeroed out. It is based on reading subtle magnetic fluctuations in the hard drive. For that reason, many data-shredding programs provide for multiple wipes with various types of random patterns of data filling. This will defeat even the spy agencies who own such equipment, and so meets the Department of Defense specifications for destruction of sensitive data. (The really top-secret stuff is physically destroyed, cut up into tiny bits—no pun intended—and then dumped into multiple land-fills.)

To better understand how this kind of disk wiping works, you need to recall that all computers operate and store information in bits of either one or zero, electrically on or off. This is the binary code. Recall also that eight of the on-or-off bits comprise a byte. A typical hard drive today has hundreds of billions of bytes. Thus if a hard drive, or any other ESI device, contains all zeros or all ones, it contains absolutely no information at all. Information can only be stored when both ones and zeros are used in the almost innumerable possible permutations. This all-zero condition does, however, tell you that the disk has been intentionally wiped. Contrary to Bissell's testimony, a computer that has been imaged, or is subject to failures of some kind, would not contain *all* zeros. Some information, some combinations of ones and zeros among the billions of bits on a hard drive, would remain. Judge Hall explains how this applies to the case as follows:

Delay found that it contained all 0's, indicating that every sector had been overwritten. Delay testified that if the drive had data on it but was failing, as Bissell testified, then data would be seen on it with Delay's forensic software, which instead recognized that the hard drive was unpartitioned and contained no data. Moreover, Seaborn's new computer had traces of other users' information on it, thus showing an inconsistent result in NCC's process of re-imaging hard drives. Even if it was consistent with NCC's policy, the fact that Seaborn's new computer showed other users' information indicates that "imaging" does not eliminate everything from a hard drive, but leaves some data from old users on it, prompting the question why Seaborn's old computer—or Schmidt's computer—did not have any evidence of other users on it. The answers provided by the defendants—a failing drive or "re-imaging"—are rejected by the court as not credible.

The irregularities in PST files that Delay uncovered is another factor that led Judge Hall to suspect that relevant evidence had been intentionally destroyed by several of the college employees. Additionally, Delay found that the Microsoft Outlook PST files, which house electronic mailboxes, of four individuals had inconsistencies "that indicate that data has been altered, destroyed or filtered." *Id.* at ¶ 6. For example, Professor Skeeter's PST file contained no deleted items and only one sent item, and the inbox and sent items contained data starting August 2004, "even though other activity is present starting in 2002." *Id.* at ¶ 8.

The lesson here is, if you are an IT tech or expert of any kind, do not try to fast-talk a federal judge with "computerese" and specious theories. It may fool your boss and many attorneys, and make you look good for a while, but it will not work in court, and could get you in serious trouble. If mistakes were made, then admit it. Do not try to cover it up with technical jargon. The best advice is to tell the truth and play it straight. Also, be careful what you say in an affidavit or expert report. You never know when you may be required to testify at trial to back it up. You will then be subject to cross-examination, sometimes by a very skilled and knowledgeable attorney, and contradicted by a well-credentialed expert. Finally, from the attorney's perspective, it is rarely a good idea to do what defense counsel did in this case, and go into an evidentiary hearing on complex IT issues without an impartial outside expert. It is too dangerous to rely solely on the client's own IT staff. As this Jane Doe opinion shows, they can "zero out" your case real fast.

JUDGE TRASH-TALKS THE GOVERNMENT FOR ITS DISCOVERY ABUSES

The U.S. Court of Federal Claims began a recent opinion imposing sanctions against the government for spoliation by quoting the old saying, "One man's trash is another man's treasure." *United Medical Supply Co., Inc. v. United States*, 2007 WL 1952680 (Fed. Cl., June 27, 2007). The saying was invoked because the government had shredded much of the plaintiff's valuable evidence. After the quote, the court immediately launched into a high-level righteous rant about the government's spoliation.

> Aside perhaps from perjury, no act serves to threaten the integrity of the judicial process more than the spoliation of evidence. Our adversarial process is designed to tolerate human failings— erring judges can be reversed, uncooperative counsel can be shepherded, and recalcitrant witnesses compelled to testify. But when critical documents go missing, judges and litigants alike descend into a world of ad hocery and half measures—and our civil justice system suffers.
>
> To guard against this, each party in litigation is solemnly bound to preserve potentially relevant evidence. In this government contract case, defendant violated that duty not once or twice, but repeatedly, over many years, and in sundry ways, leading to the destruction of many admittedly relevant documents. Most disturbingly, some of these documents were destroyed even after the court conducted its first spoliation hearing. While defendant apologizes profusely for what it claims is the "negligence" of some of its employees and for making repeated misstatements to the court as to the steps that were being taken to prevent spoliation, it, nonetheless, asseverates that the court should not—indeed, cannot—impose spoliation sanctions because defendant did not proceed in bad faith. While defendant

may be wrong in asserting that it acted in good faith, it most
certainly is wrong in thinking that it can recklessly disregard its
obligations to preserve evidence without legal consequence.
Id. at *1.

The judge describes a parade of discovery horribles, recounting in
detail the blunders and misrepresentations by the Department of Justice,
its attorneys and staff, and the Department of Defense. Although the
case involves some emails and other electronic records, the main spoliation here is from good old-fashioned shredding. Hundred of boxes of
paper documents, including email printouts, were thrown away for years
after suit was filed. My favorite horribles in the parade include:

1. Making false statements to the plaintiff and the court that a *complete* search had been made, and all responsive documents had
   been produced, when in fact the government had searched only
   eight of the 18 facilities. Defense counsel blamed that one on a
   bad paralegal. *Id.* at *3, *4, *15.
2. Sending some of the preservation notices to key players 5 to 6
   years after the suit was filed. *Id.* at *4, *12.
3. Destroying documents both before and after the preservation
   notices. *Id.*
4. Failing to preserve relevant records for five years after the government had notice of plaintiff's claim. *Id.* at *12.
5. Sending evidence to the garbage dump even after the court's
   first hearing on spoliation. *Id.*

The judge goes on to speak loudly about the need to punish the government and others for this kind of discovery spoliation. The long and
scholarly opinion speaks of the need to send a message of deterrence
and impose sanctions, even without proof of bad faith, as that is often an
elusive and difficult thing to prove. The strong words include the following that we are likely to see quoted again in the future.

Guided by logic and considerable and growing precedent, the
court concludes that an injured party need not demonstrate bad
faith in order for the court to impose, under its inherent author-

ity, spoliation sanctions. Several reasons lead to this conclusion. For one thing, it makes little sense to talk of a general duty to preserve evidence if, in fact, the breach of that duty carries no real legal ramifications. Requiring a showing of bad faith as a precondition to the imposition of spoliation sanctions means that evidence may be destroyed wilfully, or through gross negligence or even reckless disregard, without any true consequences. . . .

Second, imposing sanctions only when a spoliator can be proven to have acted in bad faith defenestrates three of the four purposes underlying such sanctions—to protect the integrity of the fact-finding process, to restore the adversarial balance between the spoliator and the prejudiced party, and to deter future misconduct—and severely frustrates the last, to punish. These objectives are hardly served if the court, in effect, is constrained to say to the injured party, "sorry about that, but there is nothing I can do, except to let you present your case, such as it remains." Indeed, while some commentators have asserted otherwise, the history of the spoliation doctrine suggests that it was not designed solely to punish those who consciously destroy inculpatory documents, but also to address the manifest unfairness inherent in the loss of relevant evidence. Even if such sanctions were once rooted in an inference of consciousness of a weak case, that is neither the controlling rationale nor the prevailing rule nowadays. Finally, adopting a bad faith standard when the court is operating under its inherent authority creates an incongruity between the sanctions available for spoliation depending upon whether—or not—a discovery regime has been established that would trigger Rule 37. This incongruity could be viewed as encouraging the earlier destruction of evidence—a race to the shredder, so to speak. . . .
Id. at *10.

It is the duty of the United States, no less than any other party before this court, to ensure, through its agents, that documents relevant to a case are preserved. Indeed, while not entering into the calculus here, a good argument can be made that, as the

have been preserved. These few exceptional cases do not justify the disruption caused in the vast majority of cases where the tapes are never needed.

The general rule of exclusion of backup tapes from a hold is tested in the rare case where it turns out the tapes should have been preserved. *Oxford House* is just such a case. Here a Topeka city commissioner was found during discovery to have deleted certain relevant email in June of 2005. The plaintiff claimed spoliation and sought sanctions. The court rejected this argument because it found that litigation was not reasonably anticipated until August of 2005, two months after the email deletion. The destruction of email before a duty to preserve arises cannot constitute spoliation.

That part is fairly cut and dried. But the plaintiff also argued that the city should have preserved its email backup tapes. Instead, even after the August hold date, the city continued its normal backup tape recycling. It continued to reuse the same tapes and thus erase the old emails and other information from the previous backups. The city was on notice of pending litigation at the time it continued to recycle the tapes, and so from a time perspective, at least, the duty to preserve had arisen. But the city did not then know that the commissioner had deleted relevant emails and the tapes might be the only place they could still be found.

This situation raises the issue of the scope of the duty to preserve; did it extend to backup tapes? Clearly the preservation duty applied to "live" ESI, to the easily accessible email on the city's computers, but did it also run to the backup tapes? Some would say yes, especially legal counsel representing a party with little electronic evidence at issue. They disregard or attempt to minimize the cost and disruption caused by the routine imposition of holds on backup tape operations. The plaintiff, Oxford House, was of that ilk, and argued that the city had a duty to preserve backup tapes, but the court did not agree.

The backup tapes used by Topeka were disaster recovery-type tapes. They were not reasonably accessible, meaning they could be accessed, but only at great cost and expense. In fact, the city estimated a cost of at least $100,000 to restore and review the tapes. Judge Sebelius in Kansas, like Judge Scheindlin in Manhattan, was right to hold that these kinds of tapes do not have to be preserved. A company should not have to stop its normal, good-faith operation of recycling disaster recovery tapes every time litigation is threatened or materializes.

The City of Topeka first opposed the plaintiff's sanctions argument on the backup tapes the same way it opposed sanctions for deletion of the live email. The city argued that the relevant emails had already been deleted from the backup tapes before August 2005, and so a duty to preserve never arose before deletion. It made this claim because the backup tapes are supposed to be recycled every six weeks. Since there was an approximate eight-week gap between the estimated time of email deletion and notice of pending litigation, the city argued that the emails in question were no longer on the backup tape in August 2005. In effect, they argued that the notice to preserve came two weeks too late, so there was no need for the court to consider whether the scope of duty included backup tapes.

Judge Sebelius recognized that it was a close question as to whether the emails would still have been on the backup tapes or not. Of course, the city argued that its normal recycling procedures had been followed, and for that reason the emails would already have been written over in six weeks. But this is a slippery slope of an argument, because it is hard to know if the exact timing of the recycling protocols were in fact followed, and the timing here was close.

If the facts alleged by the city had been proven, which is difficult to do, then once again there would have been no spoliation based on timing. The erasure of the backup tapes, just like the deletion of the emails, would have occurred before a duty to preserve arose. Then the court would not have had to decide whether the duty to preserve extended to backup tapes. But the city's argument was on shaky grounds, and apparently not well confirmed by affidavits or depositions. In any event, the judge chose to reject it, and face the issue of the scope of preservation head on. Still, in other circumstances with a more fully developed evidentiary record, this argument alone might succeed.

The court denied the plaintiff's motion for sanctions for backup tape spoliation based on the assumption that the deleted emails were still on the backup tapes in August at the time the duty arose. In the words of Magistrate Judge Gary Sebelius:

In the court's view, even if such backup tapes were conclusively shown to possess the deleted e-mail communications, "as a general rule, a party need not preserve all backup tapes even when it reasonably anticipates litigation." *Zubulake,* 220 F.R.D. at 217. When parties put a litigation hold policy on destruction of documents in response to pending litigation, "that litigation hold does not apply to inaccessible back-up tapes (e.g., those typically maintained solely for the purpose of disaster recovery), which may continue to be recycled on the schedule set forth in the company's policy." *Id.* The record in this case indicates that the backup tapes are used for disaster recovery purposes.

The decision goes on to consider the related issue of whether the city should be forced to search its current backup tapes now, almost two years after the emails in question had been deleted. The plaintiff argued that there was a chance the emails were still on the tapes in spite of their reuse. The plaintiff wanted to put the city of Topeka to the expense of undertaking the restoration and search of backup tapes on the off-chance that the emails in question had never been written over. The plaintiff argued that the emails could possibly still be on the tapes because they might have been stored at the very end of the tapes, and no subsequent backups went that far. This argument was based more on hope than on reason and was rejected by the court:

It is certain that the cost of retrieval of data would be high. However, this factor is not dispositive—consideration must also be given to the potential efficacy of a technique seeking discoverable information. The court finds such efficacy is minimal at best in the instant case. The City of Topeka continually rewrites new data over the prior date on its back-up tapes. Therefore, unless the latter back-up tape did not write as close to the end as the previous back-up tape, this information has likely already been written over. As the likelihood of retrieving these electronic communications is low and the cost high, this court further finds that the unanswered portion of Plaintiffs' Interrogatory No. 4 is unduly costly. The court thereby denies plaintiffs' motion to compel further responses to Plaintiffs' Interrogatory No. 4.

Aside from the odd procedural basis of this dispute arising from an objection to an interrogatory, the opinion itself is notable for never mentioning new Rule 37(f), which states:

> Absent exceptional circumstances, a court may not impose sanctions under these rules on a party for failing to provide electronically stored information lost as a result of the routine, good faith operation of an electronic information system.

The full commentary for Rule 37 (f) is contained in the Appendix.

You would expect a full analysis of the issues in this case to include the new "safe harbor" rule. The "exceptional circumstances" exclusion to the safe harbor is intended to apply to some situations where a duty to preserve has arisen. In this case, the plaintiff would argue that the duty arose by notice of the pending litigation. There are other circumstances in which the duty can arise and the safe harbor be lost, such as by statute or regulation requiring emails or other ESI to be retained for certain periods.

Perhaps the court did not go there because it did not have evidence that the commissioner's email deletion was a "routine, good faith operation." In any event, the court chose instead to rely upon the well-established common-law elements of spoliation. It did not go into the related but separate, and as yet largely untested, provisions of the new rule. Still, in most circumstances you would want to include the Rule 37(f) arguments in this kind of spoliation dispute.

E-MAIL WOES HIT MORGAN STANLEY AGAIN

The defendant brokerage firm in the landmark $1.45 billion *Coleman* case is under attack again, this time by NASD. Morgan Stanley is accused of misrepresentations concerning the loss of all of its e-mail in the destruction of the World Trade Center on September 11, 2001. Upon request, NASD provided me with a full copy of the disciplinary Complaint No. 2005001449202.[17]

---

17. http://www.floridalawfirm.com/Morgan.Stanley.NASD. Complaint.pdf.

I am defense-oriented by nature, and so I think it should be stressed that these are mere allegations, not adjudicated facts. The first three paragraphs of the complaint summarize the allegations as follows:

1. For a three-and-a-half-year period, from October 2001 through at least March 2005, respondent Morgan Stanley DW, Inc. (MSDW) routinely failed to provide e-mails to arbitration claimants and regulators in response to discovery obligations and regulatory inquiries. After the firm's e-mail servers in New York City were destroyed on September 11, 2001, the firm restored millions of e-mails by using back-up tapes. Many other e-mails, moved from servers onto individual users' computers, were not affected by the events of September 11. Nevertheless, MSDW routinely failed to provide pre-September 11, 2001 e-mail in numerous customer arbitration proceedings and in response to regulatory inquiries, falsely claiming that its pre-September 11, 2001 e-mail had been destroyed.

2. In addition to failing to produce e-mail in numerous arbitrations and regulatory matters, and falsely stating that such e-mail had been destroyed, MSDW later destroyed many of the same e-mails. Instead of preserving the e-mail back-up tapes that had been used to restore its servers, MSDW put those tapes back into use, overwriting and permanently erasing their contents. The firm also allowed the e-mails that had been restored to the firm's servers to be permanently deleted by users of the firm's e-mail system over an extended period of time. As a result, between September 2001 and March 2005, millions of pre-September 11, 2001 e-mails that had been available to the firm were lost.

3. By virtue of the conduct set forth herein, MSDW violated NASD rules by failing to comply with its obligations to produce documents both to claimants in discovery in arbitration proceedings and to regulators, and by falsely representing that documents in its possession did not exist. MSDW also violated the recordkeeping requirements of the federal securities laws and NASD rules by erasing millions of those same documents. MSDW also failed to establish and maintain systems and written procedures to supervise the activities of its employees and

the types of business in which it engages, which were reasonably designed to ensure compliance with the recordkeeping requirements and with its obligations to respond completely and truthfully to regulatory requests and to discovery requests in arbitration proceedings.

The disciplinary complaint purports to state three causes of action. Count One alleges violations of NASD Conduct Rule 2110, Procedural Rule 8210, and IM-10100 under the Code of Arbitration Procedure. The violations are based on allegations that Morgan Stanley provided false information and failed to produce emails in response to requests from claimants and regulators. Count Two alleges violation of section 17(a) of the Securities Exchange Act of 1934, Rule 17a-4 thereunder, and NASD Conduct Rules 2110 and 3110. The violations are based on alleged failures to preserve required books and records, namely e-mails. Count Three alleges violations of Conduct Rules 2110 and 3010(a) and (b). The violations are based on allegations that Morgan Stanley failed to establish and maintain systems and written procedures reasonably designed to preserve required records and to ensure that Morgan Stanley conducted adequate searches in response to regulatory inquiries and discovery requests for e-mail.

MORGAN STANLEY WINS TWO

Morgan Stanley recently received two favorable rulings: one the reversal of the well-known $1.5 billion *Coleman* judgment, and the other an order in an employment case by Arthur Riel, the former head of Morgan Stanley's Legal IT Department. Riel claims that he was made the scapegoat for the loss in *Coleman* and fired under pretext. The facts alleged in *Riel,* especially as they pertain to discovery of the 1,600 backup tapes that so disturbed the trial judge in *Coleman*, are especially interesting.

The big win for Morgan Stanley was the reversal by the Third District Court of Appeals in Florida. *Morgan Stanley & Co., Inc. v. Coleman (Parent) Holdings Inc. (Morgan Stanley II),* No. CA4D05-2606, Fla. Ct. App., 4th Dist. (March 21, 2007). The decision said nothing at all about e-discovery and only reversed because two out of three members of the panel felt that Coleman failed to prove damages. There was a strong dissent, and so Coleman will now almost certainly move for rehearing and *en banc* consideration. Whoever loses will likely go to the Florida Supreme Court. Although Morgan Stanley is no doubt greatly relieved by this reversal, the story is far from over. Moreover, so far at least, the e-discovery aspects of the lower court's rulings have not been reversed, or even commented on.

The other new *Morgan Stanley* decision comes from the suit by Arthur Riel, the former executive director of its Legal IT Department. *Riel v. Morgan Stanley*, 2007 U.S. Dist. LEXIS 11153 (S.D. N.Y. Feb. 16, 2007). The facts of this case are what make it interesting, and will bear watching as the pared-down suit continues. Arthur Riel and his IT team developed a searchable email archive to capture all emails to and from Morgan Stanley from January 1, 2003, forward. He was also asked to add all of Morgan Stanley's earlier emails to this archive by restoring emails from 39,000 backup tapes. The harvesting of the emails from the tapes was performed by an outside vendor, not Riel's IT team.

During the course of Riel's work, he and his team noticed some suspicious emails to and from a few management personnel wherein gifts, including sporting tickets, were offered by company vendors. Although this was not part of his assigned task, Riel pursued an investigation of these email strings and concluded that they revealed illegal misconduct, including the rigging of a technology contest. In January 2004, Riel anonymously sent copies of the emails to Morgan Stanley's chief financial officer via interoffice mail with a note that read, "Needs investigation." Apparently Riel was not too adept at maintaining his anonymity, because his supervisor later learned that these tips came from him.

A few months later, in April 2004, the Florida court in *Coleman (Parent) Holdings, Inc. v. Morgan Stanley & Co., Inc.*, No. CA 03-5045 AI (Fla. Cir. Ct.), ordered Morgan Stanley to conduct a search of its emails dating back to 1988, to produce materials by May 16, 2004, and to certify, in writing, its compliance with the order. In April 2004, the outside vendor harvesting emails from the 39,000 backup tapes became aware of still more backup tapes: a set of 1,423 "DLT" backup tapes found in a warehouse in Brooklyn, and another set of 177 old 8-millimeter backup tapes. On June 7, 2004, Riel alleges that he sent an email to two Morgan Stanley in-house lawyers notifying them that these additional 1,600 backup tapes had been discovered, and that they could contain pre-2000 emails.

At the direction of Morgan Stanley's in-house counsel, the Riel team performed searches of the email archive. The search did not include the newly discovered 1,600 backup tapes, as they had not yet been added to the archive. Riel was then called upon to sign a written certification prepared by Morgan Stanley's in-house attorneys, which certified compliance with the court order to search and produce emails. Riel's complaint alleges the following concerning this certification:

> 73. Mr. Riel had no specific information concerning the Coleman Litigation and only general information concerning the search that his Law IT team conducted on the Archive. Nor did Mr. Riel, a non-lawyer, have any understanding of Morgan Stanley's discovery obligations in the Coleman Litigation. Mr. Riel believed that the Certification operated as a confirmation that Morgan Stanley conducted a search of its Archive and that the responsive materials from that search were forwarded to Morgan Stanley's lawyers for production.
>
> 74. At the time, Mr. Riel had no understanding that he was certifying, in any sense, that all responsive e-mail from any Morgan Stanley source, including older back-up tapes, had been produced.

Still, Riel signed the erroneous court certification on June 23, 2004, and the rest, as they say, is history, leading to the $1.5 billion judgment that was just reversed.

After this certification, Riel's prior action to try to tip off management anonymously about the illegal contest-rigging email came back to bite him. On August 18, 2004, Riel was placed on paid administrative leave while his supervisors investigated the propriety of his reading the content of emails of Morgan Stanley executives while performing his IT tasks. There is no mention of an investigation into the alleged illegal activities the emails supposedly revealed.

Two months later, in October 2004, SEC investigators contacted Riel at home to question him regarding Morgan Stanley's email retention practices. Riel advised the SEC of the newly discovered 1,600 backup tapes. The SEC then provided Morgan Stanley with a "Wells Notice" advising that an action was imminent. *Carlson v. Xerox Corp.*, 392 F.

Supp. 2d 267, 279 (D. Conn. 2005). Morgan Stanley responded by blaming Riel and claiming that he never told them about these 1,600 tapes. Apparently they never received the emails Riel claims he sent about the newly discovered tapes.

Later that year, on May 16, 2005, *The Wall Street Journal* published an article, "How Morgan Stanley Botched a Big Case by Fumbling Emails." This was about the Florida case. Riel claims that Morgan Stanley attempted, in what it said to the *Journal*, to lay the blame on Riel for problems with the Florida court arising from the handling of e-mails in the document production.

Finally, on September 27, 2005, Morgan Stanley sent Riel a letter stating that he was terminated for cause for reading other employees' e-mails. Riel claims that this deprived him of 1,600 stock units and 5,000 vested stock options worth several hundred thousand dollars.

Riel sued, alleging eight counts including breach of contract, defamation in connection with the *Wall Street Journal* article, fraud, and negligence. Morgan Stanley moved to dismiss all counts except for Count Three. It alleges that Morgan Stanley breached its Executive Incentive Compensation Plan by firing Riel for cause, in bad faith, with the effect of depriving him of stock and options. Morgan Stanley's motion was granted, and thus this action will continue solely on the breach of contract claim in Count Three. Like the much larger *Coleman* case, this is a victory for Morgan Stanley, but the saga continues.

Apparently one of the key elements of Riel's case going forward will be whether Riel in fact sent an email to Morgan Stanley's attorneys advising them of the 1,600 tapes. This should be easily discoverable by the mail archive system that Riel himself established. The metadata of these emails, if in fact they exist, should reveal the truth.

SCORCHED-EARTH LITIGATION TACTICS

As a frequent ERISA litigator, I am embarrassed to report that a new e-discovery nightmare comes from that field: *Wachtel v. Health Net, Inc.,* 2006 WL 3538935, LEXIS 88563 (D. N.J., Dec. 6, 2006). This class action alleges breach of fiduciary duty by improper handling of health claims. But at this point, after five years of litigation, the merits of the case have been completely overshadowed by the improper defense tactics. The district court judge begins her 44-page opinion by observing that the case "gives new meaning to the term 'scorched earth' litigation tactics."

The opinion details just about every e-discovery violation possible, including multiple misrepresentations to the court, and reads like a handbook on what not to do, including my two personal favorites:

> (7) failing to disclose to this court or to the Magistrate Judge during three years of discovery that e-mails older than 90 days were never searched . . . .
>
> (10) keeping even their own outside counsel (other than the Epstein Becker firm) unaware of their e-mail procedures that resulted in widespread dereliction of their discovery obligations.

At page 33 of the opinion, the judge returns to the scorched-earth analogy:

> Defendants' strategy has been a concerted war to waste huge time and resources of Plaintiffs in pursuing this litigation. It gives "scorched earth litigation" a new standard of brashness. Defendants have also forced the Court to devote years to police discovery abuses over and over again. Defendants continue to ignore the Court's rulings over and over again. Defendants' persistent pattern of delay, defiance of Court Orders, evasive responses to Plaintiffs' discovery requests, and lack of candor have resulted in crushing prejudice to Plaintiffs in the form of forgetful witnesses and extraordinary expenditures of time, effort, and money. The wanton waste of judicial resources caused by Health Net, as exemplified herein, is equally staggering.

Not surprisingly, the opinion concluded by imposing severe sanctions: deeming various facts as established, striking "surprise" trial exhibits, barring defendants' use of late-designated witnesses, ordering reimbursement of plaintiffs' attorney fees and costs, appointing a discovery master to be paid for by defendants, and imposing a fine in an amount to be determined. The court did not enter the ultimate sanction of a default judgment against all defendants, but reserved ruling on that pending resolution of all class-action issues. The court also reserved ruling on whether sanctions should also be imposed on defendants' lat-

The district court buttressed its holding by reliance on the Sixth Circuit's remarks:

> The Sixth Circuit has recognized that "[o]ur system of discovery was designed to increase the likelihood that justice will be served in each case, not to promote principles of gamesmanship and deception in which the person who hides the ball most effectively wins the case." *Abrahamsen*, 92 F.3d at 428-29.

NO SPOLIATION SANCTIONS FOR "MISSING" PORN ON POLICE COMPUTERS

Just a few weeks before trial, the district court in Orlando considered an "emergency motion" for spoliation sanctions against the defendant, City of Orlando, for alleged destruction of pornographic emails on police department computers. *Floeter v. City of Orlando,* 2007 WL 486633 (M.D. Fla., Feb. 9. 2007). This is a sexual harassment and retaliation case in which the plaintiff, a male undercover drug agent for the Orlando Police Department, complained about his female supervisor's sexual advances, including viewing of X-rated emails on police department computers.[18] The plaintiff complained and was then, in his words, "disciplined and stripped of his job responsibilities."

The plaintiff filed suit in state court on March 2, 2005, and the defendant removed. As part of the plaintiff's initial disclosures, he produced sexually explicit emails that he claimed were sent to him by his supervisors at the police department. The plaintiff was deposed on December 15, 2005, and described the pornographic emails and alleged harassment. The next day the plaintiff served his first request to produce documents, including copies of all "sexually explicit or pornographic materials" emailed by one of his supervisors on police department computers. Four months, later the court ordered the city to produce these materials.

The city of Orlando's "Internet security administrator" (who knew?) then completed a search of the ESI of the key players to the litigation in the Orlando Police Department. His search included the officer's computers, the email server, and the backup tapes. (The type or accessibility

---

18.   http://www.officer.com/article/article.jsp?siteSection=5&id=33557.

of the backup tapes involved is not described, but they were not identified as disaster recovery-type backup tapes, and it is inferred that they were readily searchable.) The search by the Internet security administrator even included a "remote search" of the computers of some of the key players, which I presume means it was done surreptitiously. The administrator reported, however, that key hard drives could not be searched for various reasons, including an alleged hard drive crash and a re-imaging of another key hard drive after an upgrade to a new laptop. The re-imaging of the old drive made it forensically impossible to search for deleted or slack files. The re-imaging was standard procedure for a new computer replacement. The magistrate who heard the testimony concerning these facts found the timing of the request for a new computer, resulting as it did in the complete destruction of all deleted data on the old computer, to be "certainly suspicious."

The backup tapes the administrator searched were porn-free as to these individuals. However, by the time of the search, these tapes only went back to October 2005, seven months *after* suit was filed. This is because the city recycles its tapes every three months. Remarkably, the court reports that:

> There is no evidence that in-house nor outside counsel for the City ever issued a directive requiring that information which might be relevant to the issues in the case be preserved.
> *Id.* at fn.3.

The city reported that it had made an exhaustive search of its computers and none had the sexually explicit or pornographic materials requested. Next, mediation took place on August 15, 2006, which under governing rules is supposed to be completely secret. Not so here, however, as the opinion reports that the plaintiff at mediation told the city he had possession of more emails that he had not shown them yet, and they were clearly sent from police computers. The mediation impassed, and the city promptly made its own request for emails within the plaintiff's custody supporting his claim of a hostile work environment. The plaintiff objected, arguing that since the emails requested were disclosed at mediation, they were confidential and privileged as work product.

The city then moved to compel, and the plaintiff responded cutely that the emails were already in the city's possession. The city replied that it had looked and had not been able to find them. Based on this representation, on October 6, 2006, the court ordered the plaintiff to produce the emails and the sexually explicit materials attached thereto, and moreover, taxed the plaintiff with part of the city's costs to make the motion. (The award was, however, a mere $150.00.) Next the parties filed cross-motions for summary judgment, motions in limine related to the pornographic materials, motions to seal these x-rated documents, and other final pretrial-related motions then due under the scheduling order. After these motions were completed, the plaintiff filed the mentioned "emergency motion" related to spoliation, which led to an evidentiary hearing on January 11 and 18, 2007.

The district court magistrate judge, after hearing (and presumably also seeing) the evidence at the spoliation hearing, including the sexually explicit emails once located in the Police Department computers, noted that under Eleventh Circuit jurisdiction, negligent destruction of evidence without a showing of bad faith will not sustain an adverse inference instruction:

> "Mere negligence" in losing or destroying the records is not enough for an adverse inference, as it does not sustain an inference of consciousness of a weak case. *Bashir v. Amtrak*, 119 F.3d 929, 931 (11th Cir. 1997) (quoting *Vick v. Tex. Empl. Comm'n*, 514 F.2d 734, 737 (5th Cir. 1975).

Id. at *5.

The magistrate reviewed the evidence summarized above and concluded that the first element for a prima facie case for sanctions from spoliation, namely "that the missing evidence existed at one time," had been met. *Id.* The plaintiff proved that the pornographic emails had once been on the police officer's work computers.

The next element of spoliation is proof that "the alleged spoliator had a duty to preserve the evidence." The magistrate stated her opinion that it is still an open question in the Eleventh Circuit as to whether the "mere filing of litigation" raises a duty to preserve evidence. *Id.*, fn. 6. In this case, evidence was destroyed when the backup tapes were recycled and the hard drive wiped. The hard drive was cleaned when the new computer was issued, which occurred after the plaintiff's internal complaint of harassment but before suit was filed. The backup tapes were recycled, and thus potentially relevant pornographic emails erased, well after the complaint was served, but before a request to produce was made. The magistrate declined to determine whether a duty to preserve the backup tapes existed after the suit was filed, but inferred that there was no duty to preserve the old computer hard drive before the suit was filed. The magistrate stated she did not have to reach the duty to preserve issues because she found that the third element of spoliation was clearly not met—namely, that the "evidence is crucial to the movant being able to prove its *prima facie* case." Also, as mentioned, she found no bad faith, a precondition to the adverse inference sanction requested for the spoliation.

Although the magistrate agreed that the pornographic emails were relevant, she did not agree that they were *crucial* to the plaintiff's case. The plaintiff himself had kept "eleven sexually explicit emails" and had deposition testimony as to others. The court held that the missing emails were cumulative, and "the trier of fact does not need to actually see these emails to understand their contents." *Id.* at 6.

The magistrate also noted that she found no bad faith in the post-litigation erasure of backup tapes because this was done "as part of a long-standing City practice." Although the court found the timing of the supervisor's request for a new computer "certainly suspicious," the wiping of the hard drive of the old computer that followed was also "performed consistently with City practice," so again, no bad faith. *Id.* at 7.

The court denied the motion for sanctions, including the request for an adverse inference instruction to the jury, and would not even grant the plaintiff's request for refund of the $150 sanction he had previously paid. Still, the court noted that the evidence surrounding the alleged spoliation may be admissible at trial, and the plaintiff's counsel might be able to argue adverse inference to the jury in closing. **Note:** A news story appeared on local Orlando television in December 2006 about this lawsuit, how it led to discovery of porn on police computers, and how five police officers faced suspension as a result.[19]

---

19. http://www.local6.com/news/10479838/detail.html.

ADVERSE INFERENCE ENTERED AGAINST PLAINTIFF EMPLOYEE

In employment litigation, spoliation sanctions are usually a tactic of the employee plaintiff against the big corporate employer. The employer is the one with the vast collection of computer records where it is easy to mess up on the duty to preserve and produce. For this reason, the employer is usually the one charged with spoliation. That was certainly the case in the *Zubulake* decisions. But lately, employers have seen the value of e-discovery and their own spoliation motions. That is exactly what happened recently in Charlotte, North Carolina, where Target Stores is defending a sex discrimination claim. *Teague v. Target Corp.,* 2007 WL 1041191 (W.D. N.C., April 4, 2007). One of Target's affirmative defenses to the suit is "failure to mitigate."

In deposition, the plaintiff revealed that after she was fired, she engaged in an extensive job search on her home computer. This would tend to rebut Target's defense of failure to mitigate. She also testified that she used the computer to communicate regarding her alleged discriminatory firing and the circumstances of her discharge. The problem was, she no longer had that computer anymore. She said her home computer crashed and that her brother, who "dabbles in computers," was unable to get the hard drive to work. So she threw it away. Big mistake—because by that time she had already retained legal counsel to sue Target and had already filed charges with the EEOC. With her home computer gone, she had very few records regarding her claim. It was all pretty much a matter of her word against Target's. Still, her deposition testimony indicated that her computer, if it were still around, would have had evidence that the court held "related directly to her lawsuit against Target."

Once the employer discovered these facts, it moved for sanctions on the basis of spoliation of the computer evidence. The court found that the plaintiff had a duty to preserve the evidence, even though suit had not yet been filed, because she had retained counsel and filed EEOC charges. The destruction of the evidence by throwing away her computer was sufficient to show she had a "culpable state of mind." The motion was granted. Although the court did not find her conduct severe enough to warrant complete dismissal of the case, it was severe enough to warrant an adverse inference jury instruction. Such an inference is almost always case-dispositive.

THE CASE OF THE MIDNIGHT HACKER

One of my cases was published recently and is worthy of note. *Optowave v. Nitikin*,[20] Case No. 6:05-cv-1083-ACC-DAB, Doc. 90 (M.D. Fla. Nov. 7, 2006); now published in Westlaw (2006 WL 3231422) and LEXIS (2006 LEXIS 81345). Trial counsel Jim Foster and I call this the "Midnight Hacker" case. My law firm represented the plaintiff in a contract dispute involving the sale of equipment under the UCC. Defendant Nitikin, a computer expert, tried to fool the court and the plaintiff with a story of missing hard drives and unknown computer hackers breaking into his network in the middle of the night and erasing files.

Magistrate David Baker, who is known to be adept with computers himself, found the defendant's stories incredible. Magistrate Baker also found that the preservation letter, sent out by the plaintiff's counsel (one of our attorneys), put the defendant on notice that he should not have reformatted a key employee's hard drive when he left the company without first preserving his emails and documents. The court found that negligence alone was not sufficient for a severe spoliation sanction of default, that bad faith was also required. But the court found evidence of bad faith in this case from the intentional destruction of key emails, and for this reason entered a "practically dispositive" adverse inference that the missing emails proved the plaintiff's case.

Several months after this order was entered, the case was tried over several days, and we obtained a final judgment for our client, Optowave, a Korean corporation. The judgment awarded significant damages against the defendant, Nitikin, a citizen of Russia residing in Florida. I would love to write more about this case, but it is still on appeal to the Eleventh Circuit.

---

20.   http://ralphlosey.files.wordpress.com/2006/11/optowave.pdf.

PLAINTIFF'S E-DISCOVERY SKULLDUGGERY LEADS TO FURTHER PUNISHMENT BY THE COURT

In this case, the employee plaintiff, James Plasse, was punished again by the district court for his alteration and destruction of electronic evidence and ordered to pay the employer defendant $55,472.32. *Plasse v. Tyco Elec. Corp.,* 2006 WL 3445610 (D. Mass., Nov. 8, 2006).

This is a sequel to one of our favorite decisions in which the plaintiff's case was dismissed with prejudice as a sanction for his inartful attempt to change the dates on documents on his home computer and other e-discovery abuses. *Plasse v. Tyco Elec. Corp.,* 2006 WL 2623441 (D. Mass., Sept. 7, 2006). In *Plasse I,* a forensic examination of the plaintiff's home computer exposed his clumsy fraud. At the end of the opinion in *Plasse I,* the court invited the defendant to move for fees and costs, suggesting that further punishment was in order against Plasse.

In *Plasse II,* the court awarded one-half of the fees incurred and all of the defendant's e-discovery costs. The fees were awarded under the court's inherent equitable power to do so "against the party that has acted in bad faith, vexatiously, wantonly, or for oppressive reasons." Only one-half of the fees sought were awarded because the court found "some degree of duplication and overkill." All of the costs were awarded as punishment for the plaintiff, who tried to mislead the court by altering data on his computer. In the words of the judge, "The court will award Defendant its full costs, since retention of experts was particularly necessary to uncover Plaintiff's skullduggery."

BLOG READER COMMENT

Sounds like a real righteous dude; he should have had to pay the full amount. Oh well, next time.

BANKRUPTCY COURT IMPOSES SANCTIONS IN ADVERSARY PROCEEDING

A bankruptcy court in Florida recently considered e-discovery abuses and imposed sanctions against the defendant law firm and its attorneys. *In re Atlantic International Mortgage Co., Debtor; Steven S. Oscher, Liquidating Trustee for Atlantic International Mortgage Co., Plaintiff, v. The Solomon Tropp Law Group, P.A., et al.*, 2006 WL 2848575 (Bankr. M.D. Fla. 1006). The sanctions imposed required The Solomon Tropp Law Group and its attorneys to pay all of the debtor's costs and all fees incurred in connection with discovery in this complicated adversary proceeding in Bankruptcy Court in Tampa, Florida. The decision begins with words all too common in this type of case:

> The matter before this Court presents a deplorable scenario under which the ultimate issues raised by the pleadings are completely overcome by discovery disputes which have gained their own life.

The e-discovery disputes begin when the plaintiff finds a memo suggesting that many more emails must exist than have been produced:

> This discovery dispute arose after the Trustee discovered a post petition communication dated December 8, 1999, between Livingston and the Solomon Firm directing that all communications with him should be by email. . . . The Trustee has maintained throughout this proceeding that in accordance with these instructions, there ought to be a substantial record of electronic communications and activities between the Solomon Firm and Livingston, far more than what has been produced by the Solomon Firm pursuant to the Trustee's Request for Production and the Electronic Records Production Order.

There were a number of e-discovery abuses noted in the opinion, but perhaps the most interesting from a "geek perspective" was the one concerning the disputed use of the Forensic Toolkit software by the law firm's expert and the contradictory findings by the expert appointed by the court. Again, in Judge Paskay's words:

> On September 27, 2005, the Solomon Firm filed an Amended Affidavit by the Firm's technology manager, William Kent (Kent), in an attempt to refute the information contained in the Computer Expert's report and the Motion for Default Judgment.

(Doc. No. 344.) Not only is this Affidavit of questionable verac-
ity, but it has been totally refuted by competent evidence before
this Court. The Kent affidavit asserted that the document recovery program, Forensic Toolkit, had not been used to search for
and recover any documents related to the present adversary proceeding. However, the Computer Expert found evidence on the
Solomon Firm's computers which proved that Forensic Toolkit
had, in fact, been used to search for documents relating to Atlantic and Livingston. Responsive documents recovered by the
Solomon Firm at that time were not produced to the Trustee.

The court denied the plaintiff/debtor's demand for entry of a default
judgment against the defendant law firm, but did state that fees and costs
would be awarded against both defendant law firm and its attorneys,
holding:

Modern discovery was designed to eliminate litigation by am-
bush and surprise. Cooperation and candor by all parties are
crucial to the proper function of the discovery process; obstrep-
erous conduct and deceptive tactics designed to delay and im-
pede have no place in the discovery process. . . . This Court is
not satisfied that the Solomon Firm's conduct rises to the level
required to sustain a motion for default judgment at this time.
While the remedy of the entry of a default judgment is too dras-
tic an action under the facts presented in the hearing, this Court
is convinced that monetary sanctions are appropriate. Under
FRBP 7037(b)(2), reasonable expenses, including attorneys' fees,
may be awarded against a party, its attorney, or both. Such sanctions, when awarded against a party's attorneys, serve to "remind attorneys that service to their clients must coexist with
their responsibilities toward the court, toward the law and toward their brethren at the bar." *Devaney v. Cont'l Am. Ins. Co.*,
989 F.2d 1154, 1162 (11th Cir.1993). Based on the foregoing,
this Court is satisfied that the appropriate sanction is to impose
monetary sanctions against the Solomon Firm and its counsel,
F. Lorraine Jahn, Esq., and Michael J. McGirney, Esq., by award-

ing the Trustee his reasonable attorneys' fees and costs incurred in pursuing all discovery in this adversary proceeding.

Defendants have moved for a rehearing, so this is not the final order and could be set aside. There has been no ruling yet on the rehearing motion because, as I understand it, Judge Paskay has been ill. The plaintiffs have, however, filed motions to determine the amount of the sanctions award, wherein they seek computer expert costs of around $100,000 and fees of approximately $600,000. Plaintiffs have not argued as to how the award should be allocated.

Postscript: On August 24, 2007, Judge Paskay entered a final judgement of sanctions against defendants for discovery misconduct in the amount of $341,028.90.

Metadata 5

WHAT IS METADATA?

Metadata literally means "data about data." Many courts define the term by referring to the *Sedona Glossary of Commonly Used Terms for E-Discovery and Digital Information Management,*[1] which defines "metadata" as:

> . . . information about a particular data set or document which describes how, when and by whom it was collected, created, accessed, modified and how it is formatted. Can be altered intentionally or inadvertently. Can be extracted when native files are converted to image. Some metadata, such as file dates and sizes, can easily be seen by users; other metadata can be hidden or embedded and unavailable to computer users who are not technically adept. Metadata is generally not reproduced in full form when a document is printed.

All computer files have metadata associated or within them that provide information about the files. For instance,

---

1. http://www.thesedonaconference.org/dltForm?did=tsglossarymay05. pdf

email software includes information in email files about its author, creation date, attachments, and identities of all recipients, including those who received a copy or blind copy. Metadata even tells you if an email has been opened by a recipient. The printout of an email, which is essentially a TIFF version, may not show the blind copies, and certainly will not tell you if it has been read or not. The metadata of an email will also maintain the history of the email and its conversation thread, such as who replied and who forwarded. Also, unless it is an Outlook email stripped out of its PST file into an MSG file (as explained in the blog that follows in this chapter, *MSG Is Bad for You*), it will tell you in what folder the email was filed by its custodian.

Some programs include information within the contents of files that is hidden until you instruct the software to reveal it. This is called "embedded" information, and courts frequently refer to such information as metadata. Technically, it is not true "metadata" because it is not "data about data." It is not information about the file itself; instead, it is information within a file, but hidden for some reason. It is information that the user has created but is not visible without a command. A good example of this is the "Comments" feature in Word. Comments can be inserted into a Word document that are not visible until you use the View Command to show them. The comments are embedded into the file itself. Another example is the formula that a user can place in an Excel or other spreadsheet to calculate values within a cell. The math used to calculate the value of a spreadsheet cell is embedded in the file. Although technically "embedded data" is not "metadata," for purposes of legal analysis embedded data is treated as a form or type of metdadata because most courts, and the legal profession at large, do not grasp the distinction.

WHEN SHOULD METADATA BE PRODUCED?

The foremost metadata issue facing all parties and courts today is when metadata should be produced. The answer is found in a string of cases from 2005 to 2007.

Williams I

The key case on metadata is *Williams v. Sprint/United Management Co.*, 230 F.R.D. 640 (D. Kan. 2005). Here, terminated employees brought a class action and sought Excel spreadsheets with all metadata intact, including embedded formulae. The court held that under "emerging standards of electronic discovery," metadata ordinarily visible to users of Excel spreadsheets "should presumptively be treated as part of the 'document' and should thus be discoverable." *Id.* at 652.

The court reviewed case law, the pending new rules and commentary, and the *Sedona Principles for Electronic Document Production*, especially Principle 12, which provides that "[u]nless it is material to resolving the dispute, there is no obligation to preserve and produce metadata absent agreement of the parties or order of the court." The commentary to this principle at that time opined that "most of the metadata has no evidentiary value, and any time (and money) spent reviewing it is a waste of resources." The commentary also set forth an important caveat: "Of course, if the producing party knows or should reasonably know that particular metadata is relevant to the dispute, it should be produced."

The court accepted the Sedona Principle 12, with commentary, as an important part of the "emerging standard," but rejected Sprint's argument that this meant the Excel spreadsheets' metadata should not be produced. Instead, the court found that the Excel metadata was material to the dispute, and Sprint United should have known that and should have produced it. The actual holding then goes even further to state:

> Based on these emerging standards, the Court holds that when a party is ordered to produce electronic documents as they are maintained in the ordinary course of business, the producing party should produce the electronic documents with their metadata intact, unless that party timely objects to production of metadata, the parties agree that the metadata should not be produced, or the producing party requests a protective order. The initial burden with regard to the disclosure of the metadata would therefore be placed on the party to whom the request or order to produce is directed. The burden to object to the disclosure of metadata is appropriately placed on the party ordered to produce its electronic documents as they are ordinarily maintained because that party already has access to the metadata and is in the best position to determine whether producing it is ob-

jectionable. Placing the burden on the producing party is further supported by the fact that metadata is an inherent part of an electronic document, and its removal ordinarily requires an affirmative act by the producing party that alters the electronic document.

Until recently, it looked like, in spite of Sedona Principle 12, metadata production was indeed to be the new standard, especially since new Fed. R. Civ. P. 34(b)(2)(B) went into effect, which requires production of electronically stored files as they "are kept in the usual course of business or in a form or forms that are reasonably usable." The usual course of business is to keep files in their native format, because that is how they are used—i.e., document files created in Word, .xls files created in Excel—and native files by definition include all metadata.

Williams II

Several recent cases, along with a sequel to *Williams* itself, have, however, shown that the exact nature of the emerging standard is still in doubt. First the sequel: *Williams v. Sprint/United Management Co.*, 2006 WL 3691604 (D. Kan. Dec. 12, 2006) (*Williams II*). The spreadsheets in question in *Williams I* were produced in native format as the court ordered, but the plaintiffs wanted more. They returned to the court a year later to try to compel production in native format of all 11,000 emails produced that transmitted spreadsheets. (The judge here used a golf analogy for "native" format of "play it like it lies." See my blog post by the same name later in this chapter.) The plaintiffs argued that the original native format of the emails was needed in order for them to determine which emails transmitted which spreadsheets. The defendant had the burden to show why this native production should not be done, that it was permissible for it to have "improved their lie."

The defendant met this burden and the motion to compel was denied, primarily because the emails had already been produced in paper without objection, and a second reproduction at this date would be very burdensome, especially since the emails contained many attorney-client-privileged materials. Actually, the plaintiffs had originally objected to paper production of the email but had withdrawn their objection during one of many discovery hearings based on the defendant's assurances that it would provide Spreadsheet Reports that "would match up the transmittal e-mails with their respective attachments." The defendant argued it had done so as agreed, but the plaintiffs complained that the Spreadsheet Reports were deficient, and they were unable to match them up. The court disagreed that the Spreadsheet Reports were deficient, noted the apparent impossibility to redact privileged materials from native files, and held that since the plaintiffs had already received production in one format (paper), the new rules protected the defendant from having to produce them again in another format (native). To continue the golf analogy, the court in effect applied new Rule 34(b)(iii) to prevent the plaintiff from receiving a "mulligan," a second request. The exact wording of the court is instructive and, to a certain extent, explains and clarifies *Williams I*:

> Federal Rule of Civil Procedure 34(b)(iii), as amended on December 1, 2006, provides that "[u]nless the parties otherwise agree, or the court otherwise orders, . . . a party need not produce the same electronically stored information in more than one form." In this case, Defendant has already produced the transmittal e-mails, as well as all the attachments to those e-mails. Defendant has further created Spreadsheet Reports to correlate the transmittal e-mails to the attachments they transmitted. The Court therefore finds that under Rule 34(b)(iii), Defendant need not re-produce its RIF-related transmittal e-mails together with their attachments in native format, as requested by Plaintiffs.
>
> Defendant raises legitimate concerns about producing the transmittal e-mails with their attachments in their native format, including whether production in native format would permit the redaction or removal of privileged information in the transmittal e-mail or the attachment.
>
> Moreover, even assuming that Defendant could produce the transmittal e-mails together with their attachments in native format with the privileged information redacted, Plaintiffs have not sufficiently explained why they need the transmittal e-mails in their native format. Previously, this Court has ordered Defendant to produce the Excel RIF spreadsheets in native format, but in that instance Plaintiffs provided valid reasons for the spread-

sheets to be produced in their native format. Namely, that the contents of the spreadsheet cells could not otherwise be viewed as the cells contained formulas. Also, in many instances, the column width of the cells prevented viewing of the entire content of the cells. Here, other than arguing that ordering Defendant to reproduce the transmittal e-mails together with their attachments in native format would be more helpful to Plaintiffs in matching up the transmittal e-mails with their respective attachments, Plaintiffs fail to provide any other reason why they need the transmittal e-mails produced in their native format. For these reasons, the Court denies Plaintiffs' request for Defendant to produce all its RIF-related transmittal e-mails in native format with all attachments in native format and attached to the transmittal e-mails.

The *Williams II* court did, however, state that the plaintiffs could pose specific interrogatories to the defendant as necessary to decipher the Spreadsheet Reports and determine which emails matched with a particular spreadsheet.

Wyeth

Another court quoted *Williams I* but reached an opposite result, disallowing production of native format. *Wyeth v. Impax Laboratories, Inc.*, 2006 WL 3091331, 2006 U.S. Dist. LEXIS 79761 (D. Del., Oct. 26, 2006). The facts behind the decision are similar to those of *Williams II*. *Wyeth* declined to require metadata production, relying primarily on the failure to request metadata before the production and a local rule making TIFF and JPEG the default format of production. In effect, the court was relying on the "one format" production limitation of revised Rule 34(b), although the new rule is not mentioned in the opinion and had not yet gone into effect. The *Wyeth* court explained its ruling as follows:

Since the parties have never agreed that electronic documents would be produced in any particular format, Wyeth complied with its discovery obligation by producing image files. Further, neither party has argued that the need for accessing metadata was foreseeable or generally necessary. Finally, Impax has not demonstrated a particularized need for the metadata or database production it has requested. Therefore, this part of Impax's Motion is denied.

Wyeth apparently tries to buttress the decision with a quote from *Williams I*, that the "emerging standards of electronic discovery appear to articulate a general presumption against the production of metadata." The court correctly quotes *Williams I*, but does not point out that this was a summary of the defendant's position, which *Williams I* rejected. (*Williams II* had not yet been decided.)

Kentucky Speedway

A better-reasoned case in Kentucky district court explicitly rejects *Williams I. Kentucky Speedway, LLC v. NASCAR*, 2006 U.S. Dist. LEXIS 92028 (E.D. Ky., Dec. 18, 2006). This is an antitrust action against NASCAR in which the defendants had already spent over $3 million in 5 months responding to e-discovery requests. Then, with that background, the plaintiff asked for production of all metadata in documents already produced. (Again, note the similarities with *Williams II*, which had not yet been decided.) The plaintiff relied upon *Williams I* to try to justify this late request, but failed to make "any showing of a particularized need for the metadata." The *Kentucky Speedway* court rejected *Williams I* in this context and instead followed *Wyeth*, holding that:

> In the rapidly evolving world of electronic discovery, the holding of the *Williams* case is not persuasive. Having the benefit of the newly amended rules, advisory notes, and commentary of scholars, I respectfully disagree with its conclusion that a producing party "should produce the electronic documents with their metadata intact, unless that party timely objects . . . , the parties agree that the metadata should not be produced, or the producing party requests a protective order."
>
> Here, the parties clearly had no agreement that the electronic files would be produced in any particular format. Plaintiff did not notify defendant ISC that it sought metadata until seven months after ISC had produced both hard copy and electronic copies of its documents. . . .

To the extent that plaintiff seeks metadata for a specific document or documents where date and authorship information is unknown but relevant, plaintiff should identify that document or documents by Bates Number or by other reasonably identifying features. Responding to a request for additional information concerning specific documents would be far less burdensome to defendant and far more likely to produce relevant information.

The opinion in *Kentucky Speedway* does not answer the question of whether it would have reached the same result if the plaintiff had made the request for metadata from the beginning, and not waited until after the defendants had already spent millions of dollars to produce the same documents without metadata.

It is, however, clear from *Kentucky Speedway* that whenever a metadata production will create a substantial burden on the producing party (here it would have cost NASCAR another $500,000), the requesting party will have to provide good cause. The plaintiff's reliance on *Williams I* to support the production of metadata in all circumstances, and without a good-cause showing, was misplaced and distorts the actual holding of *Williams I* (as shown, for instance, by *Williams II*). Instead, *Williams* stands for the proposition that the producing party must object and show undue burden; the burden then shifts to the requesting party to prove good cause. The argument on metadata production is essentially the same as the inaccessibility argument under Rule 26(b)(2)(B). If you can show a real need to see the metadata, as the plaintiffs did in *Williams I* (but not *Williams II*), it may be possible to compel the production in spite of burden on the producing party. It will be a balancing test dependent upon the circumstances, and following something like the seven factors recommended by the Rules Committee for 26(b)(2)(B) analysis, and earlier in *Zubulake I* for cost shifting, but with the added dimension of the debatable feasibility of redacting privileged materials from native files.

In Re Payment

The latest word in this controversy of "emerging standards" comes out of a consolidated group of class-action cases styled *In Re Payment Card*

Interchange Fee and Merchant Discount Antitrust Litigation, 2007 U.S. Dist. LEXIS 2650 (E.D. NY., Jan. 12, 2007). As in *Kentucky Speedway, Wyeth,* and *Williams II,* the defendants here sought the production of the metadata for documents already produced without metadata. (Actually, the defendants never filed a motion to compel; they just raised the issue at a conference, and that was part of the problem.) In addition, the defendants wanted the plaintiffs to produce all metadata on documents they had not yet produced.

As to the previously produced documents, the holding here follows *Kentucky Speedway, Wyeth,* and *Williams II. In Re Payment* holds that the defendants waited too long to complain of the metadata-stripped production and implied that there had been a waiver. The lesson here is that in order to obtain metadata you may need, you should specifically ask for it to begin with, and if the production is later stripped of the metadata requested, you should immediately and vigorously object.

In Re Payment also followed *Williams I* to a certain extent, in that it ordered all future productions by the plaintiffs to include metadata. The court explained its reasons for requiring full metadata production:

> The defendants object to Individual Plaintiffs' production protocol on the grounds that, by failing to supply meta-data, it does not comply with amended Rule 34. The Advisory Committee on Civil Rules, in its notes to the 2006 amendment to Rule 34, wrote that a party responding to a discovery request may elect to produce a "reasonably usable" form of electronic data rather than produce the information as kept in the ordinary course of business. Fed. R. Civ. P. 34(b), 2006 Amendment, Advisory Committee's Note. That is precisely what the Individual Plaintiffs have done. By making that choice, however, they have run afoul of the Advisory Committee's proviso that data ordinarily kept in electronically searchable form "should not be produced in a form that removes or significantly degrades this feature."
> *Id.*

However, the same cannot be said of prospective discovery, meaning the electronic documents that the Individual Plaintiffs have not yet substantially prepared for production as searchable TIFF images. Now that the Individual Plaintiffs are aware of the defendants' objections, their argument of undue burden is weaker; indeed, they have conceded that their concerns about the burdens of producing electronic documents in native format largely disappear with respect to the documents they have not yet processed for production.

Thus this new metadata case, like *Williams I* and *II*, supports the proposition that the emerging standard requires metadata production when requested and not objected to, but at the same time emphasizes the need for early, clear requests, and prompt objections if the metadata is not provided.

BLOG READER COMMENT:

Don't you think that Principle 12 of the 2d edition of the Sedona Principles changes your conclusion fairly dramatically? And are there still lawyers out there who are not asking for metadata?

RALPH'S REPLY:

No, not dramatically, and yes, there are! The First Edition of Principle 12 was considered by all of the cases discussed here. In the meantime, the 12th Principle has been slightly edited, and I admit the revisions tend to suggest a movement toward production, but certainly not in every case, and not for all metadata. The latest version of Principle 12, the Second Edition, June 2007, states: "Absent party agreement or court order specifying the form or forms of production, production should be made in the form or forms in which the information is ordinarily maintained or in a reasonably usable form, taking into account the need to produce reasonably accessible metadata that will enable the receiving party to have the same ability to access, search, and display the information as the producing party where appropriate or necessary in light of the nature of the information and the needs of the case." Comment 12.a. to the 2007 *Sedona Principles* still says: "The extent to which metadata should be preserved in a particular case will depend on the needs of the case."

METADATA MISTAKE BY TOP SPY AGENCY

Metadata, the hidden data contained in computer files, makes many people nervous, but especially lawyers. They are uncomfortable with anything hidden, or for that matter anything poorly understood, and metadata qualifies as both. Adding to this discomfort are the horror stories, well known in the profession, of other counsel accidentally producing documents to opposing counsel that contain embarrassing metadata— for instance, a Word document containing secret comments they added, then hid, and then forgot to delete or "scrub" before production.

This can be very serious for attorneys because of their high ethical duty to maintain the secrecy of the confidential information disclosed to them by their clients. For this reason, attorneys, more than most, tend to worry about inadvertently disclosing these secrets by metadata. The concern is magnified for litigation attorneys who have opposing counsel watching their every move for mistakes. That is one of the reasons for the advent of "clawback" agreements and new Rule 26(b)(5)(B). If a privileged communication in a computer file is accidentally disclosed— say, because it was contained in metadata that they did not see—they want to get it back and prevent a waiver.

For that reason, it is especially troubling to lawyers to hear that even the best professionals at secret keeping, our country's top spies, mess up on metadata. If anyone is serious about secrecy, it is spies. Their very lives may be at stake. So if espionage professionals accidentally reveal state secrets because of metadata, then it could happen to anyone.

Metadata is by definition out of sight. And what is out of sight is out of mind, and thus easily forgotten. The latest metadata mistake story proves this point in classic "spy versus spy" fashion.

The Office of the Director of National Intelligence (DNI) is the highest intelligence agency in the United States. The DNI oversees all federal intelligence agencies, including the CIA. The size of the total U.S. intelligence budget that DNI oversees is one of the government's most closely guarded secrets.

On May 14, 2007, a senior procurement executive of DNI gave an unclassified presentation to a group of outside contractors in Colorado titled "Procuring the Future." Her PowerPoint included a slide with two graphics depicting the trend of award dollars to contractors from 1995 have to request production of the applicable operating files for that. The same holds true for the metadata of the folder structure for Outlook emails in a PST file. That information is contained only in the packing file that holds all of a user's emails, the PST file, and not contained in the individual email file itself. I wrote about this in my blog later in this chapter, *MSG Is Bad for You.*

Production in "native" format means production of computer files, or ESI, in the format in which they were originally created and maintained. *Williams v. Sprint/United*, 2006 WL 3691604 (D. Kan. 2006) (*Williams II*). (See my blog later in this chapter, *Play It Like It Lies and No Mulligans*, for more on this case.) Most of the time, this means files are produced in the format of the software application used to create the ESI. Thus, for example, if you produce a file created by Microsoft Word, this typically means production in the Microsoft Word format, wherein the file ends with the ".doc" extension. This is not necessarily always the case, however, because you can also use Microsoft Word software to save your documents in other formats—say, for instance, html format. Some people might do that for some reason, such as to facilitate posting the document on the Web.

The fundamental metadata case, *Williams v. Sprint/United*, 230 F.R.D. 640 (D. Kan. 2005) (*Williams I*), which I previously discussed at length, mentions the four most popular objections to native file production. The fact that these objections all failed in *Williams I* is testament only to their weak inapplicability to the facts and circumstances of the particular motion presented, and the opinion of Magistrate Judge Waxse. The arguments and objections were good, and this is where any practitioner would want to begin his or her analysis. These same arguments may succeed with other facts, or even in similar facts with a different judge. This is a very new and evolving area of the law. In fact, these same defendants, Sprint/United, are still presenting these same arguments in other nearly identical cases in the same court, but with a different magistrate. *Bolton v. Sprint/United,* 2007 WL 756644 (D. Kan., March 8, 2007).

So, without further ado, presented in the order in which they were summarized in *Bolton,* here are the four basic objections to native format production (with my short comments in *italics*).

1. Native production destroys metadata. When you access native files, you change their metadata. (*This is true; it is also true that there are usually ways to guard against that.*)

2. Native production can reveal privileges hidden in metadata, both attorney-client and work product. Metadata can, for instance, show such work product as when files were gathered, last opened, printed, etc., as opposed to the metadata existent pre-litigation during the relevant time period of the dispute. (*This could be true if counsel was not careful to preserve the original files, and again, there are usually ways to protect against this.*) As another example, metadata in the form of hidden comments to a word document could reveal privileged attorney communications. (*Again true, but a privilege review of the metadata would show these comments and allow them to be withheld.*)

3. The metadata in the native files is not relevant to plaintiff's claims. (*This is the strongest argument for objection to production of metadata and is in accord with the original Sedona Principle 12 commentary, which states that most metadata is useless and a waste of time to review. So, if the requesting party argues for native file format on the basis that it needs the metadata, challenge the relevance of the metadata. Unlike the plaintiffs in* Williams I, *who made a strong showing that they needed the native spreadsheets, the requesting party may be unable to show any particular need for native file production. See* Williams II, supra, *and* Wyeth v. Impax Laboratories, Inc., *2006 WL 391331 (D. Del. 2006)*).

4. It is difficult to ensure that native files have not been changed after production. (*Judge Waxse destroyed that argument in* Williams I *when he pointed out that hash values guarantee authenticity.* Williams I, supra *at 655. Also see my blog on hash in the "New Technologies" chapter. Still, if hash is not considered, variations of this argument may still be persuasive.*)

In addition, by far the best objection you can make, when the facts allow it, is that you have already made production in a non-native format, and new Rule 34(b)(iii) protects you from a second production. See, for example, *Williams II* and *In re Payment Card Interchange Fee*

Otherwise, you can easily fall into an expensive and confusing MSG e-discovery trap where important metadata is lost. So, just as you want to avoid MSG in your food, you want to avoid it in your e-discovery production too.

MSG stands for what you would think, "Message." It is the file extension used to identify a single email message. The PST extension is a Microsoft specialty that stands for "Personal Storage Table."[2] It is used to identify all of the emails (with attachments) stored by one particular user. This is how almost everyone maintains and uses their Outlook email program. They keep their email together in various folders, which make up one PST file. Indeed, this is the default procedure, although users can (assuming no administrative restrictions) separate their emails and scatter them all over their computer as many separate, unrelated emails. In this event, the different extension of MSG is used to store the individual emails.

To use a paper file comparison, Outlook by default keeps an individual user's emails in a filing cabinet. Received emails start in the Inbox folder. The user can then create various subfolders to file the emails for easier access later. It is equivalent to providing a filing cabinet to store paper letters and a virtually unlimited number of blank folders. Outlook's system is equivalent to traditional paper filing systems. Like paper files in Outlook (and other email software, such as Lotus), you label the folders yourself and file your emails in the folders you deem appropriate. This should result in some kind of rational record storage system that makes sense to the user and allows him or her to retrieve old letters/emails more easily. The folders' names and ordering system often provide useful insights into the user's thinking, and sometimes help to explain the meaning of a particular document. For instance, if a user created a folder called "Important," her decision to place a particular document in that file tells you something about the document itself, or at least about the user's attitude toward that document. So when you take a single email out of the Outlook folder, it is equivalent to removing it from a paper file folder and keeping it loose on your desk (or floor).

Parties today frequently specify the production of files in their native format so that all metadata will be preserved. Indeed, most commentators agree that native file production under the new rules, specifically Rule

---

2.   http://en.wikipedia.org/wiki/.pst

34(b)(ii), is now the default mode of production absent agreement by the parties to the contrary. (There are, by the way, many good reasons to agree to non-native file production, as long as essential metadata is still preserved, pertaining to the advantages of loaded TIFF files, redaction, and trial preparation software.) Moreover, most believe that the primary purpose behind this rule specification is to preserve metadata. Rule 34(b)(ii) states:

> (ii) if a request for electronically stored information does not specify the form or forms of production, a responding party must produce the information in a form or forms in which it is ordinarily maintained or in a form or forms that are reasonably usable.

An argument can be made that both types of Microsoft email files, individual MSG files, and collective PST files are "native" files, since they are both produced and used by Outlook. In that sense, they are both native to that software. But almost everyone ordinarily maintains their Outlook emails in the PST form, not the MSG form. Thus if a user maintains her email in PST form, the rules requires that it be produced that way. Conversely, in the rare event a user maintains his email only in MSG form, then it should be produced that way. Of course, the rule also has the alternative "forms that are reasonably usable," and so arguments will abound.

But if the parties have agreed to native production and also to the preservation of metadata, then I suggest that the Outlook files should be produced in PST format, not MSG. But before I complete the basis for this contention, further explanation of the terms might help. The *Sedona Conference Glossary* (2005) defines "native format" as follows:

> Native Format: Electronic documents have an associated file structure defined by the original creating application. This file structure is referred to as the "native format" of the document.

The recent case of *Palgut v. City of Colorado Springs*, 2006 WL 3483442 (D. Colo., Nov. 29, 2006) cites to the Judge's Guide and defines "native format" as:

"Native format" means all documents that are created in digital format (word-processing files, spreadsheets, presentations, and E-mail) have a native file format—that is, a format designed specifically for the most efficient use of the information in which this kind of software specializes.

Outlook has designed the PST format for the most efficient use of the information it creates. That is why it is the default. True, it also has an alternative MSG format, but it is not the most efficient use of the information. The most efficient use is to keep all of the emails together, organized into different folders, the way the information was originally and ordinarily maintained. Further, when you take a single email, remove it from the PST file, and put it into a stand-alone MSG format, you are stripping it of a key piece of metadata.

When Outlook emails are converted from their original PST format to MSG, the email metadata that shows where the email was located in the custodian's folders is lost. It is equivalent to taking a filing cabinet full of paper letters, wherein the correspondence is filed and placed in appropriate drawers, files, folders and subfolders, and dumping them into one big box of mixed-up, disorganized individual letters.

In short, you can see the original Outlook folder structure in a native format production of PST files, but you cannot and will never know this information in an MSG format production of email originally contained in a PST file. That makes review of the MSG production substantially more difficult and expensive than review of a PST production. Further, MSG production makes it impossible to determine what letters were originally filed together, and hides the file names created by the custodian to identify these folders. Thus, for instance, if a user created a folders labeled "hot," "unimportant," and "bogus," and then produced 100 emails from the unimportant folder, 20 from the bogus, and only 1 from the hot, this would no doubt lead to important deposition questioning.

So be wary of Outlook production in individual MSG files, which some parties may insist upon as less expensive than PST production. Instead, demand PST format, where you preserve the metadata showing the original folders. This is one of many items that savvy e-discovery lawyers will want to discuss in the initial meetings under new Rules 16 and 26.

Search and Review of ESI

6

INTRODUCTION TO SEARCH AND REVIEW

The Sixth Step in the standard e-discovery process is the search and review of what the new rules call electronically stored information. This is a key step, because this is where you separate the wheat from the chaff—where you find out what ESI is relevant to the case and may have to be produced. This is also the step where you determine if a privilege of some kind applies to a particular file, such as attorney-client or work product. If it does, then you need to exclude that ESI file from production. If you make a mistake and inadvertently produce one, you risk waiving your privilege entirely, not only for that document but possibly for all otherwise privileged documents concerning that subject matter. Obviously this step is very important, and most lawyers and companies take great pains to try to avoid accidental waivers of privilege. For that reason, this is the step where you often have teams of lawyers reviewing mountains of data. That is also why approximately 40%-60% of the overall costs of e-discovery are typically incurred in this step.

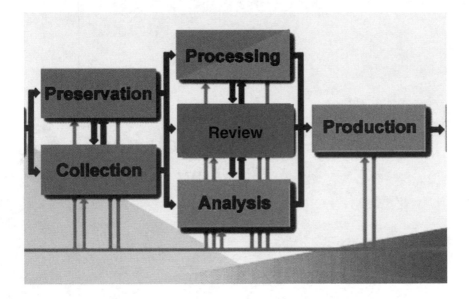

Review is frequently bifurcated to try to avoid mistakes and, at the same time, minimize costs. This first level of review pertains to responsiveness only. This is considered to be the easiest judgment call. This first-level review is often delegated to contract attorneys or paralegals, usually performed in a central location under supervision of associate attorneys and a supervising senior shareholder (on an as-needed basis), but sometimes done via third-party companies through attorneys in India and elsewhere (no kidding). The second level of review is for issue tagging and for privilege, including partial privilege, of the smaller amount of ESI determined to be responsive in the first level. Responsiveness is also double-checked. Issue tagging is also frequently performed in the first review and then double-checked in the second. The second review, especially as it pertains to privilege review, requires higher-quality reviewers and closer supervision by senior attorneys. The overall goal of any review process is to minimize the mistakes by careful supervision of reviewers, quality control reviews and spot checking.

SEDONA'S NEW COMMENTARY ON SEARCH, AND THE MYTH OF THE PHARAOH'S CURSE

The Sedona Conference has just released its *Best Practices Commentary on the Use of Search and Information Retrieval Methods in E-Discovery*

(August 2007) for public comments. A copy may be downloaded for personal use. This Best Practices Commentary, like all of the Sedona publications, was written by a committee of expert members of The Sedona Conference, who agreed upon the content and wording. This particular group is called the Search and Retrieval Sciences Project Team. Writings by committee are usually an invitation for disaster, but Sedona consistently manages to pull it off, and do a first-rate job, primarily, I think, because of the quality of its editors. The editor-in-chief for the Search Team is Jason Baron, about whom I have written several times previously, along with executive editors Richard Braman and Kenneth Withers and senior editors Thomas Allman, James Daley, and George Paul.

The Search Commentary begins by concisely stating the problems with searching high volumes of ESI. It then offers three general solutions, followed by eight specific "Practice Points." The comments contain both intellectual depth and good practical advice to all those struggling with the problems of search.

The Search Commentary is carefully considered and well written. Although I have a couple of suggestions on the comments, I fully agree with the committee's observations and solutions. Many will not. In fact, I suspect that this publication will be quite challenging to many in the legal profession, because it contradicts several well-established myths. For instance, the Search Team acknowledges that most people believe that:

> [M]anual review by humans of large amounts of information is as accurate and complete as possible—perhaps even perfect— and constitutes the gold standard by which all searches should be measured.

But the committee states that this is a *myth*! Manual review may be perfect for a few hundred pages of documents but fails miserably for a few hundred thousand, much less million or billion. So much for the gold standard.

The Search Team also makes the point, which is not controversial, that the large amounts of ESI in many lawsuits today has made the "venerated process of 'eyes only' review" both impractical and cost-prohibitive. They contend that a new consensus is forming in the legal community:

that human review of documents in discovery is expensive, time-consuming, and error-prone. There is growing consensus that the application of linguistic and mathematic-based content analysis embodied in new forms of search and retrieval technologies, tools, techniques, and process in support of the review function can effectively reduce litigation cost, time, and error rates.

This leads to **Practice Point 1** (of 8):

In many settings involving electronically stored information, sole reliance on manual search process for the purpose of finding responsive documents may be infeasible or unwarranted. In such cases, the use of automated search methods should be viewed as reasonable, valuable, and even necessary.

The automated search method of choice today is keyword search review. It involves the use of select keywords that you think the documents you seek will contain. Keyword searches also frequently include "boolean" logic and can be expanded further with fuzzy logic and stemming. You then manually search the documents located by keyword search to determine relevance. The manual review frequently leads to adjustments in the query terms and repeat of the keyword search. Most lawyers think that with this kind of iterative process, and skilled researchers, you can find most documents.

In fact, in a study done in 1985, lawyers and paralegals with special skills in this area searched a discovery database of 40,000 documents and 350,000 pages in a case involving a subway accident. David Blair & M.E. Maron, *An Evaluation of Retrieval Effectiveness for a Full-Text Document Retrieval System*, 28 COM. A.C.M. 289 (1985). At the end of the lengthy process, the legal team was confident that they had located about 75% of the relevant documents. In my experience, most attorneys think they have a similar, if not better, success rate.

Lawyers have been using keyword searches since the 1970s with Lexis and Westlaw to find case law. I was first trained in this in 1978. At that time, Westlaw and Lexis each had mandatory video (VHS) training programs leading to certification. Once certified, you could use "dumb terminals" to access mainframes over modems. It was a tremendous innovation in its day.

It was a natural extension in the 1980s and 1990s to use the same keyword search technology to locate relevant documents in large sets of ESI. Lawyers and judges quickly endorsed this legal research method to search for documents. As one judge put it, "The glory of electronic information is not merely that it saves space but that it permits the computer to search for words or 'strings' of text in seconds." *In re Lorazepam & Clorazepate*, 300 F. Supp. 2d 43, 46 (D. D.C. 2004). Keyword searching appeared to solve the problem of large volumes of electronic documents where the gold standard of "eyes only" review was not practical. It might not be "perfect" like manual searches, but it got at least 75% of the documents, and so was an acceptable alternative.

The profession today is very familiar and comfortable with keyword searching. Keyword search is the method employed by almost all lawyers when they use an automated search process. In fact, I suspect that most lawyers are not even aware that there are alternatives to keyword searches.

That is why the committee's next contention may prove very controversial: **the supposed accuracy of keyword searches is just another myth!** The Blair and Maron study in 1985 showed that, while the lawyers thought they had found at least 75% of the relevant documents, **in fact they had only located 20%.**

Can justice really be served with only 20% of the picture? Has the exploding cornucopia of ESI cursed the legal system with the pretense of real knowledge?

The Blair and Moran study, which is still the only one of its kind, led one commentator, Daniel Dabney, a lawyer and information scientist who now works for Westlaw, to equate the false confidence of computer searchers to the *Curse of Thamus*. Daniel P. Dabney, *The Curse of Thamus: An Analysis of Full-Text Legal Document Retrieval*, 78 Law Libr. J. 5 (1986). Thamus was an Egyptian pharaoh reported by Plato in his *Phaedrus Dialogue* to have criticized the invention of writing as a false substitute for real learning. Thamus condemned writing, said to be a gift from the god Theuth (aka Hermes), as a curse in disguise. The pharaoh predicted that writing would only lead to a delusionary "semblance of truth" and "conceit of wisdom." As Dabney put it in his article:

Since the mere possession of writings does not give knowledge, how are we to extract from this almost incomprehensibly large collection of written records the knowledge that we need?

Dabney argued that the Blair and Maron study proved that full-text computer-assisted retrieval was not a valid cure to the pharaoh's curse. The Sedona Search Team agrees:

> . . . the experience of many litigators is that simple keyword searching alone is inadequate in at least some discovery contexts. This is because simple keyword searches end up being both over- and under-inclusive in light of the inherent malleability and ambiguity of spoken and written English (as well as all other languages). . . .
>
> The problem of the relative percentage of "false positive" hits or noise in the data is potentially huge, amounting in some cases to huge numbers of files which must be searched to find responsive documents. On the other hand, keyword searches have the potential to miss documents that contain a word that has the same meaning as the term used in the query, but is not specified. . . .
>
> Finally, using keywords alone results in a return set of potentially responsive documents that are not weighted and ranked based upon their potential importance or relevance. In other words, each document is considered to have an equal probability of being responsive upon further manual review.

The Sedona Search Team notes that currently most e-discovery vendors and software providers continue to rely on outdated keyword searching. This is also what I am seeing. This message may come as an unwelcome challenge to many e-discovery providers and is therefore likely to be controversial.

But the Sedona Search Commentary does not end on a negative note; instead, it points to new search technologies that will significantly improve upon the dismal recall and precision ratios of keyword searches. Here is how they summarize the herald of coming good:

Alternative search tools are available to supplement simple keyword searching and Boolean search techniques. These include using fuzzy logic to capture variations on words; using conceptual searching, which makes use of taxonomies and ontologies assembled by linguists; and using other machine learning and text mining tools that employ mathematical probabilities.

This part of the new Commentary is really interesting, albeit challenging, as the team talks about alternative search tools and methods and describes many of them in detail in the Appendix.

The many incredible advances in technology over the last 20 years have created the legal morass we are in now. In our present cursed state, it is impossible to find all relevant evidence, and a mere 20% capture rate seems pretty good. The only viable solution is to fight fire with fire and find a high-tech answer. This requires a new kind of team synergy that I often talk about in this blog, a combination of science, technology and the law. The Sedona search group concludes with a similar recommendation:

> The legal community should support collaborative research with the scientific and academic sectors aimed at establishing the efficacy of a range of automated search and information retrieval methods.

The problems created by the information explosion impact all of society, not just the law. There is strong demand for new, improved search technologies, and this is becoming big business. Billions of dollars are now pouring into search technology research. For instance, in 2006 Google spent $1.23 billion, Yahoo spent $833 million, and e-Bay spent $495 million in core research and development activities. With this kind of commercial activity, there is good reason to hope that the pharaoh's curse may soon be lifted.

Blog Reader Comments:

Ken Withers

Director, Judicial Education and Content
The Sedona Conference

Thank you, Ralph, for resurrecting Dabney's "Curse of Thamus" from the tomb of academic history—I always loved the article and still have a copy in my file of important reading that I downloaded on October 24, 2000, as one of the few works exploring the intersection of law and information science and the implications of the Blair and Maron study (and as an avid reader of *Biblical Archaeology Review*, I applaud your choice of graphic illustration). I appreciate your comments and hope that your readers will submit more. All Sedona Conference papers are a "work in progress," even though we might call them "final" for the purposes of publication.

Your readers should also be aware that the research behind this most recent commentary on search and retrieval technology is very much in progress. We actively support the new "legal track" of the National Institute of Standards and Technology's annual Text REtrieval Conference (TREC) at http:/ /trec.nist.gov/. Jason Baron of the National Records and Archives Administration captains the effort, under which members of The Sedona Conference's Working Group 1 supply sample discovery-like queries and human reviewers to help evaluate the performance of a variety of cutting-edge automated text-retrieval methods in development. Membership in Working Group 1, and participation in developing these Commentaries, is open to all, and I encourage your readers to join up at http://www.thesedonaconference.org.

Keep up the good work on your excellent blog, and I hope you allow us to post URLs occasionally.

Another Blog Reader Comment

This is a brilliant post. There is no doubt that many (most? all?) searches executed against a data universe today in lit support fail in some ways. I wrote a paper for law school that discussed the need for a "feedback loop" in the e-discovery process to test the validity of the "initial assumptions" used to formulate the search criteria.

In its simplest form, this feedback loop consists of indexing and building terms lists from those documents classified by counsel as "relevant" or "privileged," and reviewing that list of terms to see if modification to the seach criteria is necessary. Additionally, metadata could be scanned to search for data custodians that might have been overlooked. I don't know any vendors that do this, or consultants that advise clients to incorporate such a process, but it only makes sense. It strengthens the discovery process and at the very least allows a greater measure of defensibility of it in the courtroom. After all, the criteria used to filter through the data universe determines what the reviewers see, and if there is a flaw in that process, then how can you be sure of the final result?

Another Blog Reader Comment

The problems of keyword search are even more pronounced in smaller and medium-sized firms across the country, many of whom are most assuredly not terribly familiar with automated electronic searches through documents. In order to be truly effective, a technology-based answer will also have to be affordable and largely "turn-key."

Even more important, as has been pointed out in this blog and in others, is that the attorneys *must* know what their clients know about the day-to-day business implementation of the digital enterprise. Many keyword searches, while seemingly intuitive and rational, can be easily defeated by the machinations of the parties. The shorthand that people often use in email or other forms of truncated digital communication, especially when used to refer to offbeat phrases such as "Project Look What the Cat Dragged In," can result in numerous variations of keywords for one independent area of interest. Whether the reliabilty of keyword search is pegged at 20% simply due to the reliability of the underlying technology or because of other external factors, clearly lawyers cannot be lulled into relying on a single "magic bullet" to meet their obligations in e-discovery. This is clearly one area where one must keep sight of the entire forest, and not focus on just the trees.

KEYWORD SEARCHES VERSUS CONCEPT SEARCHES

A recent opinion by Judge Facciola distinguishes between the two basic kinds of searches: keyword searching and concept searching. *Disability Rights Council of Greater Washington v. Washington Metropolitan Area Transit Authority,* 2007 WL 1585452 (D.D.C. June 1, 2007). The plaintiff had proposed simple keyword searching of email by people's names, but Judge Facciola suggested the parties instead consider concept searching. This is the first opinion to recognize the distinction between the two types of searches, according to Jason R. Baron, director of litigation of the National Archives and Records Administration. He wrote to me earlier today to bring this to my attention. Jason should know, as he is an expert and a strong proponent of concept searching and the iterative process. Indeed, Judge Facciola cites to his article in the opinion. Here is the operative language from *Disability Rights Council* at *9:

I bring to the parties' attention recent scholarship that argues that concept searching, as opposed to keyword searching, is more efficient and more likely to produce the most comprehensive results. *See* George L. Paul & Jason R. Baron, *Information Inflation: Can the Legal System Adapt?,* 13 RICH. J.L. & TECH. 10 (2007).

My blog on *Information Explosion and the Future of Litigation* in Chapter One reviews this article in depth. Concept searching is just one of many cutting-edge ideas discussed in Paul & Baron's article, one that I have not discussed before. It pertains to promising new software technology that may allow for far better searching than simple keyword matching. But before I go into that, a little more about the interesting *Disability Rights Council* case itself.

The defendant Transit Authority configured its Groupwise email system so that all emails were automatically deleted after only 60 days. The only exception was when a user went to the trouble to archive a particular email. These archived emails were not deleted. In practice, few Transit Authority users ever bothered to archive any of their emails, and so after 60 days almost all were deleted. Nothing wrong with such a system in principle, but the problem here is that it was not suspended when suit was filed. In fact, the defendant continued to destroy all emails for more than two years after the suit was filed—"remarkable" and "indefensible," according to the court.

The opinion begins by noting that the "safe harbor" of new Rule 37(f) was not intended to apply to this situation, at least insofar as the emails destroyed after the suit was filed are concerned. The rule requires "routine" and "good faith" operation of a system. Although it was routine destruction, the court did not consider it to have been carried out in good faith after suit was filed. That is primarily because we are talking about the destruction of live ESI—namely, email still on the system and not on backup tapes. A preservation hold should have prevented this. After the live emails are destroyed, the only place to find them is on the backup tapes. For that reason, among others, even though the court agreed with the defendant that the backup tapes were not reasonably accessible under Rule 26(b)(2)(B), it nevertheless found good cause to order that they be restored and searched at the defendant's expense. To hold other-

wise would reward the defendant for destroying relevant emails, leaving
the backup tapes as the only remaining source of the evidence. The court
rejected this at *8 with a humorous touch:

> While the newly amended Federal Rules of Civil Procedure ini-
> tially relieve a party from producing electronically stored infor-
> mation that is not reasonably accessible because of undue bur-
> den and cost, I am anything but certain that I should permit a
> party who has failed to preserve accessible information without
> cause to then complain about the inaccessibility of the only elec-
> tronically stored information that remains. It reminds me too
> much of Leo Kosten's definition of chutzpah: "that quality en-
> shrined in a man who, having killed his mother and his father,
> throws himself on the mercy of the court because he is an or-
> phan."

Judge Facciola rejected the defendant's undue burden and expense
inaccessibility arguments and granted the plaintiff's motion to compel.
He then ordered the parties to meet and discuss how the backup tapes
will be restored and, as mentioned, how to search the restored emails,
either through keyword, as plaintiff had proposed, or via concept search,
as the judge suggested might be more efficient.

Of course, keyword searches have been around for decades and are
familiar to any lawyer who has ever done computerized legal research.
You can, for instance, run a computer search of hundreds of thousands
of emails to find all emails that include one or more of a list of names, as
the plaintiff here proposed. This takes just seconds but can produce a
high percentage of irrelevant emails—ones that include the names but
have nothing to do with the case. It can also omit many relevant emails
that just do not happen to include the keywords you *guessed* a relevant
email would have (or perhaps included them but misspelled them, a problem not often found with computerized legal research).

The use of complex Boolean connectors (such as directives that one
term be within the same paragraph as another, or that an otherwise included email be excluded if it contains certain terms, such as "but not")
can sometimes improve on the search. So too can the use of so-called

"fuzzy logic." But even with the use of Boolean and fuzzy logic, these keyword searches, also known as "theoretical set" searches, are still largely guessing games. In practice, they often fail to uncover too many otherwise relevant emails without significantly reducing the irrelevant ones.

A search that creates a lot of noise—that is, one that produces too many irrelevant emails—can create very significant time and expense burdens on all the parties, but especially on the producing party. If, for instance, the search creates a list of 100,000 emails, the producing party will have to review all of these emails for possibly privileged communication before production. This is a very expensive undertaking. The clawback agreements provide some comfort, but until privilege law changes, everyone agrees that clawbacks do not obviate the need for a privilege review. It is also expensive for the receiving party, who has to spend time and money to review the irrelevant emails.

Therefore, if there is a better search method than keyword that can produce a high percentage of relevant hits and thus less noise and less wasted time for review, it is to the advantage of all parties to use it. Moreover, it is a potentially very valuable product. There are several software vendors who have created alternative search algorithms to keyword searches. All are sometimes lumped together as "concept searches." They use a variety of methods, involving such things as contextual usages, algebraic modeling and probabilistic categories. The exact formulas are usually kept secret by the software vendors for obvious reasons, but most are willing and prepared to provide expert testimony in court if necessary to justify the legitimacy of their search methods.

Paul & Baron's article at pages 26-27 summarizes the existing state of information retrieval science in a "mind-boggling" but eloquent manner:

> However, broadly speaking, information retrieval methods fall into three broad classes: set-theoretic (Boolean strings, supplemented by fuzzy search capabilities), algebraic (premised on the mathematical idea that the meaning of a document can be derived from the constituent terms in a document, and thus weighting retrieval by the proximity of a document's terms in the form of two or higher dimensional maps, as in vector space modeling), and probabilistic (using language models and Bayesian belief networks, the

latter of which involves making educated inferences about the relevance of future documents based on prior experience in reviewing documents in a given collection).

In thinking about retrieval problems, one can also supplement all of these methods by focusing on the language used by the creators of the records, which will include using taxonomies and ontologies, essentially synonyms of words and relevant classes of related words to be developed and built in at the front end of a search process to better refine the search, and to maximize both recall and precision. In contrast to strict set-based Boolean techniques, the above algebraic and probabilistic categories of search methods are often broadly termed under various forms of the heading "concept searching."

There are several vendors who offer such marvels, and it is a growing field. This is definitely something that you should look into before agreeing to simple keyword searches, especially if the volume of ESI to be reviewed is high. The concept search software fees are probably too expensive for small-volume or low-dollar cases, but they could be a huge money saver for a larger case. Most vendors will provide you with an idea of the price break point based on the byte size of the ESI. Of course, the decision should be based on more than the number of megabytes of data involved. You will also want to consider the case subject matter, the amount of money involved, and the importance and complexity of issues.

BLOG READER COMMENT

It is noteworthy—and welcome—that a court is acknowledging that there are better technologies out there than keyword search. . . . Technologies such as these are truly changing investigation, legal discovery and regulatory compliance, allowing a level of transparency never before contemplated in the legal system. In the face of federal law changes, this form of technology is something every corporate environment should consider as the software becomes more accessible and, arguably, essential.

WHEN SHOULD YOU SEARCH FOR DELETED FILES?

The district court in Tampa recently issued a discovery order involving deleted email. *Wells v. Xpedx*, 2007 WL 1200955 (M.D. Fla., April 23, 2007). The case raises the interesting issue of when you should search for deleted files, and when you should not because they are "not reasonably accessible" under Rule 20(b)(2)(B). In my view, this often hinges on whether or not the files were "double-deleted." The order in question granted the plaintiff's motion to compel a 30(b)(6) deposition of the defendant's IT representative but deferred ruling on the companion motion to compel production of deleted emails because there was an inadequate factual record to decide the issues, and for that reason the deposition was allowed.

The dispute began after defendant Xpedx produced its written records retention policy manual. The manual showed that Xpedx had introduced a new email retention policy in 2003 wherein emails were automatically deleted after 90 days unless they were specifically designated for retention. The manual explained that if an email was not designated for retention, then after 90 days the automatically deleted email could not be restored without consent of the company's legal or tax department.

Not surprisingly, the plaintiff sought a deposition to learn what this policy meant and specifically to explain the procedures for retrieval. Further, the plaintiff hoped to discover in that deposition if any emails were destroyed relating to his claims. The plaintiff also sought to compel production of all Xpedx emails related to his claims. During the hearing on the motion to compel, the plaintiff narrowed the scope of production request to any emails containing his name, Joseph Wells, in certain time periods in 2002 and 2003 by seven Xpedx employees.

The defendant opposed the deposition, arguing that it was unnecessary because it had already produced its records retention manual. This argument was not persuasive in view of the vagaries of the wording of the policy, especially since it provided for restoration of deleted emails after approval by the law or tax department. Further, a plaintiff in this position is normally permitted to inquire whether the actual practices of the company comply with the policy directives. The defendant opposed the motion to compel because it argued that *all* relevant emails had already been produced. This is a very dangerous argument, as many defendants in the past have discovered, including UBS Warburg and Morgan Stanley. After you make that kind of representation to a court, it tends to look bad if additional relevant emails are later discovered, no matter how innocent and understandable the mistake. Finally, the defendant argued that if there had been any other emails that were not specifically preserved, they would have already been deleted under its 90-day policy. Magistrate Judge Elizabeth Jenkins, who is well known in Central Florida for her good analysis and pragmatic results, begins her discussion of the email discovery dispute by noting that:

> Deleted emails are, in most cases, not irretrievably lost. *Discoverability of Electronic Data Under the Proposed Amendments to the Federal Rules of Civil Procedure: How Effective Are Proposed Protections for "Not Reasonably Accessible" Data?* 83 N.C. L. Rev. 984, 988 (2005). Deleted emails may remain on a computer hard drive, servers or retained on back-up tapes. *Id.* at 988-90.

So far, so good; but then Magistrate Jenkins goes on to hold that: "The producing party has the obligation to search available electronic systems for deleted emails and files. *Peskoff v. Faber*, No. 04-526 (HHK/JMF), 2007 U.S. Dist. LEXIS 11623, at *13 (D. D.C., Feb. 21, 2007)." There I think the opinion goes too far, or should have been better qualified and clarified to apply only to "once-deleted" emails and files, and to exclude "double-deleted" and slack space information.

First, let me explain what I mean by these terms. As most everyone by now knows, if an email in Outlook is deleted, it is not erased; it is just moved into another Outlook folder for deleted files. It is still readily accessible. Any user can change his mind and restore the email. But if an email in the Deleted Folder is deleted again—in other words, "double-deleted"—then it is no longer indexed in Outlook and no longer readily accessible (unless, as one observant reader pointed out, it is still within a double-deleted email retention period set by the Outlook administrator; usually only seven days). Of course, double-deleted files are not truly deleted yet on the hard drive, but the file markers pointing to it and identifying it have been omitted (or, in some cases, will soon be omitted). These double-deleted files still exist; they have not been erased; but, in most cases at least, they are no longer easy to find and retrieve. They exist as part of the hard drive's slack space, the unorganized areas on the hard drive that the operating system pretends are empty and available. It requires some level of forensic examination to try to locate and retrieve them. Sometimes that may be relatively easy to do, sometimes not. In fact, in some circumstances, double-deleted emails may be impossible to retrieve from the hard drive (be it server or PC) because they have been written over by other files.

The same process applies to "once-deleted" files in the Windows operating system environment. They are not removed from an index of files when first deleted; they are simply moved to a new location, the Trash directory. But if the Trash is emptied, the pointers for that file are removed, and the disk space the file occupies is considered to be available for writing new data.

So, back to the opinion, which states that a party has an "obligation to search available electronic systems for deleted emails and files." If the phrase "deleted emails and files" is construed to mean "once-deleted," then I agree completely. These files are readily accessible. But in most circumstances it would be wrong to try to stretch the meaning of this holding to also include files that have been "double-deleted," and thus require forensics to locate and restore or resort to a search of backup tapes.

In my opinion, and that of most commentators and courts that have squarely faced the issue, the obligation to search for "double-deleted" files should not arise *in all circumstances.* This duty should only arise in certain special circumstances, where, for instance, there is evidence that highly relevant emails have been double-deleted, and therefore there is good cause to go to the extra time and expense inherent in a forensic examination for such files. Most courts do not require an extraordinary search for deleted files unless special circumstances are shown to warrant such extraordinary efforts. See, for example, *Hedenburg v. Aramark American Food Services,* 2007 U.S. Dist. LEXIS 3443 (W.D. Wash., Jan. 17, 2007), discussed in my blog *Forensic Fishing Expedition Rejected* in the "New Technologies" chapter.

The facts alleged by Xpedx to oppose the deposition of its 30(b)(6) IT representative suggest that the emails sought were all "double-deleted." But it is not clear, and, in fact, that was the plaintiff's whole point. His motion to compel the deposition sought discovery of the facts surrounding these emails and deletion. The deposition should reveal whether or not the emails in question were once deleted and thus reasonably accessible under Rule 26(b)(2)(B). If they were twice-deleted, and if under Xpedx's computer system that means that they are not readily accessible, as I suspect, then an entirely different legal analysis applies to determine whether the plaintiff is entitled to compel production of these emails. If they are not reasonably accessible under Rule 26(b)(2)(B), the plaintiff would be required to make a showing of good cause sufficient to justify the extra expense of location and recovery of the double-deleted emails.

For these reasons, Judge Jenkins's order compelling the deposition makes good sense, especially when you consider she limited the deposition to four hours and permitted it to occur by phone. It also makes sense to defer ruling on the motion to compel. This motion cannot be properly determined without evidence as to whether the deleted emails are reasonably accessible, and if not, whether the facts and circumstances show good cause for them to be produced anyway, perhaps with cost sharing, as suggested by Rule 26(b)(2)(B).

BLOG READER COMMENT

But if an email in the Deleted Folder is deleted again, in other words "double-deleted," then it is no longer indexed in Outlook, and no longer readily accessible. — Just because the message is "double deleted" in Outlook does not mean that it is not accessible. I'm assuming that you are using Outlook against the Exchange server. The majority of Exchange admins will set a "Deleted Items Recovery" retention period. This means that even if the email message is "doubled deleted," it can be recovered from the Exchange server. If the user is using Outlook 2003, the email message may be recovered from its cache. (see http://www.computer performance.co.uk/exchange2003/exchange2003 _recovery_deleted_item.htm)

Other email systems have similar functionality. The GroupWise client, for example, has had a desktop cache feature for years.

I've never heard the term "double deleted," and I suggest that it is a poor term because it infers that the message is truly gone (outside of the message fragments hanging out on the hard drive).

RALPH'S REPLY

You make a point that even a double-deleted email may still be easily restored in some circumstances where it is still within an administrator-set time recovery period. This basically means that a temporary pointer still exists for the file; even though it has been double-deleted by the user, the computer delays the second deletion for a set time as a type of backup in case the fickle user changes his mind. For purposes of simplification in this blog, I assumed this second fail-safe did not apply. But I admit the example you provide could be an exception, depending on time frames, to the proposed general rule of when an email is not "reasonably accessible." Note I say in accord with the rules, not "reasonably" accessible. I do not say "not accessible." Yes, It can be accessed—most everything can be restored and accessed—but at what costs and time or effort? That is where the reasonability component comes in.

The term "deleted" itself implies that the message or file is truly gone. That should be your true gripe, and blame Microsoft, not me. The modifier "double" is easy to understand and does not imply true erasure, just that retrieval may—I would say usually is (depending only on the limited backup time quirk you mentioned)—more difficult to restore.

SHOULD YOU SAVE AND SEARCH INTERNET CACHE?

Does the duty to preserve potential evidence require you to search and save your Internet cache? A district court in Pennsylvania recently addressed this issue and, indirectly at least, said no. *Healthcare Advocates, Inc. v. Harding, Earley, Follmer & Frailey,* 2007 WL 2085358 (E.D. Pa., June 20, 2007). The court held that the defendant's automatic and unwitting deletion of cache files did not constitute spoliation and did not warrant any kind of sanctions, even though potential evidence had been destroyed. The court did not squarely hold there was no duty to preserve Internet cache per se; instead, it held that in this case, the destruction of evidence contained in the temporary cache files was accidental and was not prejudicial, so no sanctions were appropriate.

of this page, Explorer allows you to specify how many days to save "the list of websites you have visited." This is not a full cache of the Web sites visited, just a list of the addresses.

The above summary is not intended to be complete; there can be many variances, depending on browser software and other configurations. In addition, other files are cached when the Internet is used, especially for email, where copies of all emails sent and received may be stored on disk in other locations depending on the software utilized.

Back to the *Healthcare Advocates* case: it involves some very interesting facts, albeit a far-fetched complaint. I do not have all of the facts underlying this lawsuit (some are filed under seal), but from the court's opinion, it appears that this is little more than a sour grapes type of spite suit. To understand this case, you have to understand the one that preceded it. In that case, the same plaintiff, Healthcare Advocates Inc. (hereinafter HAI), sued a competitor for trademark infringement and trade secret misappropriation. HAI lost this case, in large part because of excellent lawyering by the defendant's attorneys, the law firm of Harding, Earley, Follmer & Frailey (hereinafter Harding). Harding used the very handy service found at *archive.org* called the "Wayback Machine." If you are not already familiar with this service, I suggest you check it out. The archive's Wayback Machine allows you to view prior versions of Web sites that have been saved by archive.org. It is a very good way to determine what trademarks and other materials were actually in use by a company in the past. Harding used it to find out what HAI's Web site had looked like in the past. The old versions of HAI's site proved to be very powerful evidence, and HAI lost its case by summary judgment.

So what did HAI do next? It filed yet another lawsuit, this time against its competitor's attorneys, the Harding law firm. Unbelievable, but true! What horrible thing was the law firm alleged to have done? HAI accused the firm of violating its copyrights by "hacking" the Wayback Machine to download old versions of its Web site! Never mind that there was no credible evidence of hacking, and Harding only used the archive.org repository the way any good law firm would: to find the truth and defend their client.

To add insult to injury, HAI tried to dress up this second case with charges of spoliation based solely on Harding's failure to preserve the Internet cache files of the old HAI Web pages. HAI even had the audacity to argue that the law firm should have stopped using their computers altogether so that the temporary cache files would not be lost. In their losing cross-motion for summary judgment, HAI's lawyers got carried away again and argued that Harding's failure to stop using their computers to preserve the Internet cache was such a bad act of spoliation that it "shocks the conscience." Here is the understated way the court responded to these arguments:

> The Harding firm had no reason to anticipate that using a public website to view images of another public website would subject them to a civil lawsuit containing allegations of hacking.
>
> Thus, the failure to immediately remove computers that the firm used every day, when they had no reason to believe that their actions would subject them to a lawsuit for "hacking," is not an action that shocks the conscience.

I am pleased to report that this second suit has been dismissed too, again by summary judgment. Obviously, it was a "fair use" by the law firm of the discontinued copyrighted Web pages, and not even close to a copyright infringement. Moreover, the spoliation charges were just as bad. It is not clear from the opinion, but I think that Harding knew full well about Internet cache files. It is, after all, a group of Philadelphia lawyers specializing in intellectual property law. Harding simply chose not to preserve these files because there was no reason to save them. They had already printed out all of the files and used them in evidence. Why should they also preserve the cache? The whole suit by HAI is just plain bizarre. The court agreed, and found no prejudice at all to the plaintiff from the deletion of the cache files.

There are two more things that surprise me about this case. First, Internet Archive, the nonprofit group behind www.archive.org, was joined as a defendant to the case. That is not surprising, given HAI's obvious litigiousness, but it is hard to understand why the archive group settled with HAI instead of moving for summary judgment. Apparently, they were concerned because their exclusion policy,[3] which supposedly allows any Web site to opt-out of the archive and its Wayback Machine through use of a robots.txt file,[4] did not work in this case. HAI had, for

---

3. http://www.archive.org/about/faqs.php.
4. http://www.archive.org/about/exclude.php.

obvious reasons, tried to have its site excluded from the archive before it filed the first lawsuit against its competitor, but the exclusion failed and Harding was able to get at the truth. The terms of the settlement are confidential, so we can only speculate why Internet Archive preferred to settle. The second surprising thing is that the Harding firm provided HAI with a forensic image of their computer's hard drives. It impressed the court that Harding had nothing to hide, but one wonders why they bothered.

Postscript: After this decision, the defendant moved for an award of $161,461.90 in attorney's fees. The court denied the motion, concluding somewhat surprisingly that the plaintiff's case was not frivolous, but awarding costs of $9,348.60. *Healthcare Advocates, Inc. v. Harding, Earley, Follmer & Frailey,* 2007 WL 2684016 (E.D. Pa., Sept. 10, 2007).

NONCHALANT REVIEW CAUSES WAIVER OF ATTORNEY-CLIENT PRIVILEGE

Legal counsel's "nonchalant review" of electronic records acted to waive the attorney-client privilege as to four inadvertently disclosed emails. *Gragg v. International Management Group (UK) Inc.,* 2007 WL 1074894 (N.D. N.Y., April 2007). The following facts were found to constitute a failure to take reasonable precautions to prevent inadvertent disclosure of privileged materials, justifying a waiver as to those documents. Defendant's outside counsel asked in-house counsel "to prepare and produce to him all documents relative to the proposed project." In-house counsel in turn delegated the task to a "non-attorney assistant." The assistant "then prepared and compiled in electronic format a disk containing those materials and forwarded them directly to defendant's outside counsel who in turn, without first reviewing the documents, sent the disk to plaintiff's attorney."

Defendants argued that it was reasonable for their outside counsel to rely upon in-house counsel to make the requisite privilege review and to assume that it had been accomplished before the disk was sent to him. The court was not inclined to accept this argument because there had been no discussions between the outside counsel and the non-attorney assistant who supposedly did the review, or the in-house counsel who supposedly supervised the assistant's activities. The court considered these facts and concluded:

> Given the significance of the attorney-client privilege and the potential consequences associated with a waiver of that privilege, this nonchalance leads me to conclude that reasonable precautions were not taken to prevent the disclosure of privileged materials.

*Id. at *6.* As a secondary factor, the court noted that there were only 200 emails on the CD-ROM produced, and so the task of review prior to production "would not have been particularly onerous."

Unfortunately for the defendants, the four emails in question contained litigation strategy discussions. The emails did not address the underlying transaction. The defendants argued that for this reason it was especially unfair to find a waiver based on inadvertent disclosure. The court considered fairness, but concluded that this argument was "far overshadowed by the defendant's failure to implement reasonable measures to avoid inadvertent disclosure."

The plaintiff argued that the waiver should be a full subject matter waiver, "opening the door to full disclosure including deposition of defendants' litigation attorneys." Obviously, the plaintiff was overreaching on that one, and so the court instead accepted the defendants' argument for a "more reasoned, limited waiver" extending only to the materials at issue.

Still, the plaintiff pressed to take the deposition of the defendants' in-house counsel based on attorney-client privilege waiver. The court rejected this request as an attempt to further probe defense counsel for information on their litigation strategy. The court would not permit such an attorney deposition, even if limited to the four emails where the privilege had been waived, noting that such questioning would inevitably go beyond the four emails and invade privileged attorney work product.

LOUIS VUITTON SANCTIONED FOR SANDBAGGING A SEARCH

An adverse inference and fees sanction was entered against the plaintiff, Louis Vuitton (LV), in *Louis Vuitton Malletier v. Dooney & Bourke, Inc.*,

2006 U.S. Dist. LEXIS 87096 (S.D. N.Y. Nov. 30, 2006). LV, the well-
known maker of expensive leather bags and accessories, is supposedly
the most counterfeited brand in fashion history.[5] It is no wonder they
often sue for trademark infringement.

They may still win this case, but they are off to a very shaky start.
The magistrate's 50-page order sanctioned LV for misleading the court
about e-discovery. The court also disapproved of LV's refusal to use
outside experts to help LV's IT personnel extract emails from its computer database.

In the words of Magistrate Dolinger, who seemed quite upset:

> There is no question that LV has failed to comply with its dis-
> covery obligations, misled its adversary and the court, and flouted
> a court order. . . . That application triggered a representation by
> LV that it had undertaken an appropriate search for customer
> communications about S-lock products and had no such com-
> munications. It is evident that this representation was false, and
> in the absence of any explanation by LV for this misstatement,
> we have no reason to infer that it was other than knowingly false.

So once again we see a party burned for saying it searched and had
no emails when later events show this to be false. Nothing new here. But
the court's criticism of LV's reliance solely on its IT department is unusual and no doubt will be heavily cited by vendors in the future.

The affidavit by LV's IT employee swore to the difficulties they had
in searching the emails maintained in their Kana Oracle database. In
footnote 10, the reason alleged for this difficulty was, in the words of
LV's IT employee:

> [T]he e-mails are stored in a raw format which includes both
> HTML-formatted e-mails as well as e-mails with foreign-lan-
> guage encoding.

LV went on to argue that they would have had to hire experts in both
Oracle and Lotus Notes to properly search and extract the emails. The

---

5. http://en.wikipedia.org/wiki/Louis_Vuitton.

ironic footnote 10 recounts how LV considered the $15,000 price tag for those expert services to be too expensive, and so they tried to do it themselves. As you might imagine, the work they did was deficient in the magistrate's view, not to mention late. Ultimately, LV was hammered with an adverse inference and ordered to pay the defendant's reasonable fees, which, it is safe to assume, will make the $15,000 quote seem cheap.

Postscript: The magistrate later awarded the defendant $30,220 in fees. *Louis Vuitton Malletier v. Dooney & Bourke, Inc.*, 2007 WL 1284013 (S.D. N.Y. April 24, 2007).

ARE GOVERNMENT EMPLOYEE EMAILS ALWAYS A PUBLIC RECORD?

Are all emails stored on government computers automatically public records subject to disclosure under state and federal Freedom of Information Acts (FOIA)? In a sharply divided opinion, the Arkansas Supreme Court recently said no. *Pulaski County v. Arkansas Democrat-Gazette, Inc.*, No.07-669 (Ark., July 20, 2007).[6] The majority held that it all depends upon the content of the email, not its location in a government computer. Some emails written and received by government employees are personal in nature and have no "substantial nexus" with government activities. For that reason, they are not considered public records and thus are not subject to disclosure under the Freedom of Information Act.

In this case, a newspaper requested all emails from a management employee of the county who had recently been arrested and accused of embezzling $42,000. Before his arrest and the FOIA request, the employee deleted many of his emails—deleted but not fully erased, and certainly not gone. A computer tech for the county was able to restore them. The county then produced most of his emails but withheld others that were "of a highly personal and private nature." They were emails to and from a woman with whom the accused manager was having an extramarital affair. This woman also happened to work for a company that was a vendor of the county.

---

6. http://ralphlosey.files.wordpress.com/2007/08/case-arkansas publicrecords.pdf.

The newspaper naturally wanted to see these emails and argued they must be presumed to be public records, because they were written by a government employee during working hours on government computers, and were located and maintained on government computers. The trial court agreed and held that:

> Because the emails at issue are maintained in a public office and are maintained by public employees within the scope of their employment, they are presumed to be public records according to the Freedom of Information Act.

> Based on the facts before this Court, the emails at issue are public records because they involve a business relationship of the County and are a record of the performance or lack of performance of official functions by Ron Quillin during the times when he was an employee of Pulaski County.

The county, and the girlfriend who intervened in the suit as "Jane Doe," asked the court to look at the withheld emails *in camera*. They wanted the judge to determine whether the emails in fact pertained to county business, as he presumed, or were instead just "monkey business" with no relevance to any kind of county activities, legal or illegal. The judge declined to do so, and entered an injunction giving the county 24 hours to turn over the emails to the newspaper. The county and Jane Doe immediately appealed.

The Arkansas Supreme Court reversed and remanded the case back for the judge to read the letters *in camera*. The appeals court noted that since the trial court had declined to review the emails, they were not in the record, and so it was impossible to "discern whether some emails at issue were purely business emails while other emails were purely personal in nature." The Arkansas Supreme Court held that:

> [I]n this particular case, it is necessary to conduct an *in camera* review of the e-mails to discern whether these e-mails relate solely to personal matters or whether they reflect a substantial nexus with Pulaski County's activities, thereby classifying them

as public records. *See Griffis, supra.* Both parties agree that the definition of "public records" is content-driven. The only way to determine the content of the e-mails is to examine them. In this case, no court has reviewed the e-mails at issue. Absent such a review, we have no record on which we can determine the nature and content of the requested documents.

Rather than relying on Pulaski County or Appellee to make the determination of whether the documents are public, it is necessary to have a neutral court make this decision. *See Griffis, supra.* Accordingly, we remand this case to the circuit court with instruction to conduct an *in camera* review to determine if these e-mails "constitute a record of the performance of official functions that are or should be carried out by a public official or employee" thereby making them "public records" pursuant to the FOIA. We ask the circuit court to address this matter forthwith.

The majority decision followed other courts around the country that use content-driven analysis to determine when a document is a public record for purposes of FOIA-type laws, both state and federal. *State v. City of Clearwater*, 863 So. 2d 149, 154 (Fla. 2003) (a case involving personal emails where the Florida Supreme Court held that it is absurd to classify household bills or notes about personal conversations as public records simply because they are located in a government office); *Denver Publishing Co. v. Board of County Commissioners*, 121 P.3d 190 (Colo. 2005) (a case involving sexually explicit and romantic emails where the Colorado Supreme Court held that "[a]n analysis of the messages based solely on the context in which they were created, without an explanation of the content of the messages, is insufficient to determine whether the messages are public records"); *Griffis v. Pinal County*, 215 Ariz. 1, 152 P.3d 418 at 421-22 (Ariz. 2007) (The Arizona Supreme Court held that it was absurd to apply FOIA to all email, even private email, just because it is in government computers; purpose of FOIA is to "open government activity to public scrutiny, not to disclose information about private citizens."); *Bureau of National Affairs, Inc. v. United States Department of Justice*, 742 F.2d 1484, 1486 (D.C. Cir. 1984) (personal appointment materials, such as calendars and daily agendas, are not agency records under the FOIA).

The newspaper and three justices of the Arkansas Supreme Court did not agree with this result. They thought the emails must be presumed to be public records, as in the words of dissenting Justice Tom Glaze:

> [T]he personal and professional relationship between Quillin and Doe may have affected or influenced Quillin's performance and his expenditures of county funds; the communications between them constitute a record of the performance or lack of performance of official functions carried out by a public official or employee.
>
> Under the plain language of the statute, Quillin's emails were presumed public records, because information is not exempt from the FOIA unless specifically exempted under the Act or some other statute.
>
> Because the records at issue are plainly public records, and neither the County nor Doe has rebutted the statutory presumption compelling that result, remanding the matter for an *in camera* examination is unwarranted and a complete waste of time. The majority's position unnecessarily prolongs the process and increases the expenses of a FOIA request, and in so doing needlessly infringes upon a citizen's right to obtain public records. The Freedom of Information Act simply does not require an *in camera* inspection in these circumstances, and instructing the lower court to perform such a review thwarts the rights of Arkansas' citizens to access records that, simply stated, should be public.

The minority dissenters were not concerned with the privacy rights of "Jane Doe" as to the deleted emails forensically restored from her lover's computer. They apparently felt her rights were outweighed by the public's right to know, and the newspaper's right to sell sensational stories of the romantic life of county employees accused of theft. Besides, dissenting Justice Annabelle Imber reasoned that all of these emails would eventually be made public anyway in the subsequent (she assumed) prosecution of the accused.

YAHOO REPLACES SEX AS THE #1 SEARCH QUERY ON GOOGLE

According to the Dailey Domainer, a news Web site that covers issues relating to Internet domains, "Yahoo" has recently replaced "Sex" as the most popular search term on Google.[7] Odd, isn't it? The most popular search term on Google is now the name of its biggest search competitor, Yahoo—more popular even than sex.

Sex is, by the way, very popular as a search term in all languages and countries, but according to Google Trends,[8] which monitors (and saves) every Google search ever made (but does not track or identify the persons or computers who make searches), "sex" as a search term is most popular in cities in India and Turkey. The city of Chennai, India (a/k/a Madras), today holds the record for the city making the most search requests for "sex." In fact, all of the top ten cities for this term are in Turkey and India.

---

7. http://www.dailydomainer.com/200742-why-yahoo-is-the-1-search-term-on-google-and-why-website-owners-shouldnt-rely-on-search-engines-alone.html.

8. http://www.google.com/trends?q=sex.

1. bebo
2. myspace
3. world cup
4. metacafe
5. radioblog
6. wikipedia
7. video
8. rebelde
9. mininova
10. wiki

Count yourself very tuned in, albeit immature, if you knew them all.

Google also reports the top search terms in a host of subcategories, including News, Current Events, Entertainment, and Sports. Google reports the Zeitgeist monthly, as well as annually, to help keep track of what people want.[12]

According to Google's record of every Google search made in 2006, the most popular "News" searches were:

1. paris hilton
2. orlando bloom
3. cancer
4. podcasting
5. hurricane katrina
6. bankruptcy
7. martina hingis
8. autism
9. 2006 NFL draft
10. celebrity big brother 2006

Hmmm . . . kind of makes you wonder about the emotional and intellectual maturity of the online community.

---

12. http://www.google.com/intl/en/press/zeitgeist.html.

New Technologies 7

This chapter explores some of the new technologies that have a significant impact upon e-discovery. Here we will examine such things as RAM, hash algorithms, computer maps, thumb drives, de-duplication, email guffaws, forensic exams, and data repositories.

DISTRICT COURT IN LOS ANGELES DECIDES COMPUTER RAM MEMORY MUST BE PRESERVED AND PRODUCED

Most lawyers and judges do not have a technical background, and judges and parties are reluctant to refer cases to special masters who do. As a result, courts often do not fully understand the technological issues in a case and do not grasp the many subtleties new technologies pose to a just and fair decision. This is not surprising, since their education typically only comes from competing experts in the case before them, each of whom swears that the other is wrong. This is a trend that will continue as long as innovation and new technologies continue. One hopes it will be countered by the more frequent use of special masters, but I do not see that happening yet.

This struggle came to the fore in a recent case in Los Angeles district court that rocked the e-discovery world by holding, for the first time, that the contents of a computer's Random Access Memory (RAM) are discoverable. *Columbia Pictures Indus-tries v. Bunnell*, Case No. CV 06-1093 (FMC(JCx)) (Doc. No. 176).[1] The order dated May 29, 2007, by Magistrate Judge Jacqueline Chooljian was entered in a copyright infringement case against the owners of the popular media search engine *TorrentSpy*.[2] The order has been highly criticized by computer experts and e-discovery lawyers alike for greatly expanding the legal duty to preserve and produce electronic data to the most elusive and transitory of information, that held only in a computer's RAM chips.

Many responded by asserting that this is a rogue decision and, if not reversed on appeal, could force companies and individuals to store and produce vast amounts of data that would otherwise exist only tempo-rarily on their computer's RAM hardware. Ken Withers, a director of The Sedona Conference, was quoted by CNET News[3] as stating that he feared the judge's decision may mean a "tremendous expansion" of the scope of discovery in civil litigation, creating yet another "weapon of mass discovery." By this, he means a discovery burden that could be tremendously expensive to meet and thus could be exploited by plain-tiffs and defendants alike to force the settlement of a dispute to avoid that expense.

Commentators all seem to agree that in most circumstances, if not all, it would be prohibitively burdensome for a person or company to try to preserve and produce the transitory contents of computer memory. The burdensomeness would derive not only from the expense, but also from the disruptive actions required to comply.

Moreover, many contend that an order requiring the production of RAM data necessarily requires a party to create computer records where none before existed. This goes against a fundamental legal precept that a party is required to produce only documents and electronically stored information that have already been created and stored. A party to litiga-tion is never required to generate and create new documents and infor-mation just to satisfy the curiosity of the opposing party. As Ken With-ers stated in the CNET article:

---

1. http://i.i.com.com/cnwk.1d/pdf/ne/2007/Torrentspy.pdf
2. http://www.torrentspy.com//
3. http://news.com.com/TorrentSpy+ruling+a+weapon+of+mass+discovery/2100-1030_3-6190900.html/

There's never been a requirement that (defendants) must create documents that they wouldn't ordinarily maintain for the purpose of satisfying some (plaintiff's) discovery requests.

Judge Chooljian considered this argument but rejected it, because in her view, the information already *existed* in RAM. She concluded that the defendants were not required to create new data, merely to transfer it to permanent form and preserve it.

Withers and others think the order is ill-conceived, in part because it is based on a misunderstanding of technology and computer memory. Computer memory RAM files are temporary files that are created by the computer for operational efficiency. Computer memory like this is, by nature, information designed only for very temporary storage in the memory chips. It is quickly overwritten and is always purged—literally disappears—when a computer is turned off. (Unpowered RAM chips contain no information of any kind.) The same CNET News article also quotes Dean McCarron, principal analyst at Mercury Research, as saying:

RAM is the working storage of a computer and designed to be impermanent. Potentially your RAM is being modified up to several billions of times a second. The judge's order simply reveals to me a lack of technical understanding.

In short, RAM memory is temporary and transitory, and leaves no trace or record. Still, a computer system can be designed so that information temporarily stored in RAM is copied onto a hard drive or flash memory storage, where it then becomes fixed.

Before this decision, most e-discovery attorneys I know thought that only information fixed on a storage device, such as a hard drive, flash memory or Read Only Memory (ROM) (which are permanent), CD, DVD, etc., would be considered "stored" and thus discoverable under the new rules as "Electronically *Stored* Information." See, for example, Rule 34 and commentary contained in the Appendix. This decision broadens the meaning of "stored" to include the temporary holding of information in a volatile memory chip.

The opinion concedes that computer RAM memory has never previously been adjudicated to be Electronically Stored Information (ESI) under new Rule 34. For that reason, Judge Chooljian declined to impose sanctions on defendants for failing to preserve and produce the RAM ESI in the past, but she did order its preservation and production going forward. Although the opinion concedes it is a case of first impression for construction of Rule 34, Judge Chooljian argues that her conclusion is compelled by the unique circumstances of this case and prior Ninth Circuit law, primarily *MAI Systems Corp. v. Peak Computer, Inc.*, 991 F.2d 511, 518-519 (9th Cir. 1993). The *MAI Systems* case is well known for its holding that the copying of software into RAM memory is equivalent to "affixing" it in a tangible medium for purposes of copyright law, where "fixed" is a term of art. Judge Chooljian reasoned that if information in RAM was sufficiently *fixed* to constitute a copyright infringement, then it was sufficiently *fixed* for purposes of discoverability as electronically *stored* information. Many think that is mixing apples with oranges, and Judge Chooljian simply does not grasp the subtleties involved.

In this case, the memory at issue was stored for up to six hours, but no longer, on the server for TorrentSpy. The RAM contained information as to what Web pages were downloaded, when, by whom, and other similar information. That is called a webserver log. For this particular kind of RAM data, it is not technically difficult to set up a Web server so that the log is transferred from RAM to a permanently stored file on the hard drive. Many sites are set up to do this. These Web site owners want to keep track of who visits their site, which pages are the most popular, etc.

But TorrentSpy did not set up its system that way. It did not want to have any tracking information on its users, and thus put this privacy guaranty in its user agreement. The plaintiffs in this case, Columbia Pictures Industries, et al., were frustrated by the fact that the defendants did not know who its users were and, in fact, did not want to know. The plaintiffs claimed that TorrentSpy's users were illegally downloading their copyrighted materials—their movies, music and television shows—based on information they obtained from TorrentSpy's site. The plaintiffs claimed that TorrentSpy set up its computer systems with RAM anonymity on purpose to encourage its users to steal the plaintiffs' copyrighted materials without fear of being caught.

Note that the plaintiffs do not claim that their copyrighted materials are stored on TorrentSpy's web, or that TorrentSpy's users downloaded the files from TorrentSpy. It appears to be undisputed that TorrentSpy "only" provides information on where these materials are located—usually on the computers of individuals around the world. The plaintiffs sued the TorrentSpy owners, and not the individuals who illegally downloaded the files or those who supplied the files (for free), based on theories of vicarious copyright infringement, contributory infringement, and inducement.

Here, in my view, is where an old legal axiom comes in: "Bad facts make bad law." The facts in this case are extraordinary. The judge was convinced that the webserver logs were essential to the plaintiffs' case. This is a highly unusual situation. Moreover, the tone of the opinion suggests that the judge thinks the plaintiffs are likely to prevail if they obtain these logs, that it will enable them to prove their infringement conspiracy theories. The plaintiffs have successfully argued that the defendants were hiding this crucial evidence in their RAM, and that this was an essential part of their conspiracy to steal their intellectual property.

Further, the defendants were, according to Judge Chooljian, unable to demonstrate that it would be "unduly burdensome" for them to transfer all of the webserver logs on an ongoing basis from RAM to hard drive, and thereafter to preserve and produce this evidence. The court was referring to the burden of proof placed on a party opposing discovery under new Rule 26(b)(2)(B). Under this rule, ESI is not discoverable if the party opposing discovery can show that it is "not reasonably accessible because of undue burden or cost." The defendants failed to prove undue burden or costs. If they had, then under Rule 26(b)(2)(B) the burden of proof would have shifted to the plaintiffs to provide good cause that the "not reasonably accessible" information be produced anyway. Apparently, the defendants failed because the court went entirely with the plaintiffs' expert and rejected the defendants' contrary testimony. This certainly shows the importance of credible experts.

Judge Chooljian appeared to recognize that her decision would be controversial and took some pains to note that it was not intended to serve as precedent for the routine discovery of computer memory in other cases. Her position is explained in footnote 31 at page 31 of the 35-page opinion:

> The court emphasizes that its ruling should not be read to require litigants in all cases to preserve and produce electronically stored information that is temporarily stored only in RAM. The court's decision in this case to require the retention and production of data which otherwise would be temporarily stored only in RAM is based in significant part on the nature of this case, the key and potentially dispositive nature of the Server Log Data which would otherwise be unavailable, and defendants' failure to provide what this court views as credible evidence of undue burden and cost.

The magistrate's discovery ruling was appealed to the district court judge, Florence-Marie Cooper. *Amici* appeared and advanced "weapon of mass discovery"-type arguments, urging the court not to interpret ESI to include RAM. They were all rejected, and Judge Cooper upheld the magistrate's non-final order. *Columbia Pictures Industries v. Bunnell*, Case No. CV 06-1093 (FMC(JCx)) (Doc. No. 254).[4]

Judge Cooper begins by identifying the issue:

> At the heart of Defendants' Motion for Review is the following question of first impression: is the information held in a computer's random access memory (RAM) "electronically stored information" under Federal Rule of Procedure 34?

The court then characterizes the defendants' arguments as unsupported rule construction:

> Defendants and *amici* seek to engraft on the definition of "stored" an additional requirement, that the information be not just stored, but stored "for later retrieval." They argue that "electronically stored information" cannot include information held in RAM because the period of storage, which may be as much as six

---

4. http://ralphlosey.files.wordpress.com/2007/08/case-columbiaaffirmed-o1183212.pdf

hours, is too temporary. The Court finds this interpretation of "stored" unsupported by the text of the Rule, the accompanying commentary of its drafters, or Ninth Circuit precedent involving RAM. The Court holds that data stored in RAM, however temporarily, is electronically stored information subject to discovery under the circumstances of the instant case.

The court found support for its broad interpretation of ESI in the Rules Advisory Committee Commentary to the 2006 Amendments to Rule 34 (included in the Appendix). The commentary explained that ESI was not specifically defined so that Rule 34(a)(1) would be construed "expansively" to "cover all current types of computer-based information, and flexible enough to encompass future changes and developments."

The court clearly rejected defendants' and *amici's* position that ESI requires a degree of permanency not found in RAM. The "ephemeral" argument was again rejected on the basis of the old *Mai Systems* case, which concerned whether RAM could be copyrighted, not whether it could be discovered. The court did not address the fact that some RAM lasts far less than a second. The opinion only states that in this case the time period "may be *as much as* six hours."

The argument of *amici* that this ruling creates bad precedent, opening a floodgate of e-discovery, was rejected by simply amplifying the magistrate's footnote that this ruling pertains only to this case.

In response to *amici's* concerns over the potentially devastating impact of this decision on the record-keeping obligations of businesses and individuals, the Court notes that this decision does not impose an additional burden on any website operator or party outside of this case. It simply requires that the defendants in this case, as part of this litigation, *after* the issuance of a court order, and following a careful evaluation of the burden to these defendants of preserving and producing the specific information requested in light of its relevance and the lack of other available means to obtain it, begin preserving and subsequently produce a particular subset of the data in RAM under Defendants' control.

Many contend that this does not really address the core concerns of *amici* and demonstrates instead a kind of irresponsible naiveté as to the potential impact of the decision. They contend that the general refusal in this opinion to put any kind of time duration requirement on "information" before it is considered "electronically stored information" under the rules subjects everyone to the possibility of extremely expensive preservation, search, and production of ephemeral information.

It is interesting to note how the defendant website responded to this order. Recall that the effective date of the injunction was postponed until this district court review of the magistrate's order. The injunction required that all user activities recorded in the webserver log be transferred from RAM and produced to the plaintiffs. Just after the district court order was entered but before the injunction could go into effect, the defendants excluded all users whose computers are identified as located in the United States. When you try to use the site to search for any media, you are directed to a page[5] with the following message:

TorrentSpy Acts to Protect Privacy

Sorry, but because you are located in the USA you cannot use the search features of the Torrentspy.com website. Torrentspy's decision to stop accepting US visitors was NOT compelled by any Court but rather an uncertain legal climate in the U.S. regarding user privacy and an apparent tension between U.S. and European Union privacy laws.

We hope you understand and will take the opportunity to visit one of these other fine websites: (omitted)

It will now be interesting to see how the plaintiffs and court react to this development. The latest district court order notes that the defendants' webservers are now located in the Netherlands. This was the basis of additional arguments that defendants made to reverse the magistrate's orders. They construed Netherlands law as prohibiting the production of the server log data as required by the injunction. The district court disagreed with the defendants' interpretation of Dutch law. Further, the court

---

5. http://www.torrentspy.com/US_Privacy.asp

held that even if foreign law did prohibit the disclosure, that would "not deprive an American court of the power to order a party subject to its jurisdiction to produce evidence even though the act of production may violate that [foreign]statute." It appears that this case is far from over, and the defendants have already promised to appeal to the Ninth Circuit.

HASH

51FEC3B6FCB1E7D5465575BED5DCDC1B8897AF5A

Computer hash is an encryption algorithm that forms the mathematical foundation of e-discovery. Hash provides a method for incontrovertible electronic document authentication and identification, and for that reason every e-discovery lawyer should know something about hash.

Hashing generates a unique alphanumeric value to identify a particular computer file, group of files, or even an entire hard drive. As an example, the hash of an animated GIFF file is shown above. The unique alphanumeric of a computer file is called its "hash value." Hash is also known in mathematical parlance as the "condensed representation" or "message digest" of the original message. It is more popularly known today as a "digital fingerprint." Hash is the bedrock of e-discovery because the digital fingerprint guarantees the authenticity of data and protects it against alteration, either negligent or intentional. Hash also allows for the identification of particular files and the easy filtration of duplicate documents, a process called "de-duplication" that is essential to all e-discovery document processing.

Technically, hashing is based on the substitution and transposition of data by various mathematical formulas. Thus the process is called "hashing," in the linguistic sense of "to chop and mix." The hash value is commonly represented as a short string of random-looking letters and numbers, which are actually binary data written in hexadecimal notation. Hash is commonly called a file's "fingerprint" because it represents its absolute uniqueness.

If two computer files are identical, then they will have the same hash value. Even if the files have a different name, if their contents are exactly the same, they will have the same hash. This allows for easy identification and elimination of redundant documents, the mentioned de-duplication process. But if you so much as change a single comma in a 1,000-page text, it will have a completely different hash number from the original. There are no similarities in the hash numbers based on similarities in the files. Each number is unique. That is how the math in all hashing works.

Many kinds of effective hash formulas have been invented, but two are in wide use today: the SHA-1 and MD5 algorithms. Both are very effective, in that mathematicians conjecture that it is "computationally infeasible" for two different files to produce the same hash value. That is why hashing is commonly employed in data transmissions to verify that the integrity of a file has been maintained in transmission. If you hash the file received and it does not produce the same hash value, then it has been corrupted, and at least one byte is not the same as the original. It is a guaranteed way of verifying the integrity of an electronic file.

Software to run both the SHA-1 and MD5 hash analysis of files is widely available, easy to use, and free. I use a HashTab Shell Extension to Windows, available at Beeblebrox.org.[6] The hash value of any file can be instantly determined, regardless of the type of electronic file, including graphics. For instance, the hash values of a Word document I am working on now are:

MD5: 588BCBD1845342C10D9BBD1C23294459
SHA-1: C24AE3125BFDBCE01A27FDDA21B3A7E83FAFF69E

If I change only one comma in this multipage document, all else remaining the same, the hash values are now:

MD5: 5F0266C4C326B9A1EF9E39CB78C352DC
SHA-1: 4C37FC6257556E954E90755DEE5DB8CDA8D76710

Although the two files have only this minute difference, there are no similarities in these hash values, proving that hashing will detect even the slightest file alteration.

Hashing can also be used to determine when fields or segments within files are identical, even though the entire file might be quite different. This requires special software, which is commonly available from many e-discovery vendors, for a price. This software allows you to hash only portions of a file. Thus, for instance, you can hash only the body of an

---

6. http://www.beeblebrox.org/software.php

email, the actual message, to determine whether it is identical with another email, even when the "reference" or the "to" and "from" fields are different. This allows for an important filtering process called "near deduplication."

Hash is my favorite e-discovery technology. I became fascinated by its great potential as a safeguard for electronic evidence in the future, and ended up reading and experimenting with this algorithm in depth. Ultimately, I wrote a 44-page law review article on the subject: *HASH: the New Bates Stamp,* 12 J. TECH. L. & POL'Y 1 (June 2007). Here I discuss hash at length and review just about every case that mentions it. The article has 174 footnotes to provide reference to almost everything on the subject that might be of interest to a lawyer or others in the e-discovery field. As the title suggests, I make a specific proposal in the article for the adoption of an e-discovery file naming protocol based on hash to replace the paper-oriented Bates stamp. You will also find a full copy of the article online at my blog: http://ralphlosey.wordpress.com/.

LAW REVIEW ARTICLE PUBLISHED ON THE MATHEMATICS UNDERLYING E-DISCOVERY: *HASH: THE NEW BATES STAMP*

As many people know, especially my friends in the e-discovery world, I am a real hash enthusiast. No, not the corned beef variety, and certainly not the illicit drug; I am talking about the mathematical wonder underlying e-discovery, the hash algorithm. In September 2006, I had a brainstorm on how to use the hash algorithm to replace the old-fashioned Bates stamp as a document organization and identification protocol for electronic documents. The hash stamp can not only identify all computer documents like the 100-year-old Bates stamp does for paper documents, it can also authenticate them and reveal if there have been any alterations from the original. This would serve to protect the legal profession from the ever-present danger of fraudulent manipulation of the ephemeral bits and bytes that now make up electronic evidence.

The authentication properties of hash have long been known and used in e-discovery, but there was a serious problem with also using hash as a naming protocol: hash values are way too long. An MD5 hash is 32 alphanumeric values, and the SHA 1 has 40 places. Here is an example of the shorter MD-5 hash:

5F0266C4C326B9A1EF9E39CB78C352DC

That is too long a number for humans to use to identify an electronic document. For that reason, hash was deemed impractical for use as a document-naming protocol, even though it had tremendous advantages in authenticity control. That is where I got the "big idea" last September to truncate the hash values and just use the first three and last three places. Under that system, the above hash becomes the much more manageable:

5F0.2DC

As explained further in the article, the six-place identification alone avoids collisions 98.6% of the time. In the rare event they match, the full hash values can be consulted. Credit goes to computer expert Bill Speros, an attorney consulting in litigation technology and data management, for doing the statistical study to confirm my intuition.

I got excited about the idea and wanted to promote it. I decided the best way to do this was to take my time, thoroughly research hash and related subjects, and then write a law review article on the subject. The article would not only advocate this naming idea, but also fully explain what hash was all about, and how hashing was far superior to Bates stamping for the identification and organization of large volumes of ESI.

Once I got into this project, it took on a life of its own. Over the next nine months, I ended up reading every legal case and article that in any way pertained to hash and hundreds more outside of the law on how hash was being used by scientists, spies, and mathematicians in a variety of technologies. Before I knew it, I was up to a 44-page article with 174 footnotes. Countless evenings and weekends were lost in the process. My golf handicap soared. But this near-magical encryption formula called hash can be very addicting!

I am relieved to say that the writing part of the project concluded with the article's publication in the *Journal of Technology Law & Policy* (June 2007). The article advocates the truncated hash-naming protocol, sets forth all of the case law in this area, and explains what hash is all about without actually going into the mathematics. I readily admit that is beyond me.

Although the *Journal* citation refers to this publication as the mid-year June issue, in fact it was not printed until mid-August. The law students at the University of Florida School of Law running the publication did a good job of cite checking, proofing, and otherwise making me look good. So too did my son, Adam, who is enrolled as a law student there and helped me with research. Other articles in the *Journal* on patents and copyrights are interesting too. You can order a copy of the full *Journal* for $15 by an email to mail@wshein.com or by snail mail to the *Journal of Technology Law & Policy* at 218 Bruton Geer, Gainesville, FL 32611. Help the students out and buy a full copy.

But if you just want to see the article right now, without the full law review formatting, you can download the article only—*HASH: The New Bates Stamp*[7]—which I have uploaded here as a PDF file. You may copy and forward this article to others, as long as you do so without charge and do not alter the contents.

I had never written a law review article before. So I was quite surprised when, after publication, a law professor explained to me that my task was not complete. After an article is published, it is standard procedure to then send copies of the article to as many people as possible who might be interested in the subject, and especially to judges who might cite to it. Based on this advice, I sent out a couple of hundred copies of the article to experts in the field of e-discovery, including practitioners like myself, academicians, judges, and e-discovery vendors.

I did so in the hope that they would not only use the article as a reference for all things hash, but also to promote the new naming protocol. I strongly believe that the use of hash is imperative to the future integrity of the legal system as we move from paper to electronic bits and bytes. Digital evidence is so easy to change, both intentionally and by mistake, that the legal profession needs hash to protect the authenticity of electronic evidence. The simple Bates stamp is not up to the task.

Many who received the article expressed thanks, and many vendors especially have already expressed interest in using the protocol. The first response I received, within just two days of mailing, was

---

7. http://ralphlosey.files.wordpress.com/2007/09/hasharticlelosey.pdf

from Judge John L. Carroll, dean and professor of law, Cumberland School of Law, Samford University. Although I do not know Judge Carroll, I had heard of him, and even heard him speak once on e-discovery. To my knowledge, he is now the preeminent academic authority on e-discovery. I was surprised that he responded so quickly, and even more pleased to read what he had to say. First he thanked me for the article and then said:

> I teach a seminar in e-discovery and evidence law and I am making it required reading for my students. It is really thoughtful and very well done.

I was proud to receive that and several other positive responses. But I did learn, secondhand, that at least one recipient of the article suspected commercial motives on my part and criticized the mailing for that reason. I doubt they actually read the article; they just saw a letter from a lawyer sending an article and assumed it was another pesky "white paper" pointing to some software or consulting services. But the truth is, I sell no hash software and offer no hash or hashing services. Also, as far as I know, no lawyer has ever been hired because of his or her knowledge of a mathematical formula, much less an encryption formula like hash. I just think that "truncated hash marking" is a good idea whose time has come. I really believe that lawyers need to use hash to protect the integrity of electronic evidence, and thus protect the whole system of justice in the electronic age. A bit grandiose perhaps, but that is the motivation, not the delusional hope of some commercial gain.

But this is America, and a few people apparently suspect there must be a hidden profit agenda here somewhere (not that there is anything wrong with that), so let me set the record straight. This is strictly an open source, freeware proposal. Although I appear to be the first to think of the hash truncation idea, I do not want to delay or hinder anyone else from using it. Quite the contrary; simply put, anyone can use the idea and proposal anywhere and any time they want, and they owe me nothing. I have nothing to sell.

As I explained in footnote 161 of the hash article, a few patent attorneys I talked to while researching the proposal suggested that my idea might be patentable, but I had no interest in going that route. Commercial applications and ownership claims would only interfere with and slow down the application of this idea and delay its implementation. My interest then and now is to freely disseminate and dedicate this idea into the public domain.

Someday there may well be commercial exploitations of the idea by others, which is fine. If so, this will be by e-discovery vendors and other IT document management experts with far greater technical expertise and experience in large-volume document management than I.

Anyway, this article has been a labor of love over the past year. I urge you to please download and read a copy,[8] and share it with any colleagues who might be interested.

BLOG READER COMMENTS

First off, great job on the article, Ralph. I do have a couple questions / points in response to your paper. You talk about hashing files to prove that they haven't changed. . . . For certain types of electronic archives—take Microsoft Outlook PSTs as an example—a hash of the PST file (really a container) is useful in authenticating the PST itself, but not later on when you choose to produce a single email with attachments.

Now, you could say that you should then hash the individual email and attachments . . . but the challenge here is what should you hash? You could save the email as an MSG file and hash it . . . but unfortunately, when you save an MSG file, the bits and bytes are different each time—so the same document will have a different hash. You could save a representation of the file such as RTF or HTML, but different vendors or different software versions could result in different outputs.

This can also be challenging if you must produce reviewed documents back in a PST format. Creating a PST that is a subset will obviously alter its hash, and then you also won't have a great way of referring to individual messages. Any thoughts on how your ideas can be applied to archives, specifically email archive formats?

---

8. http://ralphlosey.files.wordpress.com/2007/09/hasharticlelosey.pdf

Lastly . . . for files that contain references to other files—say, HTML and images—changing any file names will break referential integrity. This could also be the case for email archives where changing the file name of an attachment would require changing the content of the parent to keep the relationship intact. Thoughts?

RALPH RESPONDS

Greg, that is an excellent issue you raise regarding the individual emails in a PST file, part of the larger problem of unpacking and identifying files in an archive. I suppose a set of standards will need to be developed and followed by all vendors for uniformity of hash values; i.e., how to go about saving an email from the PST to MSG so that there is as little alteration as possible, and the same hash is reproduced.

I do not have a particular suggestion at this time on a standard for this. Does anyone else have any thoughts on this? Suggestions? Over time I am confident that people with greater technical expertise and experience than I have will be able to figure out good solutions to these and other problems.

COMPUTER MAPS

Computer maps are key tools in any e-discovery lawyer's arsenal. They are used to document with graphics and words the location and flow of an organization's electronically stored information. Computer maps can serve as a complete catalogue of an organization's electronic records. They are usually prepared to show networks of computers and related ESI storage devices. In a large organization, there may be separate maps for each department or business division. These maps are important, because they facilitate the clear communication of a party's inventory of ESI and the complexity of the systems involved. They provide an excellent visual summary that can be used with opposing counsel and the court to demonstrate the reasonableness of your client's preservation and collection efforts.

A computer map is more than just a complicated picture, as shown below. To be useful in the legal context, it should include detailed indexes and explanations that provide a complete inventory of an organization's ESI. The map will not only show locations but also provide information as to the types, amounts, and accessibility of ESI; the metadata associations; and the frequency, difficulties, and costs associated with restoration of inaccessible ESI such as backup tapes and the recycling schedules for these tapes. The maps should also identify the various types of CPUs and media on which the ESI is processed and stored. Ideally, the maps will provide the names and titles of all users, their actual retention and filing practices, and the external and mobile ESI devices they may use, such as laptops, thumb drives, phones, and home computers. This kind of mapping greatly facilitates the preparation and implementation of effective litigation holds and the collection, analysis, and production of ESI.

The process of mapping out where ESI is stored is much more involved than taking inventories and drawing diagrams of computers. It necessarily involves extensive interviews and analysis. Still, the diagrams—the visual maps—are, in my opinion, a key final end component of the mapping process. These visual tools are invaluable demonstrative aids to help an attorney and judge understand where and how electronic evidence is stored. This understanding allows attorneys to better supervise the preservation and search for this evidence and judges to evaluate the reasonableness of these efforts. The maps also facilitate the interviews and depositions of IT and records management personnel, as well as the key witnesses involved in a dispute. A good computer map also helps a lawyer and testifying experts to explain to the court the problems inherent in electronic evidence preservation and production, and why certain types of ESI are inaccessible and should be protected from discovery.

The complexity of today's computer networks can be readily seen by these computer maps, including the one shown below that Microsoft submitted to the Federal Rules Committee in 2004 when they were preparing the new rules on e-discovery.

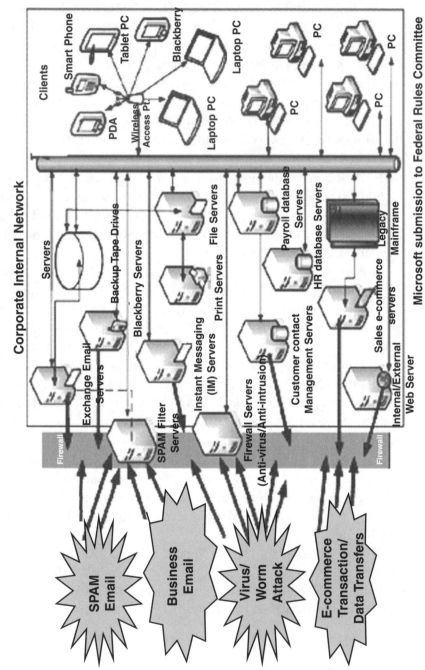

Client Server Architecture Diagram

Although most think this map illustrates a complex system, it frequently is far worse. Most medium-size to large companies have much more complex systems in each office. The beautifully drawn map on the following page shows the network of Purdue University's engineering department.[9] This network is closer in size to that of a typical office in a medium to large corporation. Since most large companies have dozens, if not hundreds, of such offices throughout the world, and the computer networks of each are usually interconnected, the total network map would be huge. It certainly could not be drawn in the kind of detail you see below. But if you imagine the map below multiplied a dozen or hundred times over, then you will get a pretty good idea of the challenges faced by e-discovery attorneys today.

9. https://engineering.purdue.edu/ECN/AboutUs/NetMaps/Maps/

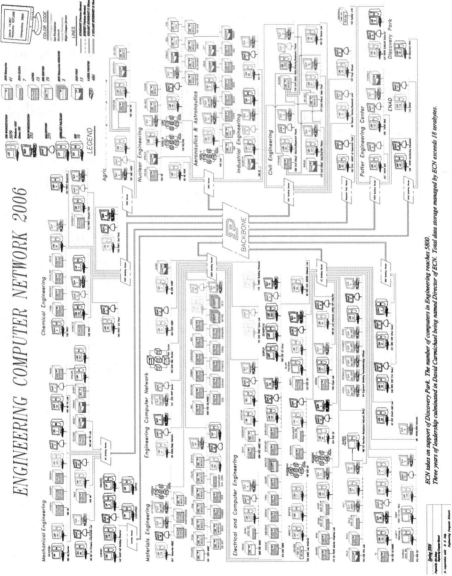

ENGINEERING COMPUTER NETWORK 2006

ECN takes on support of Discovery Park. The number of computers in Engineering reaches 5800.
Three years of leadership culminated in David Carmichael being named Director of ECN. Total data storage managed by ECN exceeds 18 terabytes.

THUMB DRIVE USED TO MISAPPROPRIATE TRADE SECRETS; 'DE-DUPLICATION' USED AS AN EXCUSE FOR NOT RETURNING ALL ESI TAKEN

An e-discovery injunction case in Houston has an interesting fact scenario involving an employee's illegal use of a "thumb drive" to misappropriate an employer's trade secrets. *Anadarko Petroleum Corp. v. Davis*, 2006 WL 3837518 (S.D. Tex., Dec. 28, 2006). It also involves what is, to my knowledge, the first successful use of a "de-duplication" defense.

A thumb drive, as you probably know, is a USB device for the flash memory storage of data. They can hold vast amounts of data in a small, hard-to-detect device. These flash memory drives are usually the size of a thumb, and thus the name.

De-duplication is the process of identifying electronically stored information files that are exactly the same and eliminating them from production. This filtration process is an important tool of efficiency in e-discovery collection and review because it is not uncommon for a computer to contain multiple copies of the same file. De-duplication is made possible though a unique mathematical algorithm, as explained in the *Hash* blog.

The employee defendant in this case, Billy Davis, used his thumb drive to take confidential information from his employer's computers on his last day of work. Davis then transferred the proprietary ESI onto his personal laptop, and from there onto his new employer's desktop computer and then onto its servers. When the former employer found out what had happened, it filed suit against both Davis and his new employer for, among other things, theft of trade secrets, and sent out a preservation letter. The three-page letter demanded the preservation of all data on the employee's and new employer's computers, including even deleted files. The employee received the letter and consulted an attorney on what to do. The attorney advised Davis to transfer all of the files back onto the thumb drive, so that he could return them—so far so good. But the attorney also supposedly advised Davis to delete all of the files on his new employer's servers and desktop and his laptop. This is the exact opposite of the preservation demanded by the plaintiff's letter (and the law).

At an emergency preliminary injunction hearing a few days after the suit was filed, Davis turned over the thumb drive to the plaintiff with the representation that this constituted all of the ESI taken. Davis also testified that he had deleted all other copies of the ESI. The defendants, both Davis and his new employer, also consented to an injunction requiring the return and full accounting of all ESI taken and a forensic examination of all of their computers to verify that all of the ESI had in fact been removed as represented.

At a later temporary injunction hearing, the plaintiff asked to have the injunction strengthened to, among other things, prohibit Davis's employment and competition on the basis of his alleged bad-faith theft of trade secrets. The judge rejected that because: 1) he believed Davis's testimony that he had never actually used the data, at least not the confidential parts; and 2) he believed Davis's testimony that he had returned all of the ESI taken. There was considerable reason to doubt that later assertion, because the plaintiff's forensic examination of its computers showed that 7.21 gigabytes had been downloaded by Davis, whereas the thumb drive returned contained only 1.14 gigabytes of data. Davis, who must have been a very credible witness, explained the missing 5 gigabytes of data with the explanation that he had eliminated all redundant, duplicate files when he loaded them back onto his thumb drive. In other words, he successfully employed a "de-duplication" defense, the first I have ever heard of in a case like this. The judge found the testimony credible and denied the injunction requested, but left the issue open upon completion of the forensic examination. Obviously, if the exam seriously impeaches Davis's testimony and shows the de-duplication excuse was a sham, the court will reconsider its ruling.

The plaintiff also sought sanctions for the spoliation that occurred in disregard of the preservation letter. The judge agreed that the ESI should not have been deleted, that it should have been preserved, but denied sanctions because he found no credible evidence of bad-faith destruction of evidence, at least not yet. In the words of the court:

> This is an unusual set of facts for a spoliation claim. In most cases in which a party asserts that the alteration or deletion of electronically stored information amounts to spoliation, the party wanted that information to remain available in the form that it

was maintained by the other party. In this case, by contrast, Anadarko specifically asked Davis and GeoSouthern to return all the electronically stored confidential and proprietary information Davis had taken from Anadarko and to prevent anyone at GeoSouthern from accessing or using that information. That request makes it necessary for GeoSouthern to make the Anadarko information Davis had placed on the GeoSouthern computer system inaccessible, which requires that such information be deleted. The second aspect that distinguishes this case from the typical spoliation case is that at the same time Davis deleted the information from the GeoSouthern computers and his own laptop, he testified that he placed the information on a thumb drive and delivered it to Anadarko. In most spoliation cases, when information is deleted, no other record of its existence is created, much less promptly produced to the other side. The third aspect that distinguishes this case is that Davis and GeoSouthern have agreed to allow Anadarko to conduct a forensic audit of their computer systems to ensure that no proprietary or confidential Anadarko information remains accessible and to ensure that Davis returned all that he took. . . . .

Anadarko asserts that it is harmed because it cannot verify that all the information Davis took has in fact been returned. Their contention is supported, at least superficially, by the discrepancy in the volume of electronically stored information Davis took compared to what he returned. . . . .

The alleged spoliation currently does not support the issuance of a broader injunction than is presently in place to protect Anadarko's trade secrets from unauthorized use or disclosure. Because the parties' computer experts are still conducting their forensic examination of GeoSouthern's and Davis's computers, the record necessary to rule on the spoliation motion and determine whether and what sanction should issue is incomplete. This court orders Anadarko to supplement its motion for sanctions within 30 days of the completion of the forensic analysis.

TOP CORPORATE OFFICERS CONTINUE TO WRITE EMBARRASSING EMAILS

Everyone in e-discovery knows that people writing emails will, much like kids on the old Art Linkletter show, "say the darndest things." Of course, instant messaging is even worse, as Congressman Mark Foley showed in his instant messages to congressional pages. Private emails and instant messages have a way of becoming public, especially when discovered in litigation and introduced into evidence at trial. There are hundreds of examples of this from past lawsuits, and the phenomenon has been widely discussed since the late 1990s. See, for instance, the scholarly observation by Kenneth Withers in his 1999 article, *Is Digital Different?*:[10]

> Much is made in the electronic discovery literature of the informal, revealing, and often embarrassing nature of e-mail. E-mail is considered the window into the corporate soul, and is therefore a highly sensitive area for discovery. The literature also notes a deep disconnect between individuals' perceptions of e-mail as private and transitory, and the reality of e-mail as a permanent and discoverable corporate record, although only rarely does the literature suggest that this phenomenon has been studied empirically in any other discipline, such as linguistics or psychology.

Since this has been known for a long time, you might think that, at the very least, senior management in businesses that are frequently involved in litigation would watch what they say. But you would be wrong, and that is why email continues to be the best field for "smoking gun" searches.

Microsoft, which was one of the first companies to be burned by email in its antitrust cases, offers the latest proof that senior corporate officers continue to say the darndest things in email. The point is proven by a horde of once-private Microsoft emails that were introduced into evidence at a trial in Iowa in December 2006. The case was a class action styled *Comes et al. v. Microsoft*. After the emails were admitted into

---

10.   http://www.kenwithers.com/articles/bileta/index.htm

evidence, the plaintiff's counsel, Roxanne Conlin,[11] a former U.S. Attorney, posted them on the Internet, just as she had done with all of the other evidence in this case. (**Note:** When this blog was originally written, all of these materials were published on the Web, and some were linked here. A few weeks later the case settled and all of the materials were removed as part of the settlement.)

Plaintiff's Exhibit 7,264, which Bates marking indicates was originally produced on June 15, 2005, and marked "Confidential," was circulated on the Net[12] as soon as it was admitted into evidence, even before the plaintiff's counsel posted it. It is an email dated January 7, 2004, from Jim Allchin to Bill Gates and Steve Ballmer. The subject line of the email is "losing our way." Mr. Allchin's email to his bosses begins like this:

> This is a rant. I'm sorry. I am not sure how the company lost sight of what matters to our customers (both business and home) the most, but in my view we lost our way.

The second paragraph of the email gets worse and he says: "*I would buy a Mac today if I was not working at Microsoft.*" This is the line that is now being widely quoted. Today Mr. Allchin is not working for Microsoft; he retired from Microsoft[13] on the day Vista was released, January 30, 2007. According to Microsoft, "Allchin was a member of the Senior Leadership Team, responsible for developing Microsoft's core direction along with Steve Ballmer and Bill Gates." No news yet on what kind of computer Jim Allchin is now using, but he did leave a humorous blog[14] on what his life after Microsoft is like.

In fairness to Microsoft and Jim Allchin, this is the reply that Jim posted on the Windows Vista Team blog when this story first broke on December 12, 2006:

---

11.   http://www.roxanneconlin.com/CM/Custom/TOCAboutRoxanne.asp

12.   *See, e.*g., http://www.groklaw.net/article.php?story=2006120913511
3443

13.   http://www.microsoft.com/presspass/exec/jim/default.mspx.

14.   http://windowsvistablog.com/blogs/windowsvista/archive/2007/01/31/
what-comes-next.aspx.

In the email, I made a comment for effect about buying a Mac if I was not working at Microsoft. Taken out of context, this comment could be confusing. Let me set the record straight:

This email is nearly 3 years old, and I was being purposefully dramatic in order to drive home a point. . . .

The spirit of being self-critical continues to flourish at Microsoft. Within Microsoft everyone considers it their duty to always put their convictions and our product quality ahead of everything else. That was the intent of my mail to Bill and Steve, and I consider it a great example of how this company can focus and do what's right for customers.

It is interesting to note that the evidence admitted was not the original email from Jim Allchin to Bill Gates, but rather an email from Allchin to another Microsoft executive, Eric Rudder,[15] sharing his private email to Gates. Again, this shows the danger of email and other electronic documents; they can easily be circulated to others without your knowledge and turn up later as part of an email chain. Email has an amazing way of surviving and appearing later, sometimes where you least expect it, despite all efforts.

FORENSIC FISHING EXPEDITION REJECTED

An employer recently tried to use e-discovery to its advantage, but did so in an unconvincing fashion, and failed. The district court rejected its motion to compel the forensic examination of the plaintiff's home computer as a mere "fishing expedition." *Hedenburg v. Aramark American Food Services*, 2007 U.S. Dist. LEXIS 3443 (W.D. Wash., Jan. 17, 2007).

Hedenburg is an employment discrimination case in which the employer sought a mirror image of the employee's personal computers. A mirror image is an exact byte-by-byte copy of an entire hard drive, including deleted files and slack space. The employer wanted the cloned drives to be examined by a computer forensic expert serving as a special

---

15. http://www.microsoft.com/presspass/exec/ericr/default.mspx. Eric Rudder still works for Microsoft. He has reported directly to Bill Gates since September 2005, when promoted to Senior Vice President leading what Microsoft calls the "Developer and Platform Evangelism division."

master. The forensic master would then prepare a report with built-in privacy safeguards to protect the employee's nonresponsive and privileged ESI along the lines set forth in *Playboy Enterprises v. Welles,* 60 F. Supp. 2d 1050 (S.D. Cal. 1999). *Playboy* is the landmark case in the area of forced forensic exams of computers.

The employer argued that forensic examinations of employees' personal computers are common in employment cases, and it was needed here to search for personal emails and Web posts that might be inconsistent with the plaintiff's claims of sexual discrimination and emotional distress. The defendant, however, failed to establish valid factual grounds for the intrusive discovery requested, and so the court easily distinguished the cases the defendant relied upon, including the seminal *Playboy* case. *Playboy* was distinguished because the defendant in *Hedenburg* made no convincing showing that the forensic exam was likely to uncover discoverable evidence, and further failed to show any kind of nexus between the claim and the computers the defendant sought to examine.

The three cases which the employer here chose to argue were interpreted and rejected by the court as follows:

> The common thread of these cases is that a thorough search of an adversary's computer is sometimes permitted where the contents of the computer go to the heart of the case. This court has in other cases permitted mirror image searches of computers where, for example, one party demonstrates the likelihood that trade secrets were forwarded to or sent by it. Here, the central claims in the case are wholly unrelated to the contents of plaintiff's computer. Defendant is hoping blindly to find something useful in its impeachment of the plaintiff.

Blind hope may be a fisherman's credo, but it is never good grounds for a forensic examination. The court concluded with an analogy of a paper files search equivalent of the electronic discovery here requested:

> Plaintiff has responded that she has made a diligent search for her computer files, and contends that she does not have additional information. Defendant essentially seeks a search war-

rant to confirm that Plaintiff has not memorialized statements contrary to her testimony in this case. If the issue related instead to a lost paper diary, the court would not permit the Defendant to search the plaintiff's property to ensure that her search was complete. The Motion to Compel is DENIED.

WORLD'S LARGEST DATA REPOSITORIES

Business Intelligence Lowdown purports to rank the "Top 10 Largest Databases in the World" as of February 2007.[16] Of course, no one really knows who has the largest repositories of data, including both paper and electronically stored information, but this article presents an educated guess. It differs substantially from a prior 2005 list of the largest databases compiled by the Winter Corporation.[17] The 2005 list ranked Yahoo[18] number one, whereas it is not even included in the 2007 list. Some of the other choices are surprising too, especially their guess as to who has the most ESI—essentially, the "weatherman." Their supposition that the tenth largest repository is the venerable Library of Congress is also almost certainly wrong, since it is generally accepted that most large corporations today have far more information stored in their computers than the equivalent of the entire paper and digital collection of the library. Still, it helps to include the library because it provides a benchmark to try to grasp the enormity of the other repositories.

Here are the rankings in reverse order, with a little detail provided on the tenth and first places:

10. Library of Congress.[19] According to the Library of Congress, it is the largest library in the world, with more than 130 million items on approximately 530 miles of bookshelves. The collections include more than 29 million books and other printed materials, 2.7 million recordings, 12 million photographs, 4.8 mil-

16. http://www.businessintelligencelowdown.com/2007/02/top_10_largest_.html
17. http://www.wintercorp.com/VLDB/2005_TopTen_Survey/2005TopTenWinners.pdf
18. http://www.yahoo.com/.
19. http://www.loc.gov/index.html.

lion maps, and 58 million manuscripts. The library expands at a rate of 10,000 items per day.[20]

9. The Central Intelligence Agency.
8. Amazon.
7. You Tube.
6. Choice Point.
5. Sprint.
4. Google.
3. AT&T.
2. National Energy Research Scientific Computing Center.[21]
1. The World Data Centre for Climate (WDCC).[22] This ESI is located on one of the world's largest supercomputers, owned by the Max Planck Institute for Meteorology and German Climate Computing Centre. The WDCC has 220 terabytes of data[23] readily accessible on the Web, including information on climate research and anticipated climatic trends, as well as 110 terabytes' (or 24,500 DVDs') worth of climate simulation data. In addition, 6 petabytes' worth of additional information are stored on magnetic tapes for easy access. According to *Business Intelligence Lowdown,* 6 petabytes is three times the amount of *all* the U.S. academic research libraries' contents combined.

20. http://en.wikipedia.org/wiki/Library_of_congress.
21. http://www.nersc.gov/.
22. http://www.ngdc.noaa.gov/wdc/.
23. http://www.mad.zmaw.de/fileadmin/extern/PI_Linux_DB_final.pdf.

Appendix

NEW RULE 16, FEDERAL RULES OF CIVIL PROCEDURE
Rule 16: Pretrial Conferences; Scheduling; Management.
(b) Scheduling and Planning. Except in categories of actions exempted by district court rule as inappropriate, the district judge, or a magistrate judge when authorized by district court rule, shall, after receiving the report from the parties under Rule 26(f) or after consulting with the attorneys for the parties and any unrepresented parties by a scheduling conference, telephone, mail, or other suitable means, enter a scheduling order that limits the time

(1) to join other parties and to amend the pleadings;

(2) to file motions; and

(3) to complete discovery.

The scheduling order may also include:

(4) modifications of the times for disclosures under Rules 26(a) and 26(e)(1) and of the extent of discovery to be permitted;

(5) provisions for disclosure or discovery of electronically stored information;

(6) any agreements the parties reach for asserting claims of privilege or protection as trial-preparation material after production;

(7) the date or dates for conferences before trial, a final pretrial conference, and trial; and

(8) any other matters appropriate in the circumstances of the case.

The order shall issue as soon as possible but in any event within 90 days after the appearance of a defendant and within 120 days after the complaint has been served on a defendant. A schedule shall not be modified except upon a showing of good cause and by leave of the district judge or, when authorized by local rule, by a magistrate judge.

Rules Committee Commentary to Rule 16

The amendment to Rule 16(b) is designed to alert the court to the possible need to address the handling of discovery of electronically stored information early in the litigation if such discovery is expected to occur. Rule 26(f) is amended to direct the parties to discuss discovery of electronically stored information if such discovery is contemplated in the action. Form 35 is amended to call for a report to the court about the results of this discussion. In many instances, the court's involvement early in the litigation will help avoid difficulties that might otherwise arise.

Rule 16(b) is also amended to include among the topics that may be addressed in the scheduling order any agreements that the parties reach to facilitate discovery by minimizing the risk of waiver of privilege or work-product protection. Rule 26(f) is amended to add to the discovery plan the parties' proposal for the court to enter a case-management or other order adopting such an agreement. The parties may agree to various arrangements. For example, they may agree to initial provision of requested materials without waiver of privilege or protection to enable the party seeking production to designate the materials desired or protection for actual production, with the privilege review of only those materials to follow. Alternatively, they may agree that if privileged or protected information is inadvertently produced, the producing party may by timely notice assert the privilege or protection and obtain return of the materials without waiver. Other arrangements are possible. In most circumstances, a party who receives information under such an arrangement cannot assert that production of the information waived a claim of privilege or of protection as trial-preparation material.

An order that includes the parties' agreement may be helpful in avoiding delay and excessive cost in discovery. See Manual for Complex Litigation (4th) § 11.446. Rule 16(b)(6) recognizes the propriety of including such agreements in the court's order. The rule does not provide the court with authority to enter such a case-management or other order without party agreement, or limit the court's authority to act on motions.

NEW RULE 26

New Rule 26: General Provisions Governing Discovery; Duty of Disclosure.

(a) Required Disclosures; Methods to Discover Additional Matter

(1) Initial disclosures. Except in categories of proceedings specified in Rule 26(a)(1)(E), or to the extent otherwise stipulated or directed by order, a party must, without awaiting a discovery request, provide to other parties:

(A) the name and, if known, the address and telephone number of each individual likely to have discoverable information that the disclosing party may use to support its claims or defenses, unless solely for impeachment, identifying the subjects of the information;

(B) a copy of, or description by category and location of, all documents, electronically stored information, and tangible things that are in the possession, custody, or control of the party and that the disclosing party may use to support its claims or defenses, unless solely for impeachment;

. . . .

(b) Discovery Scope and Limits. Unless otherwise limited by order of the court in accordance with these rules, the scope of discovery is as follows:

(2) Limitations

(A) By order, the court may alter the limits in these rules on the number of depositions and interrogatories or the length of depositions under Rule 30. By order or local rule, the court may also limit the number of requests under Rule 36.

(B) A party need not provide discovery of electronically stored information from sources that the party identifies as not reasonably accessible because of undue burden or cost. On motion to compel discovery or for a protective order, the party from whom discovery is sought must show that the information is not reasonably accessible because of undue burden or cost. If that showing is made, the court may nonetheless order discovery from such sources if the requesting party shows good cause, considering the limitations of Rule 26(b)(2)(C). The court may specify conditions for the discovery.

....

(5) Claims of Privilege or Protection of Trial Preparation Materials.

(A) Information withheld. When a party withholds information otherwise discoverable under these rules by claiming that it is privileged or subject to protection as trial preparation material, the party shall make the claim expressly and shall describe the nature of the documents, communications, or things not produced or disclosed in a manner that, without revealing information itself privileged or protected, will enable other parties to assess the applicability of the privilege or protection.

(B) Information produced. If information is produced in discovery that is subject to a claim of privilege or protection as trial-preparation material, the party making the claim may notify any party that received the information of the claim and the basis for it. After being notified, a party must promptly return, sequester, or destroy the specified information and any copies it has and may not use or disclose the information until the claim is resolved. A receiving party may promptly present the information to the court under seal for a determination of the claim. If the receiving party disclosed the information before being notified, it must take reasonable steps to retrieve it. The producing party must preserve the information until the claim is resolved.

....

(f) Conference of Parties; Planning for Discovery. Except in categories of proceedings exempted from initial disclosure under Rule 26(a)(1)(E) or when otherwise ordered, the parties must, as soon as practicable and in any event at least 21 days before a scheduling conference is held or a scheduling order is due under Rule 16(b), confer to consider the nature and basis of their claims and defenses and the possibilities for a prompt settlement or resolution of the case, to make or arrange for the disclosures required by Rule 26(a)(1), to discuss any issues relating to preserving discoverable information, and to develop a proposed discovery plan that indicates the parties' views and proposals concerning:

(1) what changes should be made in the timing, form, or requirement for disclosures under Rule 26(a), including a statement as to when disclosures under Rule 26(a)(1) were made or will be made;

(2) the subjects on which discovery may be needed, when discovery should be completed, and whether discovery should be conducted in phases or be limited to or focused upon particular issues;

(3) any issues relating to disclosure or discovery of electronically stored information, including the form or forms in which it should be produced;

(4) any issues relating to claims of privilege or protection as trial-preparation material, including – if the parties agree on a procedure to assert such claims after production – whether to ask the court to include their agreement in an order;

(5) what changes should be made in the limitations on discovery imposed under these rules or by local rule, and what other limitations should be imposed; and

(6) any other orders that should be entered by the court under Rule 26© or under Rule 16(b) and (c).

Rules Committee Commentary to Rule 26

Subdivision (a). Rule 26(a)(1)(B) is amended to parallel Rule 34(a) by recognizing that a party must disclose electronically stored information as well as documents that it may use to support its claims or defenses. The term "electronically stored information" has the same broad meaning in Rule 26(a)(1) as in Rule 34(a). This amendment is consistent with the 1993 addition of Rule 26(a)(1)(B). The term "data compilations" is deleted as unnecessary because it is a subset of both documents and electronically stored information.

Subdivision (b)(2). The amendment to Rule 26(b)(2) is designed to address issues raised by difficulties in locating, retrieving, and providing discovery of some electronically stored information. Electronic storage systems often make it easier to locate and retrieve information. These advantages are properly taken into account in determining the reasonable scope of discovery in a particular case. But some sources of electronically stored information can be accessed only with substantial burden and cost. In a particular case, these burdens and costs may make the information on such sources not reasonably accessible.

It is not possible to define in a rule the different types of technological features that may affect the burdens and costs of accessing electronically stored information. Information systems are designed to provide ready access to information used in regular ongoing activities. They also may be designed so as to provide ready access to information that is not regularly used. But a system may retain information on sources that are accessible only by incurring substantial burdens or costs. Subparagraph (B) is added to regulate discovery from such sources.

Under this rule, a responding party should produce electronically stored information that is relevant, not privileged, and reasonably accessible, subject to the (b)(2)(C) limitations that apply to all discovery. The responding party must also identify, by category or type, the sources containing potentially responsive information that it is neither searching nor producing. The identification should, to the extent possible, provide enough detail to enable the requesting party to evaluate the burdens and costs of providing the discovery and the likelihood of finding responsive information on the identified sources.

A party's identification of sources of electronically stored information as not reasonably accessible does not relieve the party of its common-law or statutory duties to preserve evidence. Whether a responding party is required to preserve unsearched sources of potentially responsive information that it believes are not reasonably accessible depends on the circumstances of each case. It is often useful for the parties to discuss this issue early in discovery.

The volume of—and the ability to search—much electronically stored information means that in many cases the responding party will be able to produce information from reasonably accessible sources that will fully satisfy the parties' discovery needs. In many circumstances the requesting party should obtain and evaluate the information from such sources before insisting that the responding party search and produce information contained on sources that are not reasonably accessible. If the requesting party continues to seek discovery of information from sources identified as not reasonably accessible, the parties should discuss the burdens and costs of accessing and retrieving the information, the needs that may establish good cause for requiring all or part of the requested discovery even if the information sought is not reasonably accessible, and conditions on obtaining and producing the information that may be appropriate.

If the parties cannot agree whether, or on what terms, sources identified as not reasonably accessible should be searched and discoverable information produced, the issue may be raised either by a motion to compel discovery or by a motion for a protective order. The parties must confer before bringing either motion. If the parties do not resolve the issue and the court must decide, the responding party must show that the identified sources of information are not reasonably accessible because of undue burden or cost. The requesting party may need discovery to test this assertion. Such discovery might take the form of requiring the responding party to conduct a sampling of information contained on the sources identified as not reasonably accessible; allowing some form of inspection of such sources; or taking depositions of witnesses knowledgeable about the responding party's information systems.

Once it is shown that a source of electronically stored information is not reasonably accessible, the requesting party may still obtain discovery by showing good cause, considering the limitations of Rule 26(b)(2)(C) that balance the costs and potential benefits of discovery. The decision whether to require a responding party to search for and produce information that is not reasonably accessible depends not only on the burdens and costs of doing so, but also on whether those burdens and costs can be justified in the circumstances of the case. Appropriate considerations may include: (1) the specificity of the discovery request; (2) the quantity of information available from other and more easily accessed sources; (3) the failure to produce relevant information that seems likely to have existed but is no longer available on more easily accessed sources; (4) the likelihood of finding relevant, responsive information that cannot be obtained from other, more easily accessed sources; (5) predictions as to the importance and usefulness of the further information; (6)

the importance of the issues at stake in the litigation; and (7) the parties' resources.

The responding party has the burden as to one aspect of the inquiry— whether the identified sources are not reasonably accessible in light of the burdens and costs required to search for, retrieve, and produce whatever responsive information may be found. The requesting party has the burden of showing that its need for the discovery outweighs the burdens and costs of locating, retrieving, and producing the information. In some cases, the court will be able to determine whether the identified sources are not reasonably accessible and whether the requesting party has shown good cause for some or all of the discovery, consistent with the limitations of Rule 26(b)(2)(C), through a single proceeding or presentation. The good-cause determination, however, may be complicated because the court and parties may know little about what information the sources identified as not reasonably accessible might contain, whether it is relevant, or how valuable it may be to the litigation. In such cases, the parties may need some focused discovery, which may include sampling of the sources, to learn more about what burdens and costs are involved in accessing the information, what the information consists of, and how valuable it is for the litigation in light of information that can be obtained by exhausting other opportunities for discovery.

The good-cause inquiry and consideration of the Rule 26(b)(2)(C) limitations are coupled with the authority to set conditions for discovery. The conditions may take the form of limits on the amount, type, or sources of information required to be accessed and produced. The conditions may also include payment by the requesting party of part or all of the reasonable costs of obtaining information from sources that are not reasonably accessible. A requesting party's willingness to share or bear the access costs may be weighed by the court in determining whether there is good cause. But the producing party's burdens in reviewing the information for relevance and privilege may weigh against permitting the requested discovery.

The limitations of Rule 26(b)(2)(C) continue to apply to all discovery of electronically stored information, including that stored on reasonably accessible electronic sources.

Subdivision (b)(5). The Committee has repeatedly been advised that the risk of privilege waiver, and the work necessary to avoid it, add to the costs and delay of discovery. When the review is of electronically stored information, the risk of waiver, and the time and effort required to avoid it, can increase substantially because of the volume of electronically stored information and the difficulty in ensuring that all information to be produced has in fact been reviewed. Rule 26(b)(5)(A) provides a procedure for a party that has withheld information on the basis of privilege or protection as trial-preparation material to make the claim so that the requesting party can decide whether to contest the claim and the court can resolve the dispute. Rule 26(b)(5)(B) is added to provide a procedure for a party to assert a claim of privilege or trial-preparation material protection after information is produced in discovery in the action and, if the claim is contested, permit any party that received the information to present the matter to the court for resolution.

Rule 26(b)(5)(B) does not address whether the privilege or protection that is asserted after production was waived by the production. The courts have developed principles to determine whether, and under what circumstances, waiver results from inadvertent production of privileged or protected information. Rule 26(b)(5)(B) provides a procedure for presenting and addressing these issues. Rule 26(b)(5)(B) works in tandem with Rule 26(f), which is amended to direct the parties to discuss privilege issues in preparing their discovery plan, and which, with amended Rule 16(b), allows the parties to ask the court to include in an order any agreements the parties reach regarding issues of privilege or trial-preparation material protection. Agreements reached under Rule 26(f)(4) and orders including such agreements entered under Rule 16(b)(6) may be considered when a court determines whether a waiver has occurred. Such agreements and orders ordinarily control if they adopt procedures different from those in Rule 26(b)(5)(B).

A party asserting a claim of privilege or protection after production must give notice to the receiving party. That notice should be in writing unless the circumstances preclude it. Such circumstances could include the assertion of the claim during a deposition. The notice should be as specific as possible in identifying the information and stating the basis for the claim. Because the receiving party must decide whether to challenge the claim and may sequester the information and submit it to the court for a ruling on whether the claimed privilege or protection applies and whether it has been waived, the notice should be sufficiently detailed so as to enable the receiving party and the court to understand the basis for the claim and to determine whether waiver has occurred. Courts will continue to examine whether a claim of privilege or protection was made at a reasonable time when delay is part of the waiver determination under the governing law.

After receiving notice, each party that received the information must promptly return, sequester, or destroy the information and any copies it has. The option of sequestering or destroying the information is included in part because the receiving party may have incorporated the information in protected trial- preparation materials. No receiving party may use or disclose the information pending resolution of the privilege claim. The receiving party may present to the court the questions whether the information is privileged or protected as trial-preparation material, and whether the privilege or protection has been waived. If it does so, it must provide the court with the grounds for the privilege or protection specified in the producing party's notice, and serve all parties. In presenting the question, the party may use the content of the information only to the extent permitted by the applicable law of privilege, protection for trial- preparation material, and professional responsibility.

If a party disclosed the information to nonparties before receiving notice of a claim of privilege or protection as trial-preparation material, it must take reasonable steps to retrieve the information and to return it, sequester it until the claim is resolved, or destroy it.

Whether the information is returned or not, the producing party must preserve the information pending the court's ruling on whether the claim of privilege or of protection is properly asserted and whether it was waived. As with claims made under Rule 26(b)(5)(A), there may be no ruling if the other parties do not contest the claim.

Subdivision (f). Rule 26(f) is amended to direct the parties to discuss discovery of electronically stored information during their discovery-planning conference. The rule focuses on "issues relating to disclosure or discovery of electronically stored information"; the discussion is not required in cases not involving electronic discovery, and the amendment imposes no additional requirements in those cases. When the parties do anticipate disclosure or discovery of electronically stored information, discussion at the outset may avoid later difficulties or ease their resolution.

When a case involves discovery of electronically stored information, the issues to be addressed during the Rule 26(f) conference depend on the nature and extent of the contemplated discovery and of the parties' information systems. It may be important for the parties to discuss those systems, and accordingly important for counsel to become familiar with those systems before the conference. With that information, the parties can develop a discovery plan that takes into account the capabilities of their computer systems. In appropriate cases identification of, and early discovery from, individuals with special knowledge of a party's computer systems may be helpful.

The particular issues regarding electronically stored information that deserve attention during the discovery planning stage depend on the specifics of the given case. See Manual for Complex Litigation (4th) § 40.25(2) (listing topics for discussion in a proposed order regarding meet-and-confer sessions). For example, the parties may specify the topics for such discovery and the time period for which discovery will be sought. They may identify the various sources of such information within a party's control that should be searched for electronically stored information. They may discuss whether the information is reasonably accessible to the party that has it, including the burden or cost of retrieving and reviewing the information. See Rule 26(b)(2)(B). Rule 26(f)(3) explicitly directs the parties to discuss the form or forms in which electronically stored information might be produced. The parties may be able to reach agreement on the forms of production, making discovery more efficient. Rule 34(b) is amended to permit a requesting party to specify the form or forms in which it wants electronically stored information produced. If the requesting party does not specify a form, Rule 34(b) directs the responding party to state the forms it intends to use in the production. Early discussion of the forms of production may facilitate the application of Rule 34(b) by allowing the parties to determine what forms of production will meet both parties' needs. Early identification of disputes over the forms of production may help avoid the expense and delay of searches or productions using inappropriate forms.

Rule 26(f) is also amended to direct the parties to discuss any issues regarding preservation of discoverable information during their conference as they develop a discovery plan. This provision applies to all sorts of discoverable information, but can be particularly important with regard to electronically stored information. The volume and dynamic nature of electronically stored information may complicate preservation obligations. The ordinary operation of computers involves both the automatic creation and the automatic deletion or overwriting of certain information. Failure to address preservation issues early in the litigation increases uncertainty and raises a risk of disputes.

The parties' discussion should pay particular attention to the balance between the competing needs to preserve relevant evidence and to continue routine operations critical to ongoing activities. Complete or broad cessation of a party's routine computer operations could paralyze the party's activities. Cf. Manual for Complex Litigation (4th) § 11.422 ("A blanket preservation order may be prohibitively expensive and unduly burdensome for parties dependent on computer systems for their day-to-day operations.") The parties should take account of these considerations in their discussions, with the goal of agreeing on reasonable preservation steps.

The requirement that the parties discuss preservation does not imply that courts should routinely enter preservation orders. A preservation order entered over objections should be narrowly tailored. Ex parte preservation orders should issue only in exceptional circumstances.

Rule 26(f) is also amended to provide that the parties should discuss any issues relating to assertions of privilege or of protection as trial- preparation materials, including whether the parties can facilitate discovery by agreeing on procedures for asserting claims of privilege or protection after production and whether to ask the court to enter an order that includes any agreement the parties reach. The Committee has repeatedly been advised about the discovery difficulties that can result from efforts to guard against waiver of privilege and work-product protection. Frequently parties find it necessary to spend large amounts of time reviewing materials requested through discovery to avoid waiving privilege. These efforts are necessary because materials subject to a claim of privilege or protection are often difficult to identify. A failure to withhold even one such item may result in an argument that there has been a waiver of privilege as to all other privileged materials on that subject matter. Efforts to avoid the risk of waiver can impose substantial costs on the party producing the material and the time required for the privilege review can substantially delay access for the party seeking discovery.

These problems often become more acute when discovery of electronically stored information is sought. The volume of such data, and the informality that attends use of e-mail and some other types of electronically stored information, may make privilege determinations more difficult, and privilege review correspondingly more expensive and time consuming. Other aspects of electronically stored information pose particular difficulties for privilege review. For example, production may be sought of information automatically included in electronic files but not apparent to the creator or to readers. Computer programs may retain draft language, editorial comments, and other deleted matter (sometimes referred to as "embedded data" or "embedded edits") in an electronic file but not make them apparent to the reader. Information describing the history, tracking, or management of an electronic file (sometimes called "metadata") is usually not apparent to the reader viewing a hard copy or a screen image. Whether this information should be produced may be among the topics discussed in the Rule 26(f) conference. If it is, it may need to be reviewed to ensure that no privileged information is included, further complicating the task of privilege review.

Parties may attempt to minimize these costs and delays by agreeing to protocols that minimize the risk of waiver. They may agree that the responding party will provide certain requested materials for initial examination without waiving any privilege or protection—sometimes known as a "quick peek." The requesting party then designates the documents it wishes to have actually produced. This designation is the Rule

34 request. The responding party then responds in the usual course, screening only those documents actually requested for formal production and asserting privilege claims as provided in Rule 26(b)(5)(A). On other occasions, parties enter agreements—sometimes called "clawback agreements"— that production without intent to waive privilege or protection should not be a waiver so long as the responding party identifies the documents mistakenly produced, and that the documents should be returned under those circumstances. Other voluntary arrangements may be appropriate depending on the circumstances of each litigation. In most circumstances, a party who receives information under such an arrangement cannot assert that production of the information waived a claim of privilege or of protection as trial-preparation material.

Although these agreements may not be appropriate for all cases, in certain cases they can facilitate prompt and economical discovery by reducing delay before the discovering party obtains access to documents, and by reducing the cost and burden of review by the producing party. A case-management or other order including such agreements may further facilitate the discovery process. Form 35 is amended to include a report to the court about any agreement regarding protections against inadvertent forfeiture or waiver of privilege or protection that the parties have reached, and Rule 16(b) is amended to recognize that the court may include such an agreement in a case-management or other order. If the parties agree to entry of such an order, their proposal should be included in the report to the court.

Rule 26(b)(5)(B) is added to establish a parallel procedure to assert privilege or protection as trial-preparation material after production, leaving the question of waiver to later determination by the court.

NEW RULE 34

New Rule 34: Production of Documents, Electronically Stored Information, and Things and Entry Upon Land for Inspection and Other Purposes.

(a) Scope. Any party may serve on any other party a request (1) to produce and permit the party making the request, or someone acting on the requestor's behalf, to inspect, copy, test, or sample any designated documents or electronically stored information – including writings, drawings, graphs, charts, photographs, sound recordings, images, and other data or data compilations stored in any medium – from which information can be obtained, translated, if necessary, by the respondent into reasonably usable form, or to inspect, copy, test, or sample any designated tangible things which constitute or contain matters within the scope of Rule 26(b) and which are in the possession, custody or control of the party upon whom the request is served; or (2) to permit entry upon designated land or other property in the possession or control of the party upon whom the request is served for the purpose of inspection and measuring, surveying, photographing, testing, or sampling the property or any designated object or operation thereon, within the scope of Rule 26(b).

(b) Procedure. The request shall set forth, either by individual item or by category, the items to be inspected, and describe each with reasonable particularity. The request shall specify a reasonable time, place, and manner of making the inspection and performing the related acts. The request may specify the form or forms in which electronically stored information is to be produced. Without leave of court or written stipulation, a request may not be served before the time specified in Rule 26(d).

The party upon whom the request is served shall serve a written response within 30 days after the service of the request. A shorter or longer time may be directed by the court or, in the absence of such an order, agreed to in writing by the parties, subject to Rule 29. The response shall state, with respect to each item or category, that inspection and related activities will be permitted as requested, unless the request is objected to, including an objection to the requested form or forms for producing electronically stored information, stating the reasons for the objection. If objection is made to part of an item or category, the party shall be specified and inspection permitted of the remaining parts. If objection is made to the requested form or forms for producing electronically stored information – or if no form was specified in the request – the responding party must state the form or forms it intends to use. The party submitting the request may move for an order under Rule 37(a) with respect to any objection to or other failure to respond to the request or any part thereof, or any failure to permit inspection as requested.

Unless the parties otherwise agree, or the court otherwise orders, (i) a party who produces documents for inspection shall produce them as they are kept in the usual course of business or shall organize and label them to correspond with the categories in the request; and (ii) if a request for electronically stored information does not specify the form or forms of production, a responding party must produce the information in a form or forms in which it is ordinarily maintained or in a form or forms that are reasonably usable; and (iii) a party need not produce the same electronically stored information in more than one form.

Rules Committee Commentary to Rule 34

Subdivision (a). As originally adopted, Rule 34 focused on discovery of "documents" and "things." In 1970, Rule 34(a) was amended to include discovery of data compilations, anticipating that the use of computerized information would increase. Since then, the growth in electronically stored information and in the variety of systems for creating and storing such information has been dramatic. Lawyers and judges interpreted the term "documents" to include electronically stored information because it was obviously improper to allow a party to evade discovery obligations on the basis that the label had not kept pace with changes in information technology. But it has become increasingly difficult to say that all forms of electronically stored information, many dynamic in nature, fit within the traditional concept of a "document." Electronically stored information may exist in dynamic databases and other forms far different from fixed expression on paper. Rule 34(a) is amended to confirm that discovery of electronically stored information stands on equal footing with discovery of paper documents. The change clarifies that Rule 34 applies to information that is fixed in a tangible form and to information that is stored in a medium from which it can be retrieved and examined. At the same time, a Rule 34 request for production of "documents" should be understood to encompass, and the response should include, electronically stored information unless discovery in the action has clearly distinguished between electronically stored information and "documents."

Discoverable information often exists in both paper and electronic form, and the same or similar information might exist in both. The items listed in Rule 34(a) show different ways in which information may be recorded or stored. Images, for example, might be hard-copy documents or electronically stored information. The wide variety of computer systems currently in use, and the rapidity of technological change, counsel against a limiting or precise definition of electronically stored information. Rule 34(a)(1) is expansive and includes any type of information that is stored electronically. A common example often sought in discovery is electronic communications, such as e- mail. The rule covers—either as documents or as electronically stored information—information "stored in any medium," to encompass future develop-ments in computer technology. Rule 34(a)(1) is intended to be broad enough to cover all current types of computer-based information, and flexible enough to encompass future changes and developments.

References elsewhere in the rules to "electronically stored information" should be understood to invoke this expansive approach. A companion change is made to Rule 33(d), making it explicit that parties choosing to respond to an interrogatory by permitting access to responsive records may do so by providing access to electronically stored information. More generally, the term used in Rule 34(a)(1) appears in a number of other amendments, such as those to Rules 26(a)(1), 26(b)(2), 26(b)(5)(B), 26(f), 34(b), 37(f), and 45. In each of these rules, electronically stored information has the same broad meaning it has under Rule 34(a)(1). References to "documents" appear in discovery rules that are not amended, including Rules 30(f), 36(a), and 37(c)(2). These references should be interpreted to include electronically stored information as circumstances warrant. The term "electronically stored information" is broad, but whether material that falls within this term should be produced, and in what form, are separate questions that must be addressed under Rules 26(b), 26(c), and 34(b).

The Rule 34(a) requirement that, if necessary, a party producing electronically stored information translate it into reasonably usable form does not address the issue of translating from one human language to another. *See In re Puerto Rico Elect. Power Auth.*, 687 F.2d 501, 504-510 (1st Cir. 1989).

Rule 34(a)(1) is also amended to make clear that parties may request an opportunity to test or sample materials sought under the rule in addition to inspecting and copying them. That opportunity may be important for both electronically stored information and hard-copy materials. The current rule is not clear that such testing or sampling is authorized; the amendment expressly permits it. As with any other form of discovery, issues of burden and intrusiveness raised by requests to test or sample can be addressed under Rules 26(b)(2) and 26(c). Inspection or testing of certain types of electronically stored information or of a responding party's electronic information system may raise issues of confidentiality or privacy. The addition of testing and sampling to Rule 34(a) with regard to documents and electronically stored information is not meant to create a routine right of direct access to a party's electronic information system, although such access might be justified in some circumstances. Courts should guard against undue intrusiveness resulting from inspecting or testing such systems.

Rule 34(a)(1) is further amended to make clear that tangible things must—like documents and land sought to be examined—be designated in the request.

Subdivision (b). Rule 34(b) provides that a party must produce documents as they are kept in the usual course of business or must organize and label them to correspond with the categories in the discovery request. The production of electronically stored information should be subject to comparable requirements to protect against deliberate or inadvertent production in ways that raise unnecessary obstacles for the requesting party. Rule 34(b) is amended to ensure similar protection for electronically stored information.

The amendment to Rule 34(b) permits the requesting party to designate the form or forms in which it wants electronically stored information produced. The form of production is more important to the exchange of electronically stored information than of hard-copy materials, although a party might specify hard copy as the requested form. Specification of the desired form or forms may facilitate the orderly, efficient, and cost-effective discovery of electronically stored information. The rule recognizes that different forms of production may be appropriate for different types of electronically stored information. Using current technology, for example, a party might be called upon to produce word processing documents, e-mail messages, electronic spreadsheets, different image or sound files, and material from databases. Requiring that such diverse types of electronically stored information all be produced in the same form could prove impossible, and even if possible could increase the cost and burdens of producing and using the information. The rule therefore provides that the requesting party may ask for different forms of production for different types of electronically stored information.

The rule does not require that the requesting party choose a form or forms of production. The requesting party may not have a preference. In some cases, the requesting party may not know what form the producing party uses to maintain its electronically stored information, although Rule 26(f)(3) is amended to call for discussion of the form of production in the parties' prediscovery conference.

The responding party also is involved in determining the form of production. In the written response to the production request that Rule 34 requires, the responding party must state the form it intends to use for producing electronically stored information if the requesting party does not specify a form or if the responding party objects to a form that the requesting party specifies. Stating the intended form before the production occurs may permit the parties to identify and seek to resolve disputes before the expense and work of the production occurs. A party that responds to a discovery request by simply producing electronically stored information in a form of its choice, without identifying that form in advance of the production in the response required by Rule 34(b), runs a risk that the requesting party can show that the produced form is not reasonably usable and that it is entitled to production of some or all of the information in an additional form. Additional time might be required to permit a responding party to assess the appropriate form or forms of production.

If the requesting party is not satisfied with the form stated by the responding party, or if the responding party has objected to the form specified by the requesting party, the parties must meet and confer under Rule 37(a)(2)(B) in an effort to resolve the matter before the requesting party can file a motion to compel. If they cannot agree and the court resolves the dispute, the court is not limited to the forms initially chosen by the requesting party, stated by the responding party, or specified in this rule for situations in which there is no court order or party agreement.

If the form of production is not specified by party agreement or court order, the responding party must produce electronically stored information either in a form or forms in which it is ordinarily maintained or in a form or forms that are reasonably usable. Rule 34(a) requires that, if necessary, a responding party "translate" information it produces into a "reasonably usable" form. Under some circumstances, the responding party may need to provide some reasonable amount of technical support, information on application software, or other reasonable assistance to enable the requesting party to use the information. The rule does not require a party to produce electronically stored information in the form it which it is ordinarily maintained, as long as it is produced in a reasonably usable form. But the option to produce in a reasonably usable form does not mean that a responding party is free to convert electronically stored information from the form in which it is ordinarily maintained to a different form that makes it more difficult or burdensome for the requesting party to use the information efficiently in the litigation. If the responding party ordinarily maintains the information it is producing in a way that makes it searchable by electronic means, the information should not be produced in a form that removes or significantly degrades this feature.

Some electronically stored information may be ordinarily maintained in a form that is not reasonably usable by any party. One example is "legacy" data that can be used only by superseded systems. The questions whether a producing party should be required to convert such information to a more usable form, or should be required to produce it at all, should be addressed under Rule 26(b)(2)(B).

Whether or not the requesting party specified the form of production, Rule 34(b) provides that the same electronically stored information ordinarily need be produced in only one form.

NEW RULE 37

New Rule 37: Failure to Make Disclosures or Cooperate in Discovery; Sanctions.

(f)* Electronically stored information. Absent exceptional circumstances, a court may not impose sanctions under these rules on a party for failing to provide electronically stored information lost as a result of the routine, good faith operation of an electronic information system.

*Note, after recent rules renumbering 37(f) has now become 37(e).

==

Rules Committee Commentary to Rule 37

Subdivision (f). Subdivision (f) is new. It focuses on a distinctive feature of computer operations, the routine alteration and deletion of information that attends ordinary use. Many steps essential to computer operation may alter or destroy information, for reasons that have nothing to do with how that information might relate to litigation. As a result, the ordinary operation of computer systems creates a risk that a party may lose potentially discoverable information without culpable conduct on its part. Under Rule 37(f), absent exceptional circumstances, sanctions cannot be imposed for loss of electronically stored information resulting from the routine, good-faith operation of an electronic information system.

Rule 37(f) applies only to information lost due to the "routine operation of an electronic information system"—the ways in which such systems are generally designed, programmed, and implemented to meet the party's technical and business needs. The "routine operation" of computer systems includes the alteration and overwriting of information, often without the operator's specific direction or awareness, a feature with no direct counterpart in hard-copy documents. Such features are essential to the operation of electronic information systems.

Rule 37(f) applies to information lost due to the routine operation of an information system only if the operation was in good faith. Good faith in the routine operation of an information system may involve a party's intervention to modify or suspend certain features of that routine operation to prevent the loss of information, if that information is subject to a preservation obligation. A preservation obligation may arise from many sources, including common law, statutes, regulations, or a court order in the case. The good faith requirement of Rule 37(f) means that a party is not permitted to exploit the routine operation of an information system to thwart discovery obligations by allowing that operation to continue in order to destroy specific stored information that it is required to preserve. When a party is under a duty to preserve information because of pending or reasonably anticipated litigation, intervention in the routine operation of an information system is one aspect of what is often called a "litigation hold." Among the factors that bear on a party's good faith in the routine operation of an information system are the steps the party took to comply with a court order in the case or party agreement requiring preservation of specific electronically stored information.

Whether good faith would call for steps to prevent the loss of information on sources that the party believes are not reasonably accessible under Rule 26(b)(2) depends on the circumstances of each case. One factor is whether the party reasonably believes that the information on such sources is likely to be discoverable and not available from reasonably accessible sources.

The protection provided by Rule 37(f) applies only to sanctions "under these rules." It does not affect other sources of authority to impose sanctions or rules of professional responsibility.

This rule restricts the imposition of "sanctions." It does not prevent a court from making the kinds of adjustments frequently used in managing discovery if a party is unable to provide relevant responsive information. For example, a court could order the responding party to produce an additional witness for deposition, respond to additional interrogatories, or make similar attempts to provide substitutes or alternatives for some or all of the lost information.

UNIFORM LAW COMMISSION'S PROPOSED UNIFORM RULES RELATING TO DISCOVERY OF ELECTRONICALLY STORED INFORMATION

NATIONAL CONFERENCE OF COMMISSIONERS
ON UNIFORM STATE LAWS

MEETING IN ITS ONE-HUNDRED-AND-FIFTEENTH YEAR
PASADENA, CALIFORNIA
JULY 27 – AUGUST 3, 2007

RULE 1. DEFINITIONS. In these rules:

(1) "Discovery" means the process of providing information in a civil proceeding in the courts of this state pursuant to [insert reference to state rules of civil procedure] or these rules.

(2) "Electronic" means relating to technology having electrical, digital, magnetic, wireless, optical, electromagnetic, or similar capabilities.

(3) "Electronically stored information" means information that is stored in an electronic medium and is retrievable in perceivable form.

(4) "Person" means an individual, corporation, business trust, estate, trust, partnership, limited liability company, association, joint venture, public corporation, government or governmental subdivision, agency, or instrumentality, or any other legal or commercial entity.

Judicial Note

The term "civil proceeding" as used in the definition of "Discovery" may need to be modified in certain states to specify that it includes civil courts with differing or limited jurisdiction within the same state. As the term is used in subsection (1), it is intended to encompass not only civil courts of general jurisdiction, but also courts of limited jurisdiction such as domestic relations and probate courts. The term is used in various rules, including Rules 3, 4 and 7.

RULE 2. SUPPLEMENTAL RULES OF DISCOVERY. Unless displaced by particular provisions of these rules, [insert reference to state rules of civil procedure] supplement these rules.

RULE 3. CONFERENCE, PLAN AND REPORT TO THE COURT.

(a) Unless the parties otherwise agree or the court otherwise orders, not later than [21] days after each responding party first appears in a civil proceeding, all parties that have appeared in the proceeding shall confer concerning whether discovery of electronically stored information is reasonably likely to be sought in the proceeding, and if so the parties at the conference shall discuss:

(1)   any issues relating to preservation of discoverable information;

(2)   the form in which each type of the information will be produced;

(3)   the period within which the information will be produced;

(4)   the method for asserting or preserving claims of privilege or of protection of the information as trial-preparation materials, including whether such claims may be asserted after production;

(5)   the method for asserting or preserving confidentiality and proprietary status of information relating to a party or a person not a party to the proceeding;

(6)   whether allocation among the parties of the expense of production is appropriate; and,

(7)   any other issue relating to the discovery of electronically stored information.

(b) If discovery of electronically stored information is reasonably likely to be sought in the proceeding, the parties shall:

(1)   develop a proposed plan relating to discovery of the information; and

(2)   not later than [14] days after the conference under subsection (a), submit to the court a written report that summarizes the plan and states the position of each party as to any issue about which they are unable to agree.

RULE 4. ORDER GOVERNING DISCOVERY.

(a) In a civil proceeding, the court may issue an order governing the discovery of electronically stored information pursuant to:

(1) a motion by a party seeking discovery of the information or by a party or person from which discovery of the information is sought;

(2) a stipulation of the parties and of any person not a party from which discovery of the information is sought; or

(3) the court's own motion, after reasonable notice to, and an opportunity to be heard from, the parties and any person not a party from which discovery of the information is sought.

(b) An order governing discovery of electronically stored information may address:

(1) whether discovery of the information is reasonably likely to be sought in the proceeding;

(2) preservation of the information;

(3) the form in which each type of the information is to be produced;

(4) the time within which the information is to be produced;

(5) the permissible scope of discovery of the information;

(6) the method for asserting or preserving claims of privilege or of protection of the information as trial-preparation material after production;

(7) the method for asserting or preserving confidentiality and the proprietary status of information relating to a party or a person not a party to the proceeding;

(8) allocation of the expense of production; and

(9) any other issue relating to the discovery of the information.

RULE 5. LIMITATION ON SANCTIONS. Absent exceptional circumstances, the court may not impose sanctions on a party under these rules for failure to provide electronically stored information lost as the result of the routine, good-faith operation of an electronic information system.

RULE 6. REQUEST FOR PRODUCTION.

(a) In a civil proceeding, a party may serve on any other party a request for production of electronically stored information and for permission to inspect, copy, test, or sample the information.

(b) A party on which a request to produce electronically stored information has been served shall, in a timely manner, serve a response on the requesting party. The response must state, with respect to each item or category in the request:

(1) that inspection, copying, testing, or sampling of the information will be permitted as requested; or

(2) any objection to the request and the reasons for the objection.

RULE 7. FORM OF PRODUCTION.

(a) A party requesting production of electronically stored information may specify the form in which each type of electronically stored information is to be produced.

(b) If a party responding to a request for production of electronically stored information objects to a specified form for producing the information, or if no form is specified in the request, the responding party shall state in its response the form in which it intends to produce each type of the information.

(c) Unless the parties otherwise agree or the court otherwise orders.

(1) if a request for production does not specify a form for producing a type of electronically stored information, the responding party shall produce the information in a form in which it is ordinarily maintained or in a form that is reasonably usable; and

(2) a party need not produce the same electronically stored information in more than one form.

RULE 8. LIMITATIONS ON DISCOVERY.

(a) A party may object to discovery of electronically stored information from sources that the party identifies as not reasonably accessible because of undue burden or expense. In its objection the party shall identify the reason for such undue burden or expense.

(b) On motion to compel discovery or for a protective order relating to the discovery of electronically stored information, a party objecting bears the burden of showing that the information is from a source that is not reasonably accessible because of undue burden or expense.

(c) The court may order discovery of electronically stored information that is from a source that is not reasonably accessible because of undue burden or expense if the party requesting discovery shows that the likely benefit of the proposed discovery outweighs the likely burden or expense, taking into account the amount in controversy, the resources of the parties, the importance of the issues, and the importance of the requested discovery in resolving the issues.

(d) If the court orders discovery of electronically stored information under subsection (c) it may set conditions for discovery of the information, including allocation of the expense of discovery.

(e) The court shall limit the frequency or extent of discovery of electronically stored information, even from a source that is reasonably accessible, if the court determines that:

(1)   it is possible to obtain the information from some other source that is more convenient, less burdensome, or less expensive;

(2)   the discovery sought is unreasonably cumulative or duplicative;

(3)   the party seeking discovery has had ample opportunity by discovery in the proceeding to obtain the information sought; or

(4)   the likely burden or expense of the proposed discovery outweighs the likely benefit, taking into account the amount in controversy, the resources of the parties, the importance of the issues, and the importance of the requested discovery in resolving the issues.

RULE 9. CLAIM OF PRIVILEGE OR PROTECTION AFTER PRODUCTION.

(a) If electronically stored information produced in discovery is subject to a claim of privilege or of protection as trial-preparation material, the party making the claim may notify any party that received the information of the claim and the basis for the claim.

(b) After being notified of a claim of privilege or of protection under subsection (a), a party shall immediately sequester the specified information and any copies it has and:

(1) return or destroy the information and all copies and not use or disclose the information until the claim is resolved; or

(2) present the information to the court under seal for a determination of the claim and not otherwise use or disclose the information until the claim is resolved.

(c) If a party that received information under subsection (b) disclosed it before being notified, the party shall take reasonable steps to retrieve the information.

RULE 10. SUBPOENA FOR PRODUCTION.

(a) A subpoena in a civil proceeding may require that electronically stored information be produced and that the party serving the subpoena or person acting on the party's request be permitted to inspect, copy, test, or sample the information.

(b) Subject to subsections (c) and (d), Rules 7, 8 and 9 apply to a person responding to a subpoena under subsection (a) as if that person were a party.

(c) A party serving a subpoena requiring production of electronically stored information shall take reasonable steps to avoid imposing undue burden or expense on a person subject to the subpoena.

(d) An order of the court requiring compliance with a subpoena issued under this rule must provide protection to a person that is neither a party nor a party's officer from undue burden or expense resulting from compliance.

ABA CIVIL DISCOVERY STANDARDS*
TECHNOLOGY SECTION EXCERPT
AUGUST 2004

*The Standards, which appear in bold face type, were adopted as ABA policy in August 1999 and revised in 2004.

The full ABA Civil Discovery Standards are available on-line at: http://www.abanet.org/litigation/discoverystandards/

VIII. TECHNOLOGY
29. Electronic Information.

    a. Identifying Electronic Information. In identifying electronic data that parties may be called upon, in appropriate circumstances, to preserve or produce, counsel, parties and courts should consider:

        i. The following types of data:

            A. Email (including attachments);

            B. Word processing documents;

            C. Spreadsheets;

            D. Presentation documents;

            E. Graphics;

            F. Animations;

            G. Images;

            H. Audio, video and audiovisual recordings; and

            I. Voicemail.

        ii. The following platforms in the possession of the party or a third person under the control of the party (such as an employee or outside vendor under contract):

            A. Databases;

            B. Networks;

            C. Computer systems, including legacy systems (hardware and software);

            D. Servers;

            E. Archives;

            F. Back up or disaster recovery systems;

            G. Tapes, discs, drives, cartridges and other storage media;

H. Laptops;

I. Personal computers;

J. Internet data;

K. Personal digital assistants;

L. Handheld wireless devices;

M. Mobile telephones;

N. Paging devices; and

O. Audio systems, including voicemail.

iii. Whether potentially producible electronic data may include data that have been deleted but can be restored.

b. Discovery of Electronic Information.

i. Document requests should clearly state whether electronic data is sought. In the absence of such clarity, a request for "documents" should ordinarily be construed as also asking for information contained or stored in an electronic medium or format.

ii. A party should specify whether electronic information should be produced in hard copy, in electronic form or, in an appropriate case, in both forms. A party requesting information in electronic form should also consider:

A. Specifying the format in which it prefers to receive the data, such as:

I. Its native (original) format, or

II. A searchable format.

B. Asking for the production of metadata associated with the responsive data—i.e., ancillary electronic information that relates to responsive electronic data, such as information that would indicate whether and when the responsive electronic data was created, edited, sent, received and/or opened.

C. Requesting the software necessary to retrieve, read or interpret electronic information.

D. Inquiring as to how the data are organized and where they are stored.

iii A party who produces information in electronic form ordinarily need not also produce hard copy to the extent that the information in both forms is identical or the differences between the two are not material.

iv. In resolving a motion seeking to compel or protect against the production of electronic information or related software, or to allocate the costs of such discovery, the court should consider such factors as:

A. The burden and expense of the discovery, considering among other factors the total cost of production in absolute terms and as compared to the amount in controversy;

B. The need for the discovery, including the benefit to the requesting party and the availability of the information from other sources;

C. The complexity of the case and the importance of the issues;

D. The need to protect the attorney-client privilege or attorney work product, including the burden and expense of a privilege review by the producing party and the risk of inadvertent disclosure of privileged or protected information despite reasonable diligence on the part of the producing party;

E. The need to protect trade secrets, and proprietary or confidential information;

F. Whether the information or the software needed to access it is proprietary or constitutes confidential business information;

G. The breadth of the discovery request;

H. Whether efforts have been made to confine initial production to tranches or subsets of potentially responsive data;

I. The extent to which production would disrupt the normal operations and processing routines of the responding party;

J. Whether the requesting party has offered to pay some or all of the discovery expenses;

K. The relative ability of each party to control costs and its incentive to do so;

L. The resources of each party as compared to the total cost of production;

M. Whether responding to the request would impose the burden or expense of acquiring or creating software to retrieve potentially responsive electronic data or otherwise require the responding party to render inaccessible electronic information accessible, where the responding party would not do so in the ordinary course of its day-to-day use of the information;

N. Whether responding to the request would impose the burden or expense of converting electronic information into hard copies, or converting hard copies into electronic format;

O. Whether the responding party stores electronic information in a manner that is designed to make discovery impracticable or needlessly costly or burdensome in pending or future litigation, and not justified by any legitimate personal, business, or other non-litigation related reason; and

P. Whether the responding party has deleted, discarded or erased electronic information after litigation was commenced or after the responding party was aware that litigation was probable and, if so, the responding party's state of mind in doing so.

v. In complex cases and/or cases involving large volumes of electronic information, the court may want to consider using an expert to aid or advise the court on technology issues

vi. The parties are encouraged to stipulate as to the authenticity and identifying characteristics (date, author, etc.) of electronic information that is not self-authenticating on its face.

2004 Comment
Subdivision(a)

Subdivision (a)(i). Standard 29(a)(i) is principally designed to provide a checklist to assist counsel in identifying types of electronic data as to which the duty to preserve may apply, once that duty has been triggered under applicable law. *See, e.g., Super Film of Am., Inc. v. UCB Films, Inc.*, 219 F.R.D. 649, 657 (D. Kan. 2004) (for purposes of Federal Rule of Civil Procedure 26, "[c]omputerized data and other electronically-recorded information includes, but is not limited to: voice mail messages and files, back-up voice mail files, e-mail messages and files, backup e-mail files, deleted e-mails, data files, program files, backup and archival tapes, temporary files, system history files, web site information stored in textual, graphical or audio format, web site log files, cache files, cookies, and other electronically-recorded information") (citation and quotations omitted).

This Standard is not intended to suggest that electronic discovery is appropriate in all cases. There may be many cases in which electronic discovery is not warranted, in light of the amount in controversy or any number of other reasons.

The deletion of the former first sentence of subdivision (a)(i) is intended to clarify that the Standards do not create or codify law but rather defer to governing substantive law. The purpose of the list provided in subdivision (a)(i) is to assist counsel in protecting client interests under whatever strictures may be imposed by governing law. It is not to suggest that every item in the list is applicable in every case or that counsel has any duty to instruct a client to preserve any, much less every, item on the list. All duties are dictated by governing state or federal law and not by this or any other of these Standards.

Subdivision (a)(ii). Just as subdivision (a)(i) provides a checklist of the types of electronic data that counsel should bear in mind, Standard 29(a)(ii) provides a checklist of platforms and places where such data may be found. As with subdivision (a)(i), subdivision (a)(ii) does not create a preservation duty. Rather, it is another reference tool intended to be consulted once the duty to preserve electronic data has accrued under local law.

Subdivision (a)(iii). Standard 29(a)(iii) is simply a reminder that, as is well established in the case law, when a preservation duty has been triggered, it may be found to apply to "deleted" information remaining on the hard drive of the computer. *Zubulake v. UBS Warburg LLC*, 217 F.R.D. 309, 313 n.19 (S.D.N.Y. 2003) ("The term 'deleted' is sticky in the context of electronic data. 'Deleting' a file does not actually erase that data from the computer's storage devices. Rather, it simply finds the data's entry in the disk directory and changes it to a 'not used' status—thus permitting the computer to write over the 'deleted' data. Until the computer writes over the 'deleted' data, however, it may be recovered by searching the disk itself rather than the disk's directory. Accordingly, many files are recoverable long after they have been deleted—even if neither the computer user nor the computer itself is aware of their existence. Such data is referred to as 'residual data.'")(internal quotations and citation omitted).

Former Subdivision (a)(ii). Former subdivision (a)(ii) has been moved to subdivision (b), where it conceptually belongs, as new subdivision (b)(i), with minor modification.

Former Subdivision (a)(iii). Former subdivision (a)(iii) has been deleted. As drafted, it appeared to create or codify a proposition of law, which is not the proper function of a Standard. Moreover, the law is evolving swiftly in the area of electronic discovery and, as stated, the deleted language is not necessarily good law. *See, e.g., Zubulake v. UBS Warburg LLC*, 217 F.R.D. 309, 324 (S.D.N.Y. 2003) ("because the cost-shifting analysis is so fact-intensive, it is necessary to determine what data may be found on the inaccessible media. Requiring the responding party to restore and produce responsive documents from a small sample of the requested backup tapes is a sensible approach in most cases").

Subdivision(b)

Subdivision (b)(i). The second sentence of subdivision (b)(i) is the former subdivision (a)(ii), with the addition of a connecting dependent clause and the insertion of the modifier "ordinarily," the latter in recognition of the fact that there may be unusual circumstances in which the stated presumption is obviously inapt. The new first sentence is added as a "best practices" reminder to counsel.

Subdivision (b)(ii). Subdivision (b)(ii) restates and expands the former subdivision (b)(i). The substantive additions are to remind counsel, first, that they have the option of specifying the format in which they wish to receive the desired data and, second, that they may want to inquire as to how the data were organized and where they were stored, since this information may be lost in electronic production.

Subdivision (b)(iii). Subdivision (b)(iii) combines the former subdivisions (b)(ii) and (b)(iv) in recognition of the fact that the factors applied by the courts in resolving motions to compel (or resist production) and motions to allocate costs are largely the same. Additionally, subdivision (b)(iii) expands the former subdivisions (b)(ii) and (b)(iv) to capture additional factors that experience and the developing case law have identified as pertinent to the court's decision. Among the authorities relied on in the recitation of factors in this subdivision are: Federal Judicial Center, Manual for Complex Litigation § 11.446 (4th ed. 2004); 7 Moore's Federal Practice §§ 37a.30-33 (3d ed. 2004); *Zubulake v. UBS Warburg LLC*, 217 F.R.D. 309 (S.D.N.Y. 2003); *Zubulake v. UBS Warburg LLC*, 216 F.R.D. 280 (S.D.N.Y. 2003); *Computer Associates International, Inc. v. Quest Software, Inc.*, No. 02-C-4721, 2003 WL 21277129 (N.D. Ill. June 3, 2003); *Medtronic Sofamor Danek, Inc. v. Michelson*, No. 01-2373-M1V, 2003 WL 21468573 (W.D. Tenn. May 13, 2003); *Dodge, Warren, & Peters Ins. Servs. v. Riley*, 130 Cal. Rptr. 2d 385 (Cal. App. 2003); *Byers v. Illinois State Police*, 2002 WL 1264004 (N.D. Ill. June 3, 2002); *Southern Diagnostic Assocs. v. Bencosme*, 833 So.2d 801 (Fla. App. 2002); *Murphy Oil USA, Inc. v. Fluor Daniel, Inc.*, 2002 WL 246439 (E.D. La. Feb. 19, 2002); *Rowe Entertainment, Inc. v. William Morris Agency*, 205 F.R.D. 421 (S.D.N.Y. Jan 16, 2002); *In re CI Host, Inc.*, 92 S.W. 3d 514 (Tex. 2002); *In re Bristol-Meyers Squibb Secs. Litig.*, 205 F.R.D. 437 (D.N.J. 2002); *McPeek v. Ashcroft*, 202 F.R.D. 31 (D.D.C. Aug. 1, 2001); McCurdy *Group, LLC v. American Biomedical Group, Inc.*, Nos. 00-6183, 00-6332, 2001 WL 536974 (10th Cir. May 21, 2001).

Subdivision (b)(iv). Subdivision (b)(iv) is the former subdivision (b)(v) unchanged.

Former Subdivision (b)(ii). Former subdivision (b)(ii), together with former subdivision (b)(iv), is contained within new subdivision (b)(iii).

Former Subdivision (b)(iii). Former subdivision (b)(iii) has been deleted. As drafted, it appeared to create or codify a proposition of law, which is not the proper function of a Standard. Moreover, the law is evolving swiftly in the area of electronic discovery and, as stated, the deleted language is not necessarily good law. *See, e.g., Zubulake v. UBS Warburg LLC*, 217 F.R.D. 309, 324 (S.D.N.Y. 2003).

Former Subdivision (b)(iv). Former subdivision (b)(iv), together with former subdivision (b)(ii), is contained within new subdivision (b)(iii).

30. Using Technology to Facilitate Discovery.
   a. In appropriate cases, the parties may agree or the court may direct that some or all discovery materials that have not been stored in electronic form should nonetheless be produced, at least in the first instance, in an electronic format and how the expenses of doing so will be allocated among the parties.
   b. A party serving written discovery requests or responses should provide the other party or parties with an electronic version of the requests or responses unless the parties have previously agreed that no electronic version is required.

2004 Comment

Subdivision (a). This change is not substantive but merely clarifying. If the data sought in discovery already exist in electronic form, there is no need for a court order requiring their production in that format. This subdivision is directed at the production in electronic format of data not currently stored electronically. The amendment makes that clear.

Subdivision (b). Subdivision (b) has been amended to interpose a presumption where previously a request was suggested. As amended, this subdivision affirmatively recommends that counsel provide adversaries with discovery requests or responses in electronic format unless the parties have previously agreed to the contrary. Because the Standard is purely precatory, it imposes no duty. Rather, it recommends a practice for counsel to consider.

31. Discovery Conferences.

a. At the initial discovery conference, the parties should confer about any electronic discovery that they anticipate requesting from one another, including:

   i. The subject matter of such discovery.

   ii. The time period with respect to which such discovery may be sought.

   iii. Identification or description of the party-affiliated persons, entities or groups from whom such discovery may be sought.

   iv. Identification or description of those persons currently or formerly affiliated with the prospective responding party who are knowledgeable of the information systems, technology and software necessary to access potentially responsive data.

   v. The potentially responsive data that exist, including the platforms on which, and places where, such data may be found as set forth in Standard 29 (a).

   vi. The accessibility of the potentially responsive data, including discussion of software, hardware or other specialized equipment that may be necessary to obtain access.

   vii. Whether potentially responsive data exist in searchable form.

   viii. Whether potentially responsive electronic data will be requested and produced:

   A. In electronic form or in hard copy, and

   B. If in electronic form, the format in which the data exist or will be produced.

   ix. Data retention policies applicable to potentially responsive data.

   x. Preservation of potentially responsive data, specifically addressing (A) preservation of data generated subsequent to the filing of the claim, (B) data otherwise customarily subject to destruction in ordinary course, and (C) metadata reflecting the creation, editing, transmittal, receipt or opening of responsive data.

xi. The use of key terms or other selection criteria to search potentially responsive data for discoverable information.

xii. The identity of unaffiliated information technology consultants whom the litigants agree are capable of independently extracting, searching or otherwise exploiting potentially responsive data.

xiii. Stipulating to the entry of a court order providing that production to other parties, or review by a mutually-agreed independent information technology consultant, of attorney-client privileged or attorney work-product protected electronic data will not effect a waiver of privilege or work product protection.

xiv. The appropriateness of an inspection of computer systems, software, or data to facilitate or focus the discovery of electronic data.

xv. The allocation of costs.

b. At any discovery conference that concerns particular requests for electronic discovery, in addition to conferring about the topics set forth in subsection (a), the parties should consider, where appropriate, stipulating to the entry of a court order providing for:

i. The initial production of tranches or subsets of potentially responsive data to allow the parties to evaluate the likely benefit of production of additional data, without prejudice to the requesting party's right to insist later on more complete production.

ii. The use of specified key terms or other selection criteria to search some or all of the potentially responsive data for discoverable information, in lieu of production.

iii. The appointment of a mutually-agreed, independent information technology consultant pursuant to Standard 32(a) to:

A. Extract defined categories of potentially responsive data from specified sources, or

B. Search or otherwise exploit potentially responsive data in accordance with specific, mutually-agreed parameters.

2004 Comment

The Federal Rules of Civil Procedure require a discovery conference at the outset of every case and prior to the filing of any discovery motion. Practices vary district by district. State court practice varies state by state, but a conference early in the case is sensible in connection with electronic discovery, regardless of whether it is compelled. Standard 31 focuses on effective use of discovery conferences to address electronic discovery issues.

Subdivision (a). Subdivision (a) focuses on the initial discovery conference. It specifies several categories of electronic discovery related matters that the parties should confer about at an initial discovery conference. It is intended to assist counsel and the court by providing a detailed array of potentially relevant issues to address. These include:

- Subject matter
- Relevant time period
- Identification of the party-affiliated persons or entities from whom electronic discovery may be sought
- Identification of those persons (including former employees) who are knowledgeable of the information systems, technology and software necessary to access potentially responsive data
- The universe of potentially responsive data that exist, including the platforms on which, and places where, such data may be found (including databases, networks, systems, servers, archives, back up or disaster recovery systems, tapes, discs, drives, cartridges and other storage media, laptops, PCs, Internet data, and PDAs)
- Accessibility issues, such as the software that may be necessary to access data
- Whether potentially responsive data exist in searchable form
- Whether potentially responsive electronic data will be requested and produced in electronic form or in hard copy
- Data retention policies
- Preservation issues, including preservation of data generated subsequent to the filing of the claim

- Possible use of key terms or other selection criteria to scour massive amounts of data for relevant information

Anticipating the privilege-related issues addressed in Standard 32, subdivision (a)(xii) suggests that the parties discuss whether they can agree on the names of unaffiliated information-technology consultants who would be capable of serving them jointly, either in a privately-retained or court-appointed capacity. In the same vein, subdivision (a)(xiii) proposes that the parties consider whether it would be desirable for them to stipulate to entry of a court order along the lines discussed in Standard 32(b) or (c).

Subdivision (b). Subdivision (b) focuses on discovery conferences relating to outstanding discovery requests (in common parlance, the "meet-and-confer"). It recognizes that there are additional issues for the parties to consider once discovery demands have been served and specific issues are on the table. Subdivision (b) anticipates a number of the privilege-related initiatives contained in Standard 32, recommending that the parties consider stipulating to a court order providing for:

- Initial production, on a without-prejudice basis, of subsets of electronic data to allow the parties to evaluate the likely benefit of production of additional data;
- The use of search terms or other selection criteria in lieu of production; or
- The appointment of an independent consultant pursuant to Standard 32

32. Attorney-Client Privilege and Attorney Work Product.

To ameliorate attorney-client privilege and work product concerns attendant to the production of electronic data, the parties should consider, where appropriate, stipulating to the entry of a court order:

a. Appointing a mutually-agreed, independent information technology consultant as a special master, referee, or other officer or agent of the court such that extraction and review of privileged or otherwise protected electronic data will not effect a waiver of privilege or other legal protection attaching to the data.

b. Providing that production to other parties of attorney-client privileged or attorney work-product protected electronic data will not effect a waiver of privilege or work product protection attaching to the data. In stipulating to the entry of such an order, the parties should consider the potential impact that production of privileged or protected data may have on the producing party's ability to maintain privilege or work-product protection vis-à-vis third parties not subject to the order.

c. Providing that extraction and review by a mutually-agreed independent information technology consultant of attorney-client privileged or attorney work-product protected electronic data will not effect a waiver of privilege or work product protection attaching to the data.

d. Setting forth a procedure for the review of the potentially responsive data extracted under subdivision (a), (b), or (c). The order should specify that adherence to the procedure precludes any waiver of privilege or work product protection attaching to the data. The order may contemplate, at the producing party's option:

   i. Initial review by the producing party for attorney-client privilege or attorney work product protection, with production of the unprivileged and unprotected data to follow, accompanied with a privilege log, or

   ii. Initial review by the requesting party, followed by:

   A. Production to the producing party of all data deemed relevant by the requesting party, followed by

   B. A review by the producing party for attorney-client privilege or attorney work product protection. Before agreeing to this procedure, the producing party should consider the potential impact that it may have on the producing party's ability to maintain privilege or work-product protection attaching to any such data if subsequently demanded by non-parties.

   The court's order should contemplate resort to the court for resolution of disputes concerning the privileged or protected nature of particular electronic data.

e. Prior to receiving any data, any mutually-agreed independent information technology consultant should be required to provide the court and the parties with an affidavit confirming that the consultant will keep no copy of any data provided to it and will not disclose any data provided other than pursuant to the court's order or parties' agreement. At the conclusion of its engagement, the consultant should be required to confirm under oath that it has acted, and will continue to act, in accordance with its initial affidavit.

f. If the initial review is conducted by the requesting party in accordance with subsection (d)(ii), the requesting party should provide the court and the producing party an affidavit stating that the requesting party will keep no copy of data deemed by the producing party to be privileged or work product, subject to final resolution of any dispute by the court, and will not use or reveal the substance of any such data unless permitted to do so by the court. 2004 Comment

Standard 32 deals with privilege and work product (collectively, "privilege") concerns. It applies in the common situation in which electronic data must be extracted for production by an information technology (IT) expert not employed by the producing party. This scenario by definition raises a risk of waiver because privileged documents are being exposed to persons outside the privilege. Standard 32 sets forth three methods to ameliorate the risk of waiver. Each would be implemented by entry of a stipulated court order.

Subdivision (a). Subdivision (a) suggests that the parties consider having the court appoint a mutually-agreed IT consultant as a special master, referee, or other officer of the court, so that the consultant's extraction and review of privileged electronic data will not effect a waiver. This approach would allow the third party consultant to pull and have access to privileged material (which may be included in any mass extraction of data) without risk that the holder of the privilege will have effected a waiver by permitting the third party to review them. Following extraction, the parties are then free to specify whatever protocol they prefer with respect to review of the data. This is addressed in subdivision (d).

Subdivision (b). Subdivision (b) addresses what is sometimes known as the "quick peek" approach to electronic discovery. Under the quick-peek scenario envisioned by subdivisions (b) and (d)(ii), the requesting party may have sufficient resources to perform or pay for the extraction, and the producing party may be inclined to allow its opponent to incur all expenses associated with doing so. At the same time, the producing party has no interest in waiving privilege. The parties therefore agree that the data will be turned over to the requesting party without review by the producing party; the requesting party will identify which documents it is interested in, and the producing party will then conduct a privilege review. Subdivision (b) captures the court order necessary to permit this procedure to proceed.

Under subdivision (b), the parties stipulate to an order providing that production of privileged electronic data will not effect a waiver. Note that this is different from the customary agreed order, which provides that inadvertent production will not effect a waiver, because parties using the subdivision (b) approach may know or be fairly certain that privileged material is contained in the mass of data to be extracted. Like that order, however, there is some question as to the effectiveness of such an order *vis-à-vis* a third party who subsequently seeks the disclosed data. Accordingly, there is an appropriate caution in the text of this subdivision and in subdivision (d)(ii).

Subdivision (c). Subdivision (c) is similar to subdivision (a) in that it envisions the use of an agreed third-party consultant. Under subdivision (c), unlike subdivision (a), that consultant is not appointed as a special master or other court officer. The court, for example, may not be inclined to appoint the consultant as a master or the parties may prefer to control the consultant directly. Subdivision (c) is also similar to subdivision (b) in that it envisions the entry of an order providing that review of intentionally-produced privileged data will not effect a waiver. But the reviewing party under subdivision (c) is an agreed-on consultant, not the opposition. As under both subdivisions (a) and (b), under subdivision (c) the parties are free to specify whatever protocol they prefer with respect to review of the data, following extraction. This is addressed in subdivision (d).

As observed in the comment to subdivision (b), *supra*, in current practice, there is no assurance that a stipulated order providing that inadvertent production does not effect a waiver will be effective against a claim of waiver asserted by a third party. Precisely the same risk is posed by the order envisaged by subdivision (c). Accordingly, it is imperative that litigants following either of these routes also have in place a confidentiality order as a second line of defense against inquisitive third parties. It is equally important that the litigants develop a protocol for, or otherwise instruct, the consultant to minimize the likelihood that the consultant will actually review (as opposed to extract) privileged material.

Subdivision (d). Subdivision (d) sets forth a pair of alternative procedures for the parties to consider with respect to the review of the data once the data have been extracted. Subdivision (d)(i) states that traditional approach, in which the extracted data are furnished to the producing party, who then conducts a review for responsiveness and privilege, and makes production of the data together with a privilege log.

Subdivision (d)(ii) identifies an unconventional approach that some parties prefer for financial reasons, as where there is an enormous amount of electronic data, little of it is likely to be either responsive or privileged, and little of that will fall in both categories. Under the (d)(ii) approach, the requesting party first reviews the data for responsiveness and provides to the producing party all data in which it is interested. The producing party then determines if any of the data in question are privileged. If so, the requesting party may not maintain copies of the privileged material unless and until a court sustains its objections to the claim of privilege. This procedure raises the risk of waiver of privilege identified in the comment to subdivision (b). Accordingly, the text of subdivision (d)(ii)(B) contains substantially the same caution as that set forth in subdivision (b).

Subdivision (e). Subdivision (e) suggests a reasonable precaution—that any IT consultant employed by the parties be required to execute an affidavit confirming that it will keep no copy of any data and will not disclose any data provided other than pursuant to the court's order or parties' agreement.

Subdivision (f). Subdivision (f) provides that, before receiving the data pursuant to subdivision (d)(ii), the requesting party is to execute an affidavit stating that it will keep no copy of data deemed by the producing party to be privileged, subject to final resolution of any dispute by the court. This precaution is appropriate in light of the trust that the producing party reposes in the requesting party under the quick-peek approach captured in subdivisions (b) and (d)(ii).

33. Technological Advances. To the extent that information may be contained or stored in a data compilation in a form other than electronic or paper, it is intended that Standards 29-32 may be consulted with respect to discovery of such information, with appropriate modifications for the difference in storage medium.

2004 Comment

Standard 33 recognizes the impracticability of keeping pace with technological change. New, non-electronic media may emerge for the creation or retention of electronic data. This Standard suggests that Standards 29-32 be consulted with respect to discovery of such data, subject to common sense modifications.

Local District Court Rules

Local Rules Governing e-Discovery
In United States District Courts

As of late 2007, at least 29 District Courts[1] have enacted some kind of special rules to address e-discovery. More are expected in the coming months, so check with my blog for the latest list. The following is a list of the Local Rules identified to date.

Arkansas: Eastern and Western Districts
Local Rule 26.1 Outline for Fed. R. Civ. P. 26(f) Report

Alaska
Local Form 26(f): Scheduling and Planning Conference Report (*see* item 4(B))
Local Rule 16.1 Pre-Trial Procedures (requiring use of Local Form 26(f) or one substantially similar)

California: Northern District
Standing Order for All Judges of the Northern District of California: Contents of Joint Case Management Statement (*see* item 6)
Local Rule 16-9 Case Management Statement and Proposed Order

---

1. http://www.uscourts.gov/courtlinks/

(requiring parties' Joint Case Management Statement to include all topics listed in Standing Order)

Colorado
Appendix F: Scheduling Order
Instructions for Preparation of Scheduling Order

Connecticut
January 19, 2007 Order Amending Local Rules
Local Rules 16(b), 26, 37 and Form 26(F)

Delaware
Default Standards for Discovery of Electronic Documents

Florida: Middle District
Civil Discovery Practice Handbook (*see* Part VII, "Technology")

Florida: Southern District
Rule 16.1 Pretrial Procedure in Civil Actions
Rule 26.1 Discovery and Discovery Material (Civil)
Appendix A: Discovery Practices Handbook (*see* Part III, in particular)

Georgia: Southern District
Rule 26(f) Report

Indiana: Northern District
Report of Parties' Planning Meeting

Indiana: Southern District
Uniform Case Management Plan (*see* Part III(K))
Rule 16.1 Pretrial Procedures (requiring use of Uniform Case Management Plan)

Iowa: Northern and Southern Districts
Scheduling Order and Discovery Plan
Instructions and Worksheet for Preparation of Scheduling Order and Discovery Plan and Order Requiring Submission of Same

Local Rule 16.1 Scheduling Order and Discovery Plan (requiring use of form)
Local Rule 26.1 Pretrial Discovery and Disclosures (requirement to submit discovery plan satisfied by submission of form Scheduling Order and Discovery Plan)

Kansas
Guidelines for Discovery of Electronically Stored Information
Initial Order Regarding Planning and Scheduling

Maryland
Suggested Protocol for Discovery of Electronically Stored Information

New Hampshire
Local Rule 26.1 Discovery Plan
Civil Form 2: Sample Discovery Plan

New Jersey
Local Rule 26.1 Discovery (*see* subpart (d))

Ohio: Southern District
Rule 26(f) Report of Parties (Western Division at Dayton)
Rule 26(f) Report of Parties (Eastern Division)

Ohio: Northern District
Default Standard for Discovery of Electronically Stored Information (Appendix K)

Pennsylvania: Eastern District
Report of Rule 26(f) Meeting
Order Governing Electronic Discovery (District Judge Timothy J. Savage)
District Judge Timothy J. Savage's Scheduling and Motion Policies and Procedures

Pennsylvania: Middle District
Local Rule 26.1 Duty to Investigate and Disclose

Pennsylvania: Western District
Local Rule 16.1.1 Scheduling and Pretrial Conferences - Generally
(*see* item (B), requiring use of Appendix B form)
Appendix B: Fed. R. Civ. P. 26(f) Report of the Parties (*see* item 11)

Tennessee: Eastern District
Form Scheduling Order (Knoxville) (Senior District Judge Leon
Jordan) (*see* Item 4(d))
Form Scheduling Order (Knoxville) (District Judge Thomas A. Varlan)
(*see* Item 4(d))
Form Scheduling Order (Chattanooga) (Magistrate Judge Susan K.
Lee) (*see* Item 5(a))

Tennessee: Western District
Form Scheduling Order (Western Division) (Magistrate Judge Diane
K. Vescovo)

Texas: Eastern District
Notice of Scheduling Conference, Proposed Discovery Order, and
Proposed Dates for Docket Control Order (Magistrate Judge John D.
Love) (*see* item 2(A))

Texas: Northern District
Miscellaneous Order No. 62 (Dallas Division, Patent Cases) (*see* item
2.1(a)(2))

West Virginia: Southern District
Report of Parties' Planning Meeting
Local Rule 16.1 Scheduling Conferences (requiring use of court's
form)

Wyoming
Local Rule 26.1 Discovery and Appendix D: Rule 26 Conference
Checklist (*see* subpart (e) of local rule)

HOW MUCH DATA DO YOU HAVE?

CD = 650 MB = 50,000 pages.

DVD = 4.7 GB = 350,000 pages.

DLT Tape = 40/80 GB = 3 to 6 million pages.
Super DLT Tape = 60/120 GB = 4 to 9 million pages.

Page Estimates:
    1 MB is about 75 pages;
    1 GB is about 75,000 pages (pick-up truck full of documents).

Average pgs. per email: 1.5 (100,099 pages per GB).
Average pgs. per word document: 8 (64,782 pages per GB).
Average pgs. per spreadsheet: 50 (165,791 pages per GB).
Average pgs. per power point: 14 (17,552 pages per GB).

For the average .PST or .NSF email file:
    100 MB .PST file is 900 emails and 300 attachments.
    400 MB .PST file is 3,500 emails and 1,200 attachments.
    600 MB .PST file is 5,500 emails and 1,600 attachments.
    A 1.00 GB .NSF file is 9,000 emails and 3,000 attachments.
    A 1.5 GB .NSF file is 13,500 emails and 4,500 attachments.

Note: Many variables will affect *all* of the actual numbers above,
including especially large image and video files, and recursive files.

Bits and Bytes Sizes:
- 8 bits are equal to 1 byte (one or two words).
- 1,024 bytes are equal to 1 kilobyte (KB).
- 1,024 kilobytes (KB) are equal to 1 megabyte (MB or Meg).
- 1,024 megabytes are equal to 1 gigabyte (GB or Gig) (truck full of paper).
- 1,024 gigabytes are equal to 1 terabyte (TB) (50,000 trees of paper).
- 1,024 terabytes are equal to 1 petabyte (PB) (250 billion pgs. of text).
- 1,024 petabytes are equal to 1 exabytes (EB) (1,000,000,000,000,000,000 bytes).

Index

A

admissibility 37–39
  five evidence rules 38
  Lorraine v. Markel American Ins. Co. 37
  treatise on the admissibility of ESI 37
American Bar Association
  civil discovery standards 23, 77, 111–12
    e discovery and technology 111
  First Annual National Institute on E-Discovery 23, 70, 96
American Society for Information and Technology 16
Ameriwood v. Liberman, 2006 WL 3825291, 2006 U.S. Dist. LEXIS
    93380 (E.D. Mo., Dec. 27, 2006) 91
Anadarko Petroleum Corp. v. Davis, 2006 WL 3837518 (S.D. Tex.,
    Dec. 28, 2006) 231-33
analysis and e-discovery 12
  relevant summary information 12
  special challenges 12
  trial preparation software 12
Arthur Andersen v. United States, 544 U.S. 696 (2005) 94, 96, 98
Association of Records Managers and Administrators 16, 102
attorney-client privilege
  erosion of 21–22
    enormous amounts of electronic documents 21
    mandatory waivers 21
    Rule 26(b)(5)(B) 21
    spoliation 21
  waiver of 200–01

B

Baron, Jason R. 15, 186
Bashir v. Amtrak, 119 F.3d 929, 931 (11th Cir. 1997) 148

F

G

Gartner research group 29

GhostSurf software 116–24

Gragg v. International Management Group (UK) Inc., 2007 WL
1074894 (N.D. N.Y., April 2007) 200-01

Griffis v. Pinal County, 215 Ariz. 1, 152 P.3d 418 at 421-22 (Ariz.
2007) 205

Grimm, Paul 18, 37–39

GTFM, Inc. v. Wal-Mart, 2000 WL 1693615 (S.D. N.Y. Nov. 9, 2000)
33, 61

H

hash algorithm 221–26
  authentication properties of 221
  document organization and identification protocol 221
  truncated hash-naming protocol 222

Healthcare Advocates, Inc. v. Harding, Earley, Follmer & Frailey, 2007
WL 2085358 (E.D. Pa., June 20, 2007) 195–200

Hedenburg v. Aramark American Food Services, 2007 U.S. Dist.
LEXIS 3443 (W.D. Wash., Jan. 17, 2007) 193, 236

Hedges, Ronald 80

Hopson v. Mayor of Baltimore, 232 F.R.D. 228, 245 (D. Md. 2006) 60

Hughes, John J. 72, 80

I

identification and e-discovery 9
  counter-e-discovery plans 9
  data sets, degree of accessibility 9
  key witnesses 9
  meet and confer sessions 9
  location of all discoverable data 9
  sources of discoverable information 9
  triggering event 9
  unreasonable requests 9

IEEE Computer Society 16

O

P

U

About the Author

Ralph C. Losey is a shareholder in the Orlando office of Akerman & Senterfitt, P.A., where he heads the firm's national electronic discovery practice group. His work includes supervision of the e-discovery aspects of major litigation handled by his firm and others; serving as national e-counsel to coordinate the discovery work of local counsel; and assisting large corporate and government clients to prepare for litigation by helping them to organize and operate their own internal e-discovery teams. His team-related services include advice on team organization and budgeting; records retention policies; litigation hold procedures; ESI identification, retrieval, search, and analysis; information management; software; hardware; and vendor selection.

He has practiced commercial and employment litigation since 1980 and has over 70 published opinions. Ralph has also been an avid computer user and technologist since 1978 and is the author of the popular multimedia Internet blog *e-Discovery Team*, found at http://ralphlosey.wordpress.com, from which this book is derived. He has been involved with electronic discovery since the 1990s and is now an active member of The Sedona Conference and other e-discovery specialty groups. He regularly lectures on e-discovery subjects in CLEs and "webinars" around the country.

Ralph was one of the first attorneys in the country with an Internet website, which he still maintains at www.FloridaLawFirm.com. He has also written and contributed to several other books and articles on e-discovery and on the Internet. He wrote chapter 3, "Your Cyber Rights and Responsibilities: The Law of the Internet," for *Que's Special Edition Using the Internet* (McMillan Publishers, third edition, 1996) and the chapter on metadata for West-Thompson's new book, *E-Discovery, a Report and Guide to the New Rules* (January 2008). Ralph has also recently written a law review article on the mathematics underlying e-discovery, "HASH: The New Bates Stamp," for the June 2007 issue of the *Journal of Technology Law & Policy*. He was certified by the Florida Bar as a mediator of computer law disputes in 1989. He received his B.A. from Vanderbilt University in 1973 and his J.D. in 1979 from the University of Florida School of Law.